The Assessment of Task Structure, Knowledge Base, and Decision Aids for a Comprehensive Inventory of Audit Tasks

The Assessment of Task Structure, Knowledge Base, and Decision Aids for a Comprehensive Inventory of Audit Tasks

Mohammad J. Abdolmohammadi
Catherine A. Usoff

QUORUM BOOKS
Westport, Connecticut • London

Library of Congress Cataloging-in-Publication Data

Abdolmohammadi, Mohammad J. (Mohammad Javad), 1950–
  The assessment of task structure, knowledge base, and decision aids for a comprehensive inventory of audit tasks / Mohammad J. Abdolmohammadi and Catherine A. Usoff.
    p. cm.
  Includes bibliographical references and index.
  ISBN 1–56720–294–2
  1. Accounting—Quality control—Standards. 2. Auditing—Quality control—Standards. 3. Financial statements. 4. Management audit. I. Usoff, Catherine A. II. Title.
  HF5626.A23 2001
  657′.45—dc21   99–089370

British Library Cataloguing in Publication Data is available.

Library of Congress Catalog Card Number: 99–089370
ISBN: 1–56720–294–2

First published in 2001

Quorum Books, 88 Post Road West, Westport, CT 06881
An imprint of Greenwood Publishing Group, Inc.
www.quorumbooks.com

Printed in the United States of America

The paper used in this book complies with the Permanent Paper Standard issued by the National Information Standards Organization (Z39.48–1984).

10 9 8 7 6 5 4 3 2 1

To our families:

Tabi, Yusef, Jacob, Yasi, and Bobby
Joe, Rebecca, and Nicholas

Contents

Illustrations

FIGURES

TABLES

Foreword

There are significant demands and expectations placed on the auditing profession by the capital markets and by other users of the financial statements, who rely on the auditor to ensure the financial information they base decisions on is reliable. Accordingly, an important concern for auditing practitioners and researchers has been the identification of methods such as staff assignment, training, and the development of decision aids for ensuring audit performance is at a high level. Previous research findings indicate that these efforts should begin with a thorough knowledge of a particular audit task such as the nature of the task (structured-unstructured) and the requisite knowledge. Nonetheless, until recently little data were compiled at the task level. This book provides an important contribution by addressing this issue. First, using audit manuals from several major public accounting firms, auditing texts, and professional manuals, the authors have compiled a comprehensive list of 433 audit tasks, divided into six phases and several sub-phases. This book extends the earlier work by Abdolmohammadi, who identified some 300 tasks. Second, data are gathered from experienced managers and partners for each of these tasks regarding degree of task structure, knowledge level needed to perform the task, and whether a decision aid would be appropriate for the task and, if so, the nature of the decision aid. Analyses are also provided comparing the responses in the 1988 study to the current one to identify temporal changes. Finally, hypotheses are tested on the relationship between task structure, requisite knowledge, and decision aid type.

The findings of this study are of benefit to several parties. Auditing practitioners may use the data to consider the proper staff assignment of personnel on various tasks, to consider the desirability of developing new decision aids, and to evaluate the need for (and level of) professional training. Researchers, particularly in the judgment and decision-making area, will also find the book to be of value in considering the appropriate experience level of participants to involve in a study examining performance on a particular task. Of importance, the book considers the construct of experience along several dimensions including general audit experience (years in auditing), staff level, and number of supervised instances of performing the task. The results of these alternative experience measures indicate for each task whether these measures are highly correlated, in which case they are essentially surrogates. In other cases they vary, indicating general years of experience is not a good measure of requisite knowledge and a task specific measure is needed. The level of reported consensus also indicates the extent to which auditors agree on the appropriate experience level for a given task. When consensus is low, the authors of this book suggest employing subjects at the upper end of the spectrum to be conservative. Finally, students will find the compilation of tasks and their knowledge level to be informative in considering the breadth and depth of auditing judgments and decisions.

In summary, the authors are to be highly commended for this comprehensive effort, which provides the most extensive documentation of audit tasks to date. I anticipate this book will be widely used and cited by researchers, as was the previous study by Abdolmohammadi, and will serve as a useful reference for practitioners.

Arnie Wright, Arthur Andersen Professor of Accounting
Boston College
Editor, *Auditing: A Journal of Practice & Theory*
November 1999

Preface

Interest in issues of task structure, knowledge base, and decision aids has been growing in the past decade. There have been calls for a better understanding of these issues at the very detailed audit task level. Task structure and the knowledge base required to perform the task are major attributes for decision aid development, for training programs, and for behavioral accounting research in general and expertise research in particular. This book therefore should interest professional auditors, auditing researchers and doctoral students in accounting and information systems programs.

The objectives of the book are to (1) develop a comprehensive inventory of audit tasks; (2) use a decision process model as a framework for collection of data from highly experienced auditors (partners and managers) on task structure, knowledge base demands, and applicable decision aids for each task; and (3) compare data collected in the current study with similar data collected in a 1988 study to reveal potential changes in experienced auditors' assessments of individual task characteristics over an eight-year period.

To accomplish the research objectives, a comprehensive inventory of audit tasks was developed based on a selected number of current Canadian and U.S. accounting firm audit manuals, auditing textbooks, and the extant audit literature; a lengthy 45-page task instrument was developed to collect data; and data were collected from a sample of managers and partners from five of the then Big Six accounting firms and one large regional accounting firm.[1] Both between-subject and within-subject designs were used to collect data. The between-subject design refers to the fact that the sample was divided into three groups of approximately equal sizes. Each group was randomly assigned to one of the three versions of the task instrument. The within-subject design refers to the fact that each subject made repeated judgments about task structure, knowledge base, and decision aids for approximately 145 audit tasks.

A rather large database was created by coding of the 1,732 variables under study (433 tasks times four judgments of task structure, years of experience, supervised instances of work, and applicable decision aids). Data were analyzed using primarily univariate analysis. The results are presented descriptively where task structure, knowledge base, and decision aid choices for every task are presented in a large number of tables. If the same task had been included in the 1988 study, comparison data are also provided. Also presented are correlation and logistic regression statistics to investigate the relationships between task structure as an independent variable and other variables. Effects of demographic variables such as firm audit methodology, respondent rank, and respondent specialty (i.e., high-tech versus others) were also analyzed, but are not reported. This is due to the fact that partition of the data by demographic variables rendered very small sample sizes that made inferences from the results unreliable.

This inventory of audit tasks is the most detailed found in the extant auditing literature. For each of 433 tasks, we present task structure, audit experience in years and the number of supervised instances of practice before an auditor is considered to be knowledgeable enough to perform the task independently, and the applicable decision aids to perform the task based on responses from 44 audit managers and partners from five Big Six and one regional accounting firm. At the individual task level, we also provide data from a 1988 study if the task description is exactly the same in both studies. Of the 433 tasks reported on with current data, there are 247 tasks for which comparison data are provided from the 1988 study. In that study, task structure and applicable decision aids were assessed

---

1. We had proposed to collect data from Canada as well as the United States. However, our repeated attempts to collect data from Canada resulted in one response from a chartered accountant and four responses from Certified General Accountants (CGAs), providing insufficient data for any meaningful analysis.

for each task, but knowledge base was measured as professional rank, rather than as years of audit experience or supervised instances.

Also provided are tests of five hypotheses on the positive correlation between task structure as an independent variable and audit experience, supervised instances of practice, professional rank of auditors, decision aids in general, and specific types of decision aids as dependent variables. All five hypotheses were supported at highly significant levels at the audit phase and aggregate levels.

This book contributes to a better understanding of these issues in the following ways:

1. It provides a review of the issues of task structure, task-specific knowledge base and decision aids.
2. It provides the most detailed inventory of audit tasks in the literature.
3. It presents data from highly experienced auditors (managers and partners) concerning the structure of each audit task.
4. It presents data on the knowledge base needed to perform each audit task in terms of general audit experience in rank and years of practice as well as the number of supervised instances of practice before an auditor is qualified to perform the task independently.
5. It presents data concerning the applicable decision aid to perform each audit task.
6. It tests hypotheses on the relationships between task structure, knowledge base, and decision aids.
7. It provides a comparison over an eight-year period of experienced auditors' assessments of individual task characteristics along structure, experience requirements, and appropriate decision aids.

Acknowledgments

This book has come to completion with support and assistance from many people, a listing of all of whom might prove to be incomplete due to our oversight. To all those who helped us we express our deepest gratitude. Special thanks are due CGA (Certified General Accountants) Canada for its initial financial support of the project and to its research director, Mr. Stephen Spector. The project was also part of a research package that was the basis for a full-year sabbatical awarded to the first author at Bentley College. We greatly appreciate the support from Bentley College, particularly that of its former president, Dr. Joseph Cronin.

In the process of compiling the inventory of audit tasks, we benefited from audit manuals of several anonymous accounting firms, the CICA (Canandian Institute of Chartered Accountants) Handbook and the Professional Engagement Manual of the CICA. We gratefully acknowledge these accounting firms and the CICA for allowing us to use their audit manuals.

This project would not have come to fruition had we not received the generous cooperation of several accounting firms and participation of their busy professionals in the study. The project required extensive time from highly experienced audit managers and partners. Our deepest appreciation to the anonymous accounting firms and their professionals whose participation made this project possible.

Our graduate assistants, Lien Le, Lynette Grenlay, and Cherie Nelson provided invaluable assistance in compiling the inventory of audit tasks, the development of the research instrument, coding of the data in electronic form, data validation, and data analysis. We thank them for their dedication, quality work under a tight schedule, and professionalism. Alba Becton, Jeanne DiBona, Florence Jones, Dawn Maly, and Ursula Pike provided secretarial support at various stages of this project and Mr. Donald Brown of Bentley College's Media Services assisted us in developing a professionally crafted research questionnaire. We thank them all for their significant contributions to this book.

Last, but certainly not least, we thank our families to whom we dedicate this work. Our spouses exhibited understanding and support for our efforts in working on this project and in many ways our children silently tolerated the time we took away from them to work on this book. We thank you for this and we love you!

Chapter 1

Introduction

This chapter provides a discussion of the motivation and history of the research study reported in this book. In the first section, we discuss the motivation for the study. This is followed by a statement of the research objectives. The benefits expected from this study are described in the third section followed by a short history of this line of research in the fourth section. The chapter ends with a summary of the research results.

MOTIVATION

Recent behavioral research in auditing has emphasized the need for consideration of task specific complexity and knowledge base and has called for further research regarding specification of these performance variables.[1] For example, two researchers provided evidence that the interaction between task complexity and experience level explains the

---

1. See F. Choo, 1989, "Expert-Novice Differences in Judgment/Decision Making Research," *Journal of Accounting Literature* 8, pp. 106–136; J. S. Davis and I. Solomon, 1989, "Experience, Expertise, and Expert-Performance Research in Accounting," *Journal of Accounting Literature* 8, pp. 150–164; S. Bonner and N. Pennington, 1991, "Cognitive Processes and Knowledge as Determinants of Auditor Expertise," *Journal of Accounting Literature* 10, pp. 1–50; and R. Libby, 1995, "The Role of Knowledge and Memory in Audit Judgment," in R. H. Ashton and A. H. Ashton (eds.), *Judgment and Decision Making Research in Accounting and Auditing* (New York: Cambridge University Press), pp. 176–206 for extensive reviews of this literature.

mixed experience effect results reported in the auditing literature.[2] The author of a detailed review of the literature on the effects of ability, knowledge, and experience on performance called for specifying the knowledge needed in performing audit tasks at very detailed level.[3] This literature leads to a conclusion that tasks need to be analyzed at the highest level of detail for specification of task complexity and the knowledge base needed to perform each task.

One model of the auditing process identifies 28 distinct steps for the purpose of assessing the structure of the audit methodology of 14 large accounting firms.[4] Other researchers further subdivided the 28 step audit model into 60 audit steps to study the perceptions of practicing auditors on difficulty and criticalness of each step.[5] The authors concluded that, "to identify the benefits of audit research to practice, it would be desirable to distinguish among sub-parts of each audit phase, rather than to simply focus on a particular phase."[6] We note that many accounting firms have changed their audit approach to a more strategic focus in recent years. For example, KPMG Peat Marwick has adopted a strategic approach called Business Measurement Process (BMP) and Deloitte and Touche has a system called Audit System/2.[7] Although the auditor may put less emphasis on some audit processes (e.g., tests of details) and more emphasis on other processes (e.g., the strength of control systems), the operational details of the audit have remained largely unchanged under new strategic approaches. Therefore, the potential benefits of studying the auditing process at a detailed task level have not lessened significantly over time.

The decision aids literature also indicates a need for analysis of the task at the most detailed level. One article suggested a model of task complexity and decision aids where there is a positive correlation

---

2. M. J. Abdolmohammadi and A. Wright, 1987, "An Examination of the Effects of Experience and Task Complexity on Audit Judgments," *The Accounting Review* 62 (1), pp. 1–13.

3. R. Libby, 1995, "The Role of Knowledge and Memory in Audit Judgment," pp. 176–206.

4. B. E. Cushing and J. K. Loebbecke, 1984, "The Implications of Structured Audit Methodologies," *The Auditor's Report* 8 (Summer), pp. 1, 10, 13.

5. See W. C. Chow, A. H. McNamee, and R. D. Plumlee, 1987, "Practitioners' Perceptions of Audit Step Difficulty and Criticalness: Implications for Audit Research," *Auditing: A Journal of Practice and Theory* 6 (2), pp. 123–133.

6. Ibid., p. 131.

7. A. R. Bowrin, 1998, "Review and Synthesis of Audit Structure Literature," *Journal of Accounting Literature* 17, p. 64.

between task complexity and decision aid type.[8] The auditing literature has interpreted this model to mean that while routine tasks can be automated, decision support systems and knowledge-based expert systems are useful for more complex audit tasks.[9] More recent literature has presented evidence that the choice of decision aid type for a task is dependent on a number of factors such as the auditors' electronic data processing specialty[10] and that the task-structure/decision-aid-type contingency does not completely map onto the auditing domain.[11] These results indicate a need for further investigation of the factors involved in identification of the appropriate decision aid for various audit tasks.

OBJECTIVES

This book is designed to serve five distinct objectives. The first objective is to develop a comprehensive inventory of detailed audit tasks. The second is to classify these tasks by their levels of task structure using Herbert Simon's model of the decision process as a framework.[12] This model is discussed in Chapter 2. The third objective is to provide evidence concerning the knowledge base needed to perform each task. The issues related to knowledge base demands are discussed

---

8. P. G. W. Keen and M. S. Scott-Morton, 1978, *Decision Support Systems: An Organizational Perspective* (Reading, Mass: Addison-Wesley).

9. See, for example, W. F. Messier Jr. and J. V. Hansen, 1984, "Expert Systems in Accounting and Auditing: A Framework and Review," in S. Moriarity and E. Joyce (eds.), *Decision Making and Accounting: Current Research* (University of Oklahoma), pp. 182–202; W. F. Messier Jr. and J. V. Hansen, 1987, "Expert Systems in Auditing: The State of the Art," *Auditing: A Journal of Practice and Theory* 7 (1), pp. 94–105; M. J. Abdolmohammadi, 1987, "Decision Support and Expert Systems in Auditing: A Review and Research Directions," *Accounting and Business Research* 17 (66), pp. 173–185; and W. F. Messier Jr., 1995, "Research in and Development of Audit Decision Aids," in R. H. Ashton and A. H. Ashton (eds.), *Judgment and Decision Making Research in Accounting and Auditing* (New York: Cambridge University Press), pp. 207–228.

10. M. J. Abdolmohammadi, 1991a, "Factors Affecting Auditor's Perceptions of Applicable Decision Aids for Various Audit Tasks," *Contemporary Accounting Research* 7(2), pp. 535–548.

11. M. J. Abdolmohammadi, 1991b, "A Test of the Relationship between Task Structure and Decision Aid Type in Auditing" in *Auditing: Advances in Applied Behavioral Research*, L. A. Ponemon and D. R. L. Gabhart (eds.), (New York: Springer-Verlag Publishing), pp. 131–142.

12. The original source for this model is H. Simon, 1960, *The New Science of Management* (New York: Harper and Row).

in Chapter 3. Briefly, we define knowledge base in terms of the years of audit experience, professional rank, and the number of supervised instances of practice before an auditor is qualified to perform a task independently. The fourth objective is to provide data concerning the type of decision aid applicable to perform each task. Issues related to applicable decision aids are discussed in Chapter 4. The final objective is to test several research hypotheses about the positive relationship between task structure as an independent variable and audit experience, professional rank, supervised instances of practice, and decision aids as dependent variables. These research hypotheses are developed in Chapters 3 and 4.

BENEFITS OF A COMPREHENSIVE STUDY OF AUDIT TASKS

This research can be beneficial in auditing in four important areas as described below. The first benefit is that the task level data on the knowledge base required to perform the task independently should help behavioral auditing researchers as they study various phenomena at the detailed task level. The second benefit is that the task level structure data should provide valuable, systematic information for decision aid development efforts. The third benefit relates to professional training programs. Knowledge of specific tasks should assist in developing training programs for various levels of auditors. Finally, the comprehensive, organized description of audit tasks will be useful for auditing students at the undergraduate and graduate level.

The literature reviewed indicates that task structure, knowledge base, and appropriate decision aids need to be investigated at a highly detailed task level to assist in understanding of expertise and the development of decision aids and training programs in auditing. This study provides a data base on complexity, knowledge base, and appropriate decision aids for a comprehensive inventory of audit tasks.

Guide for Behavioral Researchers

Identification of the complexity of audit tasks and the requisite knowledge base to perform those tasks is useful as a guide for behavioral researchers, particularly in the area of research on audit expertise. Recent behavioral research has particularly emphasized the importance of task-specific knowledge in a variety of research settings.[13] An article reporting the results of a questionnaire completed

---

13. See, for example: M. J. Abdolmohammadi and A. Wright, 1987, "An Examination of the Effects of Experience and Task Complexity on Audit

by highly experienced auditors reported that auditors view knowledge as the most important attribute of expertise.[14] Thus, the complexity and knowledge base demands of tasks are important issues of research in auditing from a behavioral research perspective. Many studies consider expertise to be equivalent to or the natural result of general audit experience. The authors of one article, however, point out that this common assumption may not be justified.[15] In other words, just because an auditor has general audit experience, one should not assume that he or she can be considered expert in all audit tasks. One way to support valid use of experience as a surrogate for expertise is to document that an auditor would have had ample opportunity to perform the *particular* task under study by the time he or she has reached the current experience level. Accordingly, we will provide evidence at the individual task level concerning general audit experience as well as the number of supervised instances of practice before an auditor is qualified to perform a task independently.

For a comprehensive inventory of audit tasks (433 in total), we provide data on the years of experience required to perform the task independently. We also asked highly experienced auditors to indicate the number of times the task should be performed with supervision before the auditor would be able to perform the task independently. For 247 of the tasks, we also provide data on the professional rank at which an auditor is expected to perform the task. Having data on these experience measures (required practice as well as time on the job and rank) should be very useful to auditing researchers, as well as professional auditors. For research that involves specific tasks it may

---

Judgments;" A. H. Ashton, 1991, "Experience and Error Frequency Knowledge as Potential Determinants of Audit Expertise," *The Accounting Review* 66 (2), pp. 218–239; J. Bédard. and M. T. H. Chi, 1993, "Expertise in Auditing," *Auditing: A Journal of Practice and Theory* 12 (Supplement), pp. 21–45; S. E. Bonner, 1990, "Experience Effects in Auditing: The Role of Task-Specific Knowledge," *The Accounting Review* 65 (1), pp. 72–92; S. Bonner and B. Lewis, 1990, "Determinants of Auditor Expertise," *Journal of Accounting Research* 28 (Supplement), pp. 1–20; S. Bonner and N. Pennington, 1991, "Cognitive Processes and Knowledge as Determinants of Auditor Expertise," pp. 1–50; D. M. Frederick and R. Libby, 1986, "Expertise and Auditors' Judgments of Conjunctive Events," *Journal of Accounting Research* 24 (2), pp. 270–290; R. Libby, 1995, "The Role of Knowledge and Memory in Audit Judgment," pp. 176–206.

14. M. J. Abdolmohammadi and J. Shanteau, 1992, "Personal Attributes of Expert Auditors," *Organizational Behavior and Human Decision Processes* 53 (2), pp. 158–172.

15. S. Bonner and N. Pennington, 1991, "Cognitive Processes and Knowledge as Determinants of Auditor Expertise," pp. 1–50.

be important to ask auditor-participants how many times they have performed a particular task as well as how many years of experience and what rank they have before considering them to be knowledgeable about a particular task. Having more than one dimension of experience should provide justification for using particular levels of auditors for research depending on what auditing tasks are being studied.

In addition to the benefit provided by the average experience levels reported for each of the detailed auditing tasks, the variance in the responses for each task will provide valuable information. For an individual task, respondents from different firms may provide highly variable responses to the questions of what professional rank, how many years of experience, and how many supervised instances are required for an auditor to perform the task independently. For tasks where there is wide variation, audit researchers may not be justified in using the average experience level required to support using that level of auditor as valid subjects for their studies. The variance of responses will be important for researchers to take into account. Valid research participants for tasks with high variance responses may have to be chosen from the high end of the experience/rank spectrum of responses for that task. Given better and more detailed information about the experience requirements for tasks will provide better justification for those doing auditing behavioral work to use the specific levels of auditors that they use.

Benefit to Decision Aid Research and Development

Decision aid development in auditing is, in part, dependent upon the structure of the task under investigation.[16] A study reported that despite the heavy emphasis on decision aid development in auditing in recent years, there is no systematic model to identify audit tasks for decision aid development.[17] Such developments are still done largely on a one-task-at-a-time basis. Use of a systematic model to collect data from experienced auditors will be beneficial in decision aid research and development efforts in auditing.

---

16. P. G. W. Keen and M. S. Scott-Morton, 1978, *Decision Support Systems: An Organizational Perspective.*

17. M. J. Abdolmohammadi, 1991a, "Factors Affecting Auditor's Perceptions of Applicable Decision Aids for Various Audit Tasks," pp. 535–548.

Guidance for Training Programs

Finally, identification of the requisite knowledge base for a given task (and the appropriate decision aid for the task) has implications for development of staff training programs in accounting firms.[18] For example, while the less complex tasks may be learned with relative ease, more complex tasks need to be identified for development of training programs tailored specifically to the knowledge base demands of the task. The authors of a review paper have stated that, "we find a strong relation between the learning environment and performance, which suggests that performance is probably poor in some tasks because auditors have not had good opportunities to acquire knowledge."[19]

The message from some of the evidence is that task specific training may be necessary for performance because outcome feedback is not sufficient.[20] The authors concluded, "Tasks that receive mainly outcome feedback but show good performance by experts (e.g., identifying controls that should be in place) are those for which there is extensive, well-developed theory. Conversely, tasks that receive a large amount of feedback but show poor performance by experts (e.g., developing specific expectations about the balance of each account) are those with virtually no instruction because there are no well-developed theories of task performance. The lack of theories prohibits learning from outcome feedback."[21] Identification of the nature of the audit tasks (e.g., complexity) at a highly detailed level is useful in developing theories (and thus training material) to provide training to auditors.

As some researchers have argued, one of the objectives of judgment and decision-making research in auditing is training enhancement.[22] Training (and decision aids) can be used as alternatives to learning from experience which has implications for lowering the cost of performing a task and developing expertise on the task. Given more

---

18. C. E. Grease, 1984, "Accounting for Change," *World* 18, pp. 16–17; and J. R. Keith, 1985, "Expert Systems in Auditing: A Practitioner's Perspective" (paper presented at the 1985 Price Waterhouse Auditing Symposium, Lake Tahoe).

19. S. Bonner and N. Pennington, 1991, "Cognitive Processes and Knowledge as Determinants of Auditor Expertise," p. 27.

20. S. Bonner and N. Pennington, 1991, "Cognitive Processes and Knowledge as Determinants of Auditor Expertise," pp. 1–50.

21. Ibid., p. 36

22. I. Solomon and M. D. Shields, 1995, "Judgment and Decision Making Research in Auditing," in R. H. Ashton and A. H. Ashton (eds.), *Judgment and Decision Making Research in Accounting and Auditing* (New York: Cambridge University Press), pp. 137–175.

opportunities to practice the task, as well as "timely, accurate, complete and useful feedback,"[23] contributes to a high quality learning environment and therefore better performance on the task.

The literature reviewed indicates that task structure, knowledge base, and appropriate decision aids need to be investigated at a highly detailed task level to assist in understanding of expertise and the development of decision aids and training programs in auditing. This study provides a data base on complexity, knowledge base, and appropriate decision aids for a comprehensive inventory of audit tasks.

Benefits to Students

Because the audit task inventory is so comprehensive it should be useful for auditing classes and training programs. The inventory provides a detailed level description of what students will be expected to do in their future careers. The knowledge base data informs them when they will be expected to be performing specific parts of the audit.

A SHORT HISTORY OF THIS AREA OF STUDY

A systematic documentation and test of the interaction between task complexity and audit judgment was started in the mid-1980s. Two researchers used a large sample of auditors of varying experience levels as well as auditing students who made various audit judgments on several audit tasks.[24] These tasks were classified by their levels of task structure through an independent survey of 88 managers and partners in several of the then Big Eight accounting firms. The authors used this classification to investigate the effects of experience on audit judgments.

These authors found that while experience made a difference in audit judgment for unstructured and some of the semi-structured tasks, it did not make a difference in judgment of experienced and inexperienced participants for the structured audit tasks. This research was then supported by the KPMG Peat Marwick Research Opportunities in Auditing program to compile an inventory of audit tasks and to classify them by their level of task structure, experience level (defined as professional rank) and applicable decision aids. This

---

23. S. Bonner and N. Pennington, 1991, "Cognitive Processes and Knowledge as Determinants of Auditor Expertise," p. 37.

24. M. J. Abdolmohammadi and A. Wright, 1987, "An Examination of the Effects of Experience and Task Complexity on Audit Judgments," pp. 1–13.

work resulted in compilation of 332 audit tasks, various aspects of which have been reported in several articles.[25]

To compile this inventory of audit tasks, auditing texts, professional standards and audit manuals were consulted. A general framework in which the audit process was divided into five phases was used.[26] Adding financial reporting issues, the project resulted in six phases: Orientation, Understanding Control Structure, Tests of Controls, Substantive Tests, Forming Opinion, and Financial Statement Reporting. This framework was then expanded to include audit tasks from the audit manuals of three international accounting firms as well as the auditing literature and an auditing text.[27]

The current study (hereafter referred to as the 1996 study) builds on the previous one (hereafter referred to as the 1988 study), but differs from it in several important ways.[28] The first is that a more comprehensive search of the audit manuals, auditing texts, and the authoritative literature (e.g., the Canadian Institute of Chartered Accountants [CICA] Handbook[29]) was undertaken than for the previous study. This search resulted in an identification of 433 tasks as compared with the 332 in the previous study. Second, the proxy for experience used in the previous study was the auditors' professional

25. M. J. Abdolmohammadi, 1991a, "Factors Affecting Auditor's Perceptions of Applicable Decision Aids for Various Audit Tasks," pp. 535–548; M. J. Abdolmohammadi, 1991b, "A Test of the Relationship Between Task Structure and Decision Aid Type in Auditing," pp. 131–142; M. J. Abdolmohammadi and M. S. Bazaz, 1991, "Identification of Tasks for Expert Systems Development in Auditing," *Expert Systems With Applications* 3 (1), pp. 99–108; and M. J. Abdolmohammadi, 1999, "A Comprehensive Taxonomy of Task Structure and Knowledge Base Demands in Auditing" *Behavioral Research in Accounting* 11, pp. 51–92.

26. This framework is described in W. L. Felix, Jr. and W. R. Kinney Jr., 1982, "Research in the Auditor's Opinion Formulation Process: State of the Art," *The Accounting Review* 57 (2), pp. 245–271.

27. While it was desirable to consult more audit manuals than the three used in the study, in a personal conversation with Professor James Loebbecke (who along with Professor Barry Cushing had studied the audit manuals of the 14 largest accounting firms in B. E. Cushing and J. K. Loebbecke, 1986, "Comparison of Audit Methodologies of Large Accounting Firms,") he indicated that they all cover essentially the same audit tasks, although different methods of organization and wording are used to define the tasks.

28. The dates of the studies refer to the year in which data were collected for the studies.

29. Canadian Institute of Chartered Accountants, 1994, *CICA Handbook, Volume I and II* (Toronto: Canadian Institute of Chartered Accountants).

rank. Through the review process, it became obvious that some reviewers had difficulty with this definition on the ground that it is a more gross definition than the years of audit experience. In the current study, we collected data on experience in two different ways: years of audit experience and the number of supervised instances of a task before the auditor is viewed as experienced enough to perform the task independently.

In addition to providing a more current, more comprehensive audit task inventory as a result of the study along with experienced auditors' assessments of those tasks along task structure, knowledge base, and decision aids, we also provide a comparison with data from the previous study. As indicated below and in more detail in Chapters 7 and 8, there were not many significant differences in assessments of the tasks over the eight-year period.

A SUMMARY OF FINDINGS

The method of research is described in Chapter 6. We collected data from 44 managers and partners of several offices of the then Big Six accounting firms as well as a regional office in northeastern United States. We attempted to collect data from Canadian firms as well, but failed to collect a sufficient number of responses for meaningful statistical analysis. Specifically, after several attempts, we received only one response from a Big Six office in Canada and only four responses from Canadian Certified General Accountants. Consequently, we limited our study to the participants from the United States although we included the response from the Big Six Canadian office. Overall, the participating auditors possessed 9.48 years of experience with a 4.96 standard deviation. Their experience ranged from 4 to 24 years.

To achieve research objective number one, an inventory of 433 audit tasks was compiled as described and presented in Chapter 5. Chapter 7 provides descriptive data at the individual task level. Detailed data on task structure, experience level, supervised instances, and decision aid choices of subjects are presented in Tables 7.1 to 7.48 to satisfy research objectives two to four. Tables in Chapter 8 present correlation analysis and logistic regression results to investigate the hypothesized relationships between task structure, audit experience, supervised instances of practice, and decision aids to satisfy the fifth, and final, research objective. Where possible, comparison data are provided from the 1988 study, at the individual task level, by audit phase, and in the aggregate.

For the aggregate data by audit phase and for the audit tasks taken as a whole, strong support was found for all hypotheses. Namely, the correlation coefficients were all positive and the logistic regressions were significant at the .01 level (with one exception that was at the .03 level) for the task-structure/experience, task-structure/supervised-instances, and task-structure/decision-aids relationships. However, significant variations in the level of significance were observed between audit phases that indicated analysis at the individual task level within each phase of the audit was warranted.

Task-specific analyses reported in tables 7.1 to 7.48 revealed three general observations. First, in general, as the assessed degree of task structure increases, the coefficient of variation decreases indicating that there is more consensus among auditors for less structured tasks than for more structured tasks. Second, there were very few significant differences in assessed task structure from 1988 to 1996. Notable differences were in the Investments subphase of substantive tests where the tasks were judged to be less structured in 1996 and the Forming Opinion and Financial Reporting phases where some tasks were considered to be more structured in 1996 than in 1988. Third, the significant differences in task structure over time were generally consistent with changing perceptions about decision aid applicability for those tasks. A discussion of the conclusions and implications of these results is provided in Chapter 9.

Chapter 2

Task Structure

In this chapter we first provide a motivation for the study of task structure. We then discuss how the concept of task structure relates to the broader construct of task complexity. We then provide some discussion of task models that might be used in conjunction with the comprehensive task inventory for future research on auditing tasks. Finally, we describe a particular model of task structure that provides the basis for the current study. In Chapter 3 we hypothesize that task structure will be related to the level of experience required to perform a specific task. In Chapter 4, hypotheses are presented that relate to the expected relationship between task structure and the perceived suitability of various decision aids to perform the task.

THE IMPORTANCE OF TASK STRUCTURE

For several reasons the current study focuses on task structure as opposed to difficulty or complexity. One motivation for providing structure assessments at a detailed task level was provided by a recent review paper on the subject of audit structure.[1] The author finds that looking at the overall structure of the audit firm may not provide very useful guidance in studying how auditors make specific decisions. Accordingly, the author concludes that "firm-level measures of structure may not be sufficient when examining specific tasks, and researchers may need to become familiar with firm-specific policies and employ task-level structure measures in future studies." The

---

1. A. R. Bowrin, 1998, "Review and Synthesis of Audit Structure Literature," *Journal of Accounting Literature* 17, pp. 40–71.

task structure data then will benefit researchers who study auditor behavior and decision making in the context of specific auditing tasks.

In addition to reporting on the task structure data for its own merit, having the data allows us to explore the relationship between structure and other important aspects of the auditing tasks. For example, the level of task structure has been associated with auditors' experience level.[2] Previous research indicates that as the task becomes less structured the level of experience required to perform the task independently increases[3] and that performance differences are more pronounced for less structured tasks.[4] The level of task structure has also been associated with the task's appropriateness for decision aid development.[5]

TASK COMPLEXITY AND TASK STRUCTURE

Task structure generally relates to how well specified the task is.[6] A relatively recent review paper[7] in the auditing literature indicates that task structure is one component of task complexity with task difficulty being the other component. The author presented her own

---

2. M. J. Abdolmohammadi and A. Wright, 1987, "An Examination of the Effects of Experience and Task Complexity on Audit Judgments," *The Accounting Review* 62 (1), pp. 1–13 is frequently cited as a reason for expecting that auditors with differing levels of experience will perform differently in unstructured tasks.

3. See M. J. Abdolmohammadi, 1999, "A Comprehensive Taxonomy of Task Structure and Knowledge Base Demands in Auditing," *Behavioral Research in Accounting* 11, pp. 51–92.

4. M. J. Abdolmohammadi and A. Wright, 1987, "An Examination of the Effects of Experience and Task Complexity on Audit Judgments," pp. 1–13

5. See, for example,   G. A. Gorry and M. S. Scott-Morton, 1971, "A Framework for Management Information Systems," *Sloan Management Review* (Fall), pp. 55–70; P. G. W. Keen and M. S. Scott-Morton, 1978, *Decision Support Systems: An Organizational Perspective* (Reading, Mass: Addison-Wesley); M. J. Abdolmohammadi, 1991a, "Factors Affecting Auditor's Perceptions of Applicable Decision Aids for Various Audit Tasks," *Contemporary Accounting Research* 7 (2), pp. 535–548 and M. J. Abdolmohammadi, 1991b, "A Test of the Relationship between Task Structure and Decision Aid Type in Auditing" in *Auditing: Advances in Applied Behavioral Research*, L. A. Ponemon and D. R. L. Gabhart (eds.), (New York: Springer-Verlag Publishing), pp. 131–142.

6. H. Simon, 1973, "The Structure of Ill-Structured Problems," *Artificial Intelligence*, pp. 181–201.

7. See S. E. Bonner, 1994, "A Model of the Effects of Audit Task Complexity" *Accounting, Organizations and Society* 19 (3), pp. 213–234.

version of a task complexity model to help readers understand how task complexity affects audit task performance. A review paper[8] in the more general management literature describes various types of task models that have been presented by researchers. One of the simpler models[9] describes task complexity by the number of alternatives and the number of attributes to consider for each alternative. A very detailed model[10] measures task complexity by evaluating three constructs: component complexity, coordinative complexity and dynamic complexity. These models, intended to measure task complexity, also include elements of task structure. A task that has few alternatives or few components is naturally more structured than one that has more alternatives or more components. Another model[11] offers a way to think about tasks strictly in terms of their structure, by considering the nature of the Intelligence, Design, and Choice phases of the decision process.

TASK MODELS

Task complexity is multifaceted and multidefinitional.[12] A review paper in the management domain[13] provides several candidates for task complexity characterization according to three approaches found in the literature. The author lists these approaches as: (1) a psychological perspective, (2) an interaction between the task and the task performer, and (3) based purely on the objective characteristics of the task.[14] Table 2.1 summarizes these perspectives.

Those who take a purely psychological view to the study of task complexity are interested in the task performer's psychological

8. D. J. Campbell, 1988, "Task Complexity: A Review and Analysis," *Academy of Management Review* 13 (1), pp. 40–52.

9. J. Payne, 1976, "Task Complexity and Contingent Processing in Decision-Making: An Information Search and Protocol Analysis," *Organizational Behavior and Human Processing* 16, pp. 300–316.

10. R. E. Wood, 1986, "Task Complexity: Definition of the Construct," *Organizational Behavior and Human Decision Processes* 37, pp. 60–82.

11. H. Simon, 1960, *The New Science of Management* (New York: Harper and Row).

12. For a discussion along these lines, see S. Bonner and N. Pennington, 1991, "Cognitive Processes and Knowledge as Determinants of Auditor Expertise," *Journal of Accounting Literature* 10, pp. 1–50.

13. D. J. Campbell, 1988, "Task Complexity: A Review and Analysis," pp. 40–52.

14. Ibid., p. 40.

Table 2.1
Categories of Task Complexity Models

Perspective	Definition
1. Psychological view	Task difficulty is determined by the person's feelings about the task.
2. Person-task interaction	Task difficulty depends on person's abilities compared to task requirements.
3. Objective task characteristics	Task difficulty is determined by measuring some objective characteristic(s) of the task and comparing it to other tasks measured in the same way.

reaction to the task. For example, the subjects may be asked how challenging they felt the task was. The person's subjective feelings about the task determine its level of complexity in this type of research. One of the interests in this line of research is to determine how the perceived complexity of the task affects the task performer's motivation.

The second approach looks at the interaction between the abilities of the person performing the task and the complexity of the task. A task would be considered to be more, or less, complex depending on the level of specific abilities required by the task compared to the level of those specific abilities possessed by the task performer.

The third view of task complexity is based on objective characteristics of the tasks. We provide some limited discussion below of specific task models that may be used in future research that studies task complexity at a more detailed level. These models would be classified under this third view of task complexity.

Typology of Complex Tasks

In a review article in the management research literature,[15] the author presents a "typology of complex tasks" based on the objective characteristics of tasks. Sixteen task "types" are described, based on the presence or absence of four common task characteristics:

---

15. Ibid., p. 45.

1. multiple potential ways (i.e. paths) to arrive at desired end-state;
2. multiple desired outcomes (i.e. end-states) to be attained;
3. conflicting interdependence among paths to multiple desired outcomes; and
4. uncertain or probabilistic linkages among paths and outcomes.

The least complex task has none of the complexity dimensions listed above while the most complex task has all four dimensions. Examples of the 16 combinations of these dimensions include judgment tasks, problem tasks, and fuzzy tasks. Judgment tasks are described as requiring the performer to determine which information cues to consider, how to weight the cues, and then how to combine the cues to arrive at a judgment. Problem tasks are characterized by many potential paths to a well-specified desired outcome. For these tasks, there may be uncertainty as to how each path is related to the desired outcome. Fuzzy tasks have more than one desired outcome and multiple paths to achieve them.

Alternatives and Attributes

Another candidate for characterizing task complexity is based on the number of alternatives from which one may choose and the number of attributes to be considered.[16]   Using this model, a subsequent study[17] explored the effect of task complexity on the choice of various decision heuristics. The study varied tasks on the two dimensions suggested, number of attributes and number of alternatives, as well as in terms of time pressure imposed on the person making the choice. Considering the cost/benefit trade-off of making a decision (or choice), one would choose a less effortful decision strategy (some type of decision heuristic) as long as the outcome is not of a noticeably lower quality than a more effortful strategy.

The authors approached the study of this phenomenon from two perspectives. First, they used computer simulation to test the effects of using less effortful decision heuristics as opposed to more effortful

16. J. Payne, 1976, "Task Complexity and Contingent Processing in Decision-Making: An Information Search and Protocol Analysis," pp. 300–316.

17. J. Payne, J. Bettman, and E. Johnson, 1988, "Adaptive Strategy Selection and Decision Making," *Journal of Experimental Psychology* 16 (3), pp. 534–552.

normative decision strategies. They found that heuristics provided comparable accuracy for much less effort in many instances. When the element of time pressure was added, decision heuristics were more successful than normative strategies. With many of the decision heuristics, a decision can be made more quickly than with the normative strategy. If one does not have time to complete the normative strategy, the response from a truncated normative strategy is of much lower quality than the choice resulting from the decision heuristic.

The second phase of the study was to investigate how actual decision makers fared in comparing heuristics to normative approaches. They found that decision makers did vary their decision making strategies depending on the characteristics of the task: number of alternatives, number of attributes, and amount of time pressure. The task used for this study involved choosing between several gambles where the number of gambles to choose from and the number of payoffs within each gamble were varied. The authors concluded that people adapt decision strategies to the task and its environment. Based on simulation results showing minimal degradation of accuracy for substantial savings, the authors also concluded that adaptation can be beneficial.

A Detailed Model of Task Complexity

A detailed model[18] dedicated to explaining task complexity was intended to define tasks independently of the person performing the task and the environment surrounding the task. Such an approach provides the benefit of being able to study tasks per se. The author argues that this approach is the only one that offers construct validity. The advantage is that one can develop a characterization of the task that can be used consistently in various environments and with various persons performing the task. When tasks are studied within context (combining the effects of the environment and the task performer with those of the task), theoretical models become highly complex in nature. An alternative approach is to determine the complexity of the task itself and then to study the effects of the environment and the task performer incrementally.

The model is expected to be general enough to apply to all types of tasks (mechanical as well as judgment tasks). Tasks are described as consisting of three elements: products, required acts, and information

---

18. R. E. Wood, 1986, "Task Complexity: Definition of the Construct," pp. 60–82.

cues.[19] The product must be explicitly and specifically stated as the desired result of the acts.

The model defines three types of task complexity: component, coordinative, and dynamic.[20] Component complexity of a task is measured by summing over all subtasks the number of information cues used. The larger the number of cues, the more complex the task. The second type, coordinative complexity, is measured by summing over all acts required by a task, the number of precedence relationships that exist. If some acts must be performed before others or one act provides input into a subsequent act within the same task, then coordinative complexity is increased. Where there are interactions between the acts, coordinative complexity is also increased. The relationship between the acts and the product also influences coordinative complexity. If the relationship between performance of the acts and the resulting product are subject to random effects there is more coordinative complexity than if performing the acts definitely results in attainment of the product.

The third type of task complexity is dynamic complexity which measures the magnitude of the impact of outside influences on the relationships between acts and the product. The measure of dynamic complexity is the sum of changes in the component and coordinative complexity over time. An additional term may be added to capture the predictability of the changes over time. The less predictable the changes in component and coordinative complexity, the higher is the measure of dynamic complexity and, therefore, the more complex the task.

For tasks that can be analyzed in this way, conclusions may be drawn about different outcomes achieved across studies. The effect of the complexity of the task may be separated from the effects of other factors such as the knowledge and skill level of the person performing the task as well as environmental factors such as time pressure. Without a way to measure the objective complexity of the task itself, it is difficult to properly attribute differences in performance across tasks to the various factors involved. Four models (the three described above and Simon's model) based on objective task characteristics are summarized in Table 2.2.

---

19. Ibid., p. 64.
20. Ibid., p. 66.

Table 2.2
Task Models Based on Objective Task Characteristics

Source	Description
Campbell (1988)	Number of paths to achieve desired outcome(s), relationship between paths, and relationship between paths and outcome(s) determine task complexity.
Payne (1976) Payne et al. (1988)	Number of alternatives and number of attributes to consider in making choice determine task complexity.
Wood (1986)	Products, desired acts and information cues are studied to determine component, coordinative, and dynamic complexity for each task.
Simon (1960)	Intelligence, design and choice phases of decision are analyzed to determine whether task is structured, semistructured or unstructured.

Simon's Model

Simon's characterization of tasks is described by three decision phases: Intelligence, Design, and Choice.[21]   In the first phase, Intelligence, the person scans the environment to find the decision that must be made. This phase involves understanding the problem and its context in order to define the problem. The second phase, Design, consists of gathering information about the problem, developing various alternative courses of action and identifying their consequences. The third phase, Choice, is where the person chooses one of the alternative courses of action developed in the design phase based on an analysis of the data, or a synthesis of the literature. These phases of the decision process are depicted in Table 2.3.

Table 2.3 provides a way to translate Simon's three decision phases into steps that can be taken by a task performer. Within the Intelligence phase, one is expected to identify the problem, identify the objectives to be satisfied in solving the problem, develop key words that will allow the person to collect relevant data related to the problem, and to develop a structure for the problem by breaking it down into understandable components.

Within the Design phase, one is expected to collect data about the problem or to research the problem in the professional literature, to put any quantitative data into a form that will be appropriate for

---

21. The origins of this framework were presented in H. Simon, 1960, *The New Science of Management*.

Table 2.3

Decision Phases according to Simon's Model of the Decision Process

Decision Phase	Steps in the Process	Purpose
A. Intelligence	1. Identify the problem.	Determine the nature of the problem.
	2. Identify objectives.	Specify detailed objectives of the problem.
	3. Develop key words.	Begin the search process.
	4. Structure problem.	Break the problem into structured components.
B. Design	1. Gather data.	Collect data about the problem.
	2. Code data.	Code the data into a form useful for analysis.
	3. Generate alternatives.	Identify alternative courses of action.
	4. Determine consequences. of the alternatives.	Quantify the risks and values related to the alternative courses of action.
C. Choice	1. Analyze data or synthesize literature.	Use a quantitative or qualitative process to make sense of the data and the literature.
	2. Choose among alternatives.	Make a choice among alternatives.
	3. Explain choice.	Communicate the reasons for the choice.
	4. Develop implementation plan.	Present a practical, step-by-step implementation plan.

Source: Adapted from M. J. Abdolmohammadi and R. McQuade, *Applied Research in Financial Reporting: Text and Cases* (New York: Irwin/McGraw-Hill, forthcoming).

analysis, to identify alternative courses of action that could be taken to solve the problem and to quantify the risks and benefits associated with each alternative course of action to assist the decision maker in the next phase, Choice.

In the final phase of the decision process, Choice, the decision maker follows the steps of analyzing the data or synthesizing the professional literature, choosing among alternative courses of action, explaining the reasons for the particular choice, and developing an implementation plan. This is where quantitative or qualitative data analysis is performed to make sense of data or evidence from the literature, as a means of assisting in making a choice among alternatives. From this vantage point, the decision maker communicates the reasons for the choice and presents a practical, step-by-step implementation plan.

SELECTED RESEARCH USING TASK COMPLEXITY

Operationally, empirical studies of task complexity have been heavily influenced by early models of task structure and complexity.[22] Several studies have been based on a fairly simple model that defines complexity as a function of the number of alternative courses of action and the number of attributes in each alternative.[23] In fact, in a paper on decision models,[24] the authors stated that the most common and successful manipulation of task complexity is changing the number of alternative courses of action. Several studies provide empirical evidence that the number of alternatives has a significant impact on decision making behavior. For example, in one study[25] the number of alternative brands and the attributes within each brand were varied to study the information processing strategies of decision makers in their purchasing choices. Another study[26] found that of various dimensions of complexity examined (the number of brands, the number of attributes, the variability of information on the attributes, and the dominance of attributes), the number of brands had the greatest impact on the subjects' consumer decision making behavior.

Similar results have been reported in the auditing literature. In one study,[27] the researchers operationalized task complexity by varying the number of companies to consider in choosing the company with the highest bond rating. They found that auditors took more

22. For example, J. March and H. Simon, 1958, *Organizations* (New York: Wiley); and H. Simon, 1960, *The New Science of Management.*

23. J. Payne, 1976, "Task Complexity and Contingent Processing in Decision-Making: An Information Search and Protocol Analysis," pp. 300–316.

24. R. S. Billings and S. A. Marcus, 1983, "Measures of Compensatory and Noncompensatory Models of Decision Behavior: Process Tracing versus Policy Capturing," *Organizational Behavior and Human Performance* 31 (1), pp. 331–352.

25. C. Kim and M. Khoury, 1987, "Task Complexity and Contingent Information Processing in the Case of Couple's Decision Making," *Academy of Marketing Science* 15 (3), pp. 32–43.

26. M. L. Ursic and J. G. Helgeson, 1990, "The Impact of Choice Phase and Task Complexity on Consumer Decision Making, " *Journal of Business Research* 21, pp. 69–90.

27. L. Paquette and T. Kida, 1988, "The Effects of Decision Strategy and Task Complexity on Decision Performance," *Organizational Behavior and Human Decision Processes* 41, pp. 128–142.

time and made less accurate decisions as the number of alternative companies in the experiment increased. A subsequent study confirmed these findings.[28]

A review article on audit task complexity[29] has defined complexity in terms of the amount and clarity of input, processing, and output of the task. These components of the decision process are in general, similar to the intelligence, design and choice phases in Simon's model of the decision process. For example, the input component of the model considers the amount and clarity of cues which can be viewed as similar to the intelligence component in Simon's model where cues related to the problem are considered to classify it as well-defined, reasonably defined or ill-defined. Similarly, the amount and clarity of the number of alternatives and cues in the processing component is similar to the number of alternative courses of action considered in the design component of Simon's model. Finally, in the output component of the model the amount and clarity of the number of goals and solutions are considered. Simon's model includes this in the choice component where judgment and/or insight is used in choosing among alternative courses of action.

Based on Simon's characterization of task complexity,[30] an auditing study[31] hypothesizes that experience effects would be positively related to task complexity. The researchers expected that experience effects would be significantly greater for unstructured tasks than for structured tasks. Six auditing tasks were incorporated into three cases for which subjects made judgments. The tasks had been previously classified by experienced auditors as belonging to a structured, semistructured, or unstructured category. In the same survey, these auditors indicated the level of experience required for each task.

The authors studied the responses of experienced versus inexperienced subjects and their performance on two unstructured tasks, three semistructured tasks and one structured task. Experienced subjects were identified as those who had at least the requisite experience level to perform the task independently (as determined in the aforementioned survey). Inexperienced subjects

28. T. Kida, J. Cohen, and L. Paquette, 1990, "The Effect of Cue Categorization and Modeling Techniques on the Assessment of Cue Importance," *Decision Sciences* 21, pp. 357–372.

29. S. E. Bonner, 1994, "A Model of the Effects of Audit Task Complexity," pp. 213–234.

30. H. Simon, 1960, *The New Science of Management*.

31. M. J. Abdolmohammadi and A. Wright, 1987, "An Examination of the Effects of Experience and Task Complexity on Audit Judgments," pp. 1–13.

were those who did not have the required experience level. The results show a significant difference in judgments made between experienced (managers and partners) and inexperienced (students, seniors and supervisors) subjects for unstructured tasks. There were significant differences for two of the semistructured tasks and marginally significant differences for the third semistructured task. The results related to the structured task are not meaningful since the decision in the task depended directly on the outcome of the semistructured task and there was high variability in the decisions made across experience levels for that task.

Another study[32] provided data on levels of task difficulty (and criticalness) for 60 audit tasks. They asked over 350 auditors from Big Eight, national and other auditing firms for their *perceptions* about the difficulty of each task. The authors observe that tasks for which auditors must evaluate and aggregate information were considered more difficult than those for which they had to gather information or apply some statistical procedure. The results of the study are not based on objective characteristics of the tasks. The data, however, could be compared to that obtained from objective analyses of tasks to provide further insight into the nature of auditing tasks.

POTENTIAL APPLICATIONS OF TASK COMPLEXITY MODELS IN AUDITING RESEARCH

Based on the objective description of tasks using a "typology of complex tasks,"[33] many auditing tasks would be classified as judgment, problem or fuzzy tasks. One auditing researcher described judgment task elements as including "task predictability, the number of cues, the intercorrelations of the cues, the distribution of validities, and several other characteristics."[34] This definition provided in the auditing literature is consistent with a more general description of judgment tasks as requiring the performer to determine which pieces of information to consider, how to weigh the information, and then

---

32. W. C. Chow, A. H. McNamee, and R. D. Plumlee, 1987, "Practitioners' Perceptions of Audit Step Difficulty and Criticalness: Implications for Audit Research," *Auditing: A Journal of Practice and Theory* 6 (2), pp. 123–133.

33. See D. J. Campbell, 1988, "Task Complexity: A Review and Analysis," pp. 40–52.

34. R. H. Ashton, 1982, *Human Information Processing in Accounting* (Sarasota, Fla.: American Accounting Association), p. 186.

how to combine them to arrive at a judgment.[35] Typically some of the difficulty arises due to the relationship between the various pieces of information (e.g., are they consistent, contradictory, and/or correlated?) and the relationship between each piece of information and the resulting outcomes.

Some auditing tasks may be classified as problem tasks, having many potential paths to a well-specified desired outcome. For problem tasks, it may not be evident how each path is related to the desired outcome. In addition to the characteristics they share with problem tasks (multiple paths to achieve the desired goal), fuzzy tasks have more than one desired outcome.

The psychology literature[36] indicates that using decision heuristics may be more beneficial, on a cost-benefit basis, than having the decision maker perform the task using a normative strategy. A normative strategy may take more time but may not provide commensurately more benefit. These studies also found that when there was time pressure, as there frequently is in an audit, the use of decision heuristics resulted in more accurate outcomes than using a normative strategy that had to be truncated due to time constraints. One implication of this research for auditing relates to the design of decision aids. For certain auditing tasks, low cost (low effort) decision strategies may be employed with adequate resulting levels of accuracy. The risk in applying psychological research results to problems in the auditing domain is that contextual factors in the auditing domain may preclude using simplified decision heuristics for some situations. Given that tasks could be identified as suitable for successful application of decision heuristics, savings (and increased accuracy when there is time pressure) may be achieved.

To understand the effect of auditor choice strategies, one must consider the effects on both cost and benefit aspects. To move forward in improving the audit process in light of increasing pressure to reduce the cost of the audit, this type of research may prove fruitful. Heuristic strategies for making choices in the auditing domain may be pursued more aggressively and implemented, resulting in less processing time and acceptable effectiveness levels. There is the potential for much research to be done in this area creating a need for extensive and detailed analysis of the very specific auditing tasks as provided by the current study.

---

35. See D. J. Campbell, 1988, "Task Complexity: A Review and Analysis," pp. 40–52.

36. J. Payne, J. Bettman, and E. Johnson, 1988, "Adaptive Strategy Selection and Decision Making," pp. 534–552.

A more advanced model[37] provides an opportunity to greatly advance knowledge of auditing tasks. As discussed earlier, the objective characterization of task complexity should allow for more systematic study of tasks. Auditing tasks could be analyzed according to Wood's model to determine their overall level of complexity. For example, one of the tasks listed in the Orientation phase of the task inventory is "the performance of analytical review of interim financial statements to identify potential accounting or auditing problems affecting current year." The product of this task would be a listing of potential accounting or auditing problems. The acts required to produce this product consist of identification of problems and performance of analytical review. For this example, the third characteristic, information cues, would consist of the financial information that provides the input for analytical review.

To measure component complexity, one would consider each ratio or financial result being compared as part of analytical review and the number of information cues going into each comparison. There is a fair degree of coordinative complexity associated with analytical review since it is the pattern of financial results and ratios that is important to understanding the potential accounting and auditing problems rather than just the sum of the ratios themselves. Dynamic complexity relates to the effect outside factors have on the interpretation of comparative financial information to inform potential accounting or auditing problems. For each individual auditing task, the analysis would be substantial to determine the elements of complexity according to Wood's model but such an analysis could be performed for a limited number of tasks at a time. By determining the sources of complexity: component, coordinative and/or dynamic, auditing researchers would gain more insight into the nature of auditor ability and performance. One would be able to identify what type of complexity contributes more to the source of difficulty of various auditing tasks.

SIMON'S (1960) MODEL AND TASK STRUCTURE

The decision phases described by Simon (1960) are useful for a classification of judgment and decision making tasks by their level of structure: structured, semistructured, or unstructured.[38]   By

---

37. See R. E. Wood, 1986, "Task Complexity: Definition of the Construct," pp. 60–82.

38. G. A. Gorry and M. S. Scott-Morton, 1971, "A Framework for Management Information Systems," pp. 55–70.

considering the nature of the task within the three decision phases, one can classify tasks along a structured to unstructured continuum. Table 2.4 shows the relationship between decision phases and the levels of task structure.[39]

Structured tasks are those for which the problem is well defined in the Intelligence phase, alternative solutions are very limited in the Design phase, and very little judgment is needed to make a final choice at the Choice phase of the decision process. These tasks are generally "simple" and "programmable." An example of these tasks is the computation of depreciation expense for an equipment where all aspects of the problem are specified (e.g., use straight line method of depreciation for a five year property with no salvage value).

In unstructured tasks, the problem is ill-defined at the Intelligence phase, and/or the alternative solutions may be numerous at the Design phase, thus requiring the decision maker to use considerable judgment and insight to choose an alternative at the Choice phase of the decision process. These tasks are viewed as highly "complex" and "nonprogrammable" or "unstructured." An example of these tasks is the determination of the type of an audit report (unqualified, qualified, adverse, or disclaimer) to issue for a financially troubled client.

Somewhere between the "programmable to nonprogrammable" or "structured to unstructured" continuum are tasks with a medium level of structure. These tasks may be called "semiprogrammable" or

Table 2.4
Decision Phases and Task Characteristics

Decision Phase	TASK STRUCTURE		
	Structured	Semistructured	Unstructured
Intelligence: Problem is	well defined	reasonably defined	ill defined
Design: Alternatives are	well specified	limited, specified	numerous
Choice: Requires	no judgment	some judgment	judgment and insight

39. The discussion here is based on P. G. W. Keen and M. S. Scott-Morton, 1978, *Decision Support Systems: An Organizational Perspective*; and H. Simon, 1960, *The New Science of Management*.

"semistructured." The problem in these tasks is reasonably defined at the Intelligence phase, alternative solutions are limited and specified at the Design phase, leaving some judgment to the decision maker in choosing among the alternatives at the Choice phase of the decision process. An example of semistructured tasks is the internal control evaluation in auditing.

Appropriateness of Simon's Model for the Current Study

Since the purpose of this study is to relate auditing task structure to knowledge base requirement and type of decision aid, Simon's model provides the best characterization of tasks for this purpose. For a very practical reason, the evaluation made for each task in the current study had to be fairly simple. Because each participating auditor was evaluating a large number of tasks (144 or 145 tasks in the 1996 study and 332 tasks in the 1988 study), the assessment metric had to be easily understood as well as easily applied to each individual task. Since structure has been frequently associated with the suitability of a task for decision aid development, a straight forward, well-established framework such as Simon's is the best candidate for the purpose of the current study. In Chapter 3, we discuss the expected relationships between task structure and knowledge base and provide related research hypotheses. The discussion and research hypotheses in Chapter 4 relate to the relationship between task structure and a suitable decision aid.

Chapter 3

Task-Specific Knowledge Base

General audit experience has traditionally been viewed as the basis for superior performance in various audit tasks. For example, some behavioral studies have focused on audit experience, measured in number of years of practice, as a proxy for knowledge. The rationale has been that auditors improve their general audit knowledge through experience that results in superior performance. Recent auditing research, however, has provided only partial support for this view. For example, research indicates that while experienced auditors perform semi-structured and unstructured tasks more effectively and efficiently than inexperienced auditors, the experienced and inexperienced auditors do not differ in their performance of structured tasks.[1] In fact, a stream of new research indicates that task-specific knowledge, rather than general audit knowledge, is needed for superior performance.[2] A conclusion from this line of research is that while auditors with more years of experience have more knowledge in general, most of the explanatory power for

---

1. See M. J. Abdolmohammadi and A. Wright, 1987, "An Examination of the Effects of Experience and Task Complexity on Audit Judgments" *The Accounting Review* 62 (1): 1–13.

2. For a detailed review of these studies see R. Libby, 1995, "The Role of Knowledge and Memory in Audit Judgment" in R. H. Ashton and A. H. Ashton (eds.), *Judgment and Decision Making Research in Accounting and Auditing* (New York: Cambridge University Press), pp. 176–206.

performance on specific tasks is provided by variables which reflect task-specific training and experience.[3]

In this chapter, we discuss the issues related to a knowledge base for auditing and the determinants of superior performance on auditing tasks. First, we present a simple model that specifies the links between experience, knowledge, and performance. Next, we review auditing research that has explored the nature of the links in this model. In the third section we discuss the relationship between experience and expertise and what may promote the development of expertise or superior performance in the auditing domain. The final section is the conclusion to the chapter where two research hypotheses for the relationship between task structure (as discussed in Chapter 2) and knowledge base are specified.

A MODEL OF TASK PERFORMANCE

A model of the relationship among experience, knowledge, and ability, and their impact on performance is provided in Figure 3.1.[4] According to the model, an auditor must have both experience (Link 1) and an appropriate level of ability (Link 2) which allows him or her to gain knowledge. The knowledge the auditor has, as well as his or her ability, then determine how well the auditor will perform the task (Links 3 and 4).

Many of the research studies on auditor judgment explicitly measure the level of experience in years and assume that the participating auditors have acquired the appropriate knowledge during that time and have an adequate level of ability. Therefore, the researcher typically expects that certain levels of experience will result in higher levels of performance. Without considering the links made explicit in the model, researchers may not be justified in assuming that more experience automatically leads to better performance. Whether these links can be assumed to exist depends on the variation that exists in auditor ability levels at the same level of experience. Since ability affects both knowledge acquisition (Link 2) and performance (Link 4) directly, variance in ability levels for

---

3. For a discussion of this argument see S. Bonner and B. Lewis, 1990, "Determinants of Auditor Expertise," *Journal of Accounting Research* 28 (Supplement), p. 16.

4. Much of this discussion here is based on a review paper by R. Libby and J. Luft, 1993, "Determinants of Judgment Performance in Accounting Settings: Ability, Knowledge, Motivation, and Environment," *Accounting, Organizations and Society* 18 (5), pp. 425–450.

Figure 3.1
Model of the Relationship between Experience and Task
Performance

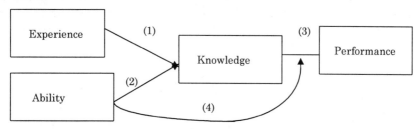

Source: Adapted from R. Libby, 1995, "The Role of Knowledge and Memory in Audit Judgment," in R. H. Ashton and A. H. Ashton (eds.), *Judgment and Decision Making Research in Accounting and Auditing* (New York: Cambridge University Press), pp. 176–206; and R. Libby and J. Luft, 1993, "Determinants of Judgment Performance in Accounting Settings: Ability, Knowledge, Motivation, and Environment," *Accounting, Organizations and Society* 18 (5), pp. 425–450.

auditors of similar years of experience could greatly affect performance.

Link (1), between experience and knowledge, may also be subject to variation. Auditors have different experiences within their lengths of service with the firm depending on the types of clients they may have had and the amount and type of audit specialization. Different experiences may provide knowledge bases that are unique enough to also result in varied performance levels among auditors with the same number of years of experience. For example, in an archival study of one accounting firm, experienced auditors did not show a possession of higher levels of error frequency knowledge as compared with inexperienced auditors.[5] On the other hand, an investigation of archival data from another accounting firm indicated that auditors engaged in the central research unit gain in efficiency and effectiveness with years of experience.[6]

It is important to note that many environmental and motivational factors influence ability and knowledge as determinants of performance. For example, decision aids used as part of an overall audit technology environment, can mitigate deficiencies in abilities

---

5. See A. H. Ashton, 1991, "Experience and Error Frequency Knowledge as Potential Determinants of Audit Expertise," *The Accounting Review* 66 (2), pp. 218–239.

6. See S. Salterio, 1994, "Researching for Accounting Precedents: Learning, Efficiency, and Effectiveness," *Contemporary Accounting Research* 11 (Fall), pp. 515–542.

and knowledge or improve these determinants of performance. Similarly, motivational factors such as accountability and performance-based bonus plans can improve an auditor's overall performance. The purpose of this chapter is not to enumerate, or discuss these factors.[7] However, we do discuss issues related to decision aids in detail in Chapter 4.

RESEARCH RELATED TO TASK PERFORMANCE

The auditing research that relates to the model presented in Figure 3.1 focuses mainly on the links among experience, knowledge and performance. There have been mixed results in the auditing research as to whether auditors of different levels of experience perform at significantly different levels. Recent research seems to support the idea that the relationship between experience and performance is dependent on the task itself and the task environment. Researchers, for example, have provided evidence that one reason for these mixed results may be that many studies have not matched the level at which auditors normally perform the tasks with the audit tasks investigated.[8]

The variation may also be due to different components of tasks benefiting from experience. One study focused on two specific auditing tasks, a control risk assessment and an analytical procedure risk assessment (assessment of detection risk for analytical review procedures) and two components of each task, cue selection and cue weighting. For cue selection, both experienced and inexperienced auditors performed better in selecting relevant cues for control risk assessment than for analytical procedure risk assessment. Experienced auditors performed better than inexperienced auditors in one firm only on the cue selection for the analytical review procedures risk. The experienced auditors in that firm also performed better than the experienced auditors in the other firm on the same task. An interesting observation is that the firm whose experienced auditors had superior performance had a decision aid (i.e., an environmental factor) that included guidance on identifying relevant cues for performing analytical review procedures. This study

---

7. The interested reader is referred to Libby and Luft, 1993, "Determinants of Judgment Performance in Accounting Settings," pp. 435–444, for a detailed discussion of environmental and motivational factors that influence ability and knowledge as determinants of performance.

8. See M. J. Abdolmohammadi, 1999, "A Comprehensive Taxonomy of Task Structure and Knowledge Base Demands in Auditing," *Behavioral Research in Accounting* 11, pp. 51–92.

concluded that the decision aid provided auditors with training that allowed them to gain *expertise* as they gained experience.[9] This study provided evidence that, all else being equal, the task environment had a significant influence on performance. In a second experiment, the author found differences in cue weighting agreement between experienced and inexperienced auditors. The difference between the two types of auditors' performance was larger for the more complex task, analytical review procedures assessment than for the less complex task of control risk assessment.

The results from this study indicate that the same type of task (cue selection) produces different performance results due to experience, depending on the setting. Experience related effects were found for cue selection, in one task (analytical review procedures) for one firm, but not for the other task (internal control assessment). The effect of experience was accentuated in the cue weighting process for the analytical review procedures, but not for the internal control assessment. These results indicate a need for more research at a detailed level to determine the effects of experience on performance in auditing tasks. The specific components of the task (cue selection versus cue weighting), and availability of firm guidance were shown to affect performance of experienced versus inexperienced auditors.

Another study attempted to identify, for four specific tasks, the effect of general audit experience on performance. The authors posit that factors that are more specific than general audit experience should explain significant variation in performance. They test for the effect of knowledge and ability as well as years of audit experience. The authors assessed knowledge and ability that were specifically related to the tasks. In addition, general problem solving ability was tested by the use of a portion of the Graduate Record Examination (GRE).[10]

The authors found that general audit experience explained very little of the variation in performance. The very specific measures of knowledge and ability were much better predictors of superior performance than was general audit experience. This study provides a model for future researchers to build toward theory development related to auditor knowledge and expertise. A reanalysis of the data in this study by two other researchers provided full support for the experience-knowledge link (Link 1) and the knowledge-performance

---

9. See S. E. Bonner, 1990, "Experience Effects in Auditing: The Role of Task-Specific Knowledge," *The Accounting Review* 65 (1), pp. 72–92.

10. See S. Bonner and B. Lewis, 1990, "Determinants of Auditor Expertise," pp. 1–20.

link (Link 3), but only partial support for the ability-knowledge link (Link 2).[11]

A question that has attracted research in the past is under what conditions do auditors gain knowledge which leads to better performance? Two researchers used the analytical review procedure of ratio analysis in audit planning to test this question. They found that the best influences on knowledge come from practice with explanatory feedback. Explanatory feedback provides the task performer with an explanation of why the outcome occurred; by relating task properties to the outcome. If the task performer has only outcome feedback, he or she may infer a relationship that is not correct. When they apply their own explanation during future performance of the task, poor performance may result.[12]

Explanatory feedback provides the task performer with the correct relationship which allows him or her to make better decisions in the future and to improve performance on the task. The analytical review procedure task studied by the researchers was complex enough to benefit from explanatory feedback. For more simple tasks, the task performer may be able to infer the correct rules from outcome feedback only. The researchers also found that initially providing instructions about how to perform the task, having the subject perform the task and then providing outcome feedback resulted in gains in knowledge that were comparable to providing explanatory feedback. These results further support the model depicted in Figure 3.1 implying that both ability and experience affect knowledge which influences performance.

EXPERIENCE AND EXPERTISE

As the discussion in the last section implies, the results of studies investigating the relationship between experience and expertise are mixed. It is not clear under what conditions experience and expertise can be assumed to be equal, and what conditions make them different. Recently, researchers have called for identification of specific tasks where experience alone results in the acquisition of

---

11. See R. Libby and H. T. Tan, 1994, "Modeling the Determinants of Audit Expertise," *Accounting, Organizations and Society* 19, pp. 701–716.

12. See S. Bonner and P. Walker, 1994, "The Effects of Instruction and Experience on the Acquisition of Auditing Knowledge," *The Accounting Review* 69 (1), pp. 157–178.

expertise (superior performance) in the task.[13] In partial response to this call, two authors analyzed the results of many audit studies and found that tasks with a good learning environment (adequate feedback, preferably outcome feedback) result in effective acquisition of expertise. Having been exposed to a particular task several times will only result in acquiring expertise if the task conditions are conducive to improving ability and increasing knowledge as a result of repeated performance of the task. An adequate learning environment was found to be a critical factor in those studies where "experts" (defined by the researcher, typically measured by years of experience) have been found to perform better than others. [14]

For *some* tasks, then, it is acceptable to equate experience with expertise. Some auditing tasks used in previous research studies (e.g., assessing inherent risk of accounting systems and identifying controls that should be in place) have already been identified as providing the necessary learning environment to make that assumption.[15] For these tasks, it may be appropriate to say that auditors with so many years of experience may be considered to be experts on that particular task. When such an assumption is being made for a new task, however, the researcher should determine whether the task contains the learning components specified above.[16] As a validity check, performance on the task should be measured to verify that there is a significant difference in the performance of those with more experience compared to those with less experience.[17]

The discussion above addresses those tasks where auditors with more task-specific experience perform better than auditors with less task-specific experience. Researchers have attempted to identify the elements of those tasks and task environment that are conducive to years of experience or practice with the task resulting in superior performance. For other tasks, where superior performance has not been observed even for very experienced auditors, *true* expertise (e.g., superior ability and knowledge base) may be the determining factor.

---

13. For example, see J. S. Davis and I. Solomon, 1989, "Experience, Expertise, and Expert-Performance Research in Accounting," *Journal of Accounting Literature* 8, pp. 150–164.

14. See S. Bonner and N. Pennington, 1991, "Cognitive Processes and Knowledge as Determinants of Auditor Expertise," *Journal of Accounting Literature* 10, pp. 1–50.

15. Ibid.

16. Ibid.

17. J. S. Davis and I. Solomon, 1989, "Experience, Expertise, And Expert-Performance Research in Accounting," pp. 150–164.

There is less research in this area than in exploring the differences in performance between those with more and less experience.

Two researchers have compared expertise research in auditing with other domains.[18] This comparison is important to determine what aspects of auditing expertise are representative of expertise in general and what aspects are unique to auditing. There is very limited evidence in the auditing research to draw conclusions about whether expert auditors exhibit the same behaviors as experts in general. Findings in auditing research that are consistent with conclusions from expertise studies in other domains are that expert auditors have more knowledge in particular auditing tasks and they are able to make more and stronger connections between concepts than novice auditors. They seem to be better able to identify the relevant information needed than novice auditors.

In well-understood auditing tasks, expert auditors perform better than novice auditors. Compared with experts in other domains (e.g., experienced radiologists), however, experienced auditors do not have the opportunity to experience decision-making events hundreds of times. The lack of *extensive* repeated experiences may contribute to the lack of well-developed schema for some portions of the audit. These areas are likely those where the expert auditors have been found to *not* significantly outperform novice auditors. By considering what is generally known about expertise and the characteristics of the audit domain that make it similar to other domains, the theory of expertise in auditing can progress more quickly than if those generalizations are not recognized and applied.

These researchers also have criticized the practice by some of equating experience and expertise. They recognize the role of ability and practice in the development of superior performance in a way that is consistent with the model in Figure 3.1. In a discussion of this research, a noted psychologist characterizes experts as not only having superior domain knowledge and ability (cognitive skills and decision strategies), but he also identifies particular psychological traits that experts possess. He also argues that task type (e.g., dynamic versus static) has an effect on superior performance by experts.[19] The psychological traits aspect of expertise simply implies that an expert must act like an expert. To find evidence in the auditing domain, this psychologist collaborated with an accounting

---

18. See J. Bédard and M. T. H. Chi, 1993, "Expertise in Auditing," *Auditing: A Journal of Practice and Theory* 12 (Supplement), pp. 21–45.

19. See J. Shanteau, 1993, "Discussion of Expertise in Auditing," *Auditing: A Journal of Practice and Theory* 12 (Supplement), pp. 51–56.

professor in a survey of three levels of auditors (managers and partners, senior and supervisor auditors, and auditing students) to determine what attributes participants considered important for "expert decision makers in auditing." When asked to list what attributes are most important, 57% of all respondents listed "knowledge." Approximately one-third of all respondents listed experience as being among the most important attributes for expert decision makers. [20]

These researchers also provided a list of twenty attributes for participants to rank. Overall, participants ranked "knows what's relevant," "assumes responsibility," and "current knowledge" as the three most important attributes of expert decision makers. Knowledge and experience were therefore perceived to be two of the most important ingredients to attaining expert status in auditing.

In a follow up study, researchers collected data from industry experts in one auditing firm about attributes they considered important to expertise. Participants were asked an open-ended question, to "list as many characteristics as they deemed relevant to describe a top industry specialist" and to rank their responses on a scale from 1 (extremely important) to 5 (minimally important).[21] The experts were also asked to rate 25 characteristics provided to them in terms of importance for auditing experts to possess. For this second task, they were to also specify to what category they believed the characteristic belonged. To summarize the findings of this study, Table 3.1 shows categories of expert characteristics and some of the most important characteristics identified by expert auditors within each category. Because some of the important characteristics are psychological traits and cognitive abilities, it may be appropriate to focus on *selecting* auditors with "expert" characteristics and providing the appropriate training to gain domain knowledge. Other researchers have also found characteristics that are important to expertise in auditing that were not studied before. For example, in one study, tacit managerial knowledge such as managing self and

20. See M. J. Abdolmohammadi and J. Shanteau, 1992, "Personal Attributes of Expert Auditors," *Organizational Behavior and Human Decision Processes* 53 (November), pp. 158–172.

21. See M. J. Abdolmohammadi, J. Searfoss, and J. Shanteau, 1998, "A Framework for Analysis of Characteristics of Audit Experts" (working paper, Bentley College).

Table 3.1
Summary of Findings Related to Expert Attributes

Type Of Attribute	Examples Of Attributes Belonging To Category
1. Knowledge	Current knowledge, experience, communicates expertise
2. Psychological traits	Persistent, self confident, assumes responsibility
3. Interpersonal skills	Communication skills, good team member
4. Cognitive abilities	Problem solver, perceptive
5. Decision strategies	Good decision maker, makes exceptions (more than one way to solve problem)
6. Task/Business	Technical skills, profitable

Source: Adapted from M. J. Abdolmohammadi, J. Searfoss, and J. Shanteau, 1998, "A Framework for Analysis of Characteristics of Audit Experts" (working paper, Bentley College).

managing others was found to be a characteristic of auditing expertise.[22]

CONCLUSION AND RESEARCH HYPOTHESES

The direction of the auditing research on experience and expertise appears to be heading toward more detailed studies of specific tasks. The early behavioral auditing research resulted in inconsistent findings about the nature of the role of experience in performance level on auditing tasks. A major issue relating to task-specific knowledge is when it would normally be acquired and whether experience is a good proxy for it. Researchers generally agree that "people get better on a task with practice."[23] This statement indicates that task-specific knowledge improves by firsthand encounters with the task. Broadly defined however, experience includes not only first hand encounters, but also secondhand encounters such as discussions

---

22. See H. T. Tan and R. Libby, 1997, "Tacit Managerial versus Technical Knowledge as Determinants of Audit Expertise in the Field," *Journal of Accounting Research* 35 (1), pp. 97–113.

23. See, for example, D. M. Neves and J. R. Anderson, 1981, "Knowledge Compilation: Mechanisms for the Automatization of Cognitive Skills," in *Cognitive Skills and Their Acquisition*, J. R. Anderson (ed.) (Hillsdale, N.J.: Lawrence Erlbaum Associates).

of other audits with colleagues, reading formal audit guides, and training.[24] Together, the firsthand and the secondhand experiences provide the main ingredients of task-specific knowledge. Consequently, we collected data for this book on both the years of experience (general audit experience) and the number of supervised instances of practice (specific experience) to perform each task to test the hypotheses listed in the next section. Other researchers have argued, and provided evidence on professional rank as a proxy for task-specific knowledge.[25]

SIMON'S MODEL AS THE BASIS FOR HYPOTHESES DEVELOPMENT

As discussed in Chapter 2, Simon's model of the decision process describes tasks by their nature in three activities (Intelligence, Design, and Choice). Based on the nature of these activities contained in a task, it can be classified along a programmed-nonprogrammed continuum. Programmed decisions are those which occur routinely and therefore a procedure has been developed for executing them. Nonprogrammed decisions on the other hand, occur less frequently and are unstructured. It is difficult to establish a procedure for them that would be successful every time. Another characteristic that Simon associates with nonprogrammed decisions is that they are "consequential."[26] If the outcome of the decision is very important and has a potentially large impact, the decision would not be "programmable" because it requires careful and thoughtful human judgment. Some nonprogrammed tasks may have components that are programmable; however to complete the task, significant reasoning or problem-solving skills are necessary. Predetermined rules or procedures are not appropriate or adequate for completing these tasks.

Simon's characterization of tasks has resulted in much follow up research. For example, management information systems designers have used the Simon model to provide a framework for thinking about tasks along a structured-unstructured continuum replacing

---

24. See R. Libby, 1995, "The Role of Knowledge and Memory in Audit Judgment," pp. 176–206.

25. See the database in M. J. Abdolmohammadi, 1999, "A Comprehensive Taxonomy of Task Structure and Knowledge Base Demands in Auditing," pp. 51–92. Data from this database are used to provide comparative analyses in Chapters 7 and 8.

26. See H. Simon, 1960, *The New Science of Management* (New York: Harper and Row), p. 6.

Simon's programmable and nonprogrammable terms. At one end of the spectrum, tasks are labeled as unstructured if all three phases of the decision (intelligence, design and choice) are unstructured. A structured task, on the other hand, is one where all three phases are structured. Semistructured tasks consist of combinations where one or more phases is structured *and* one or more phases is unstructured.[27] These researchers consider the classification of tasks along the structured-unstructured continuum to be transitory. As time passes and people become more experienced and knowledgeable about a task, they specify various elements of the task better and thus make the task more structured.

Hypotheses on the Relationship between Knowledge Base and Task Structure

A research team addressed the issue of different experience requirements for different auditing tasks and how that may cause the mixed performance results that have been found in previous research. These authors reviewed the literature and reported that some studies have found that student surrogates and novice auditors perform as well as more experienced auditors on some tasks while other studies indicate that experienced auditors make very different judgments than novice auditors and students. The mixed results led the researchers to develop a way to sort out the results to offer an explanation. They adopted Simon's model of the decision process to describe tasks along a structured-unstructured continuum and performed a study to explain the effects of this classification on audit judgments. The results of their study showed that experience effects were not found for structured auditing tasks, but experience effects were found for unstructured, and some semistructured tasks. Specifically, more experienced auditors performed better than nonexperienced auditors on unstructured and semistructured tasks.[28]

Similarly, a more recent research study indicates that it makes sense for firms to assign more experienced auditors to those tasks that require more judgment (unstructured tasks) and to assign less experienced auditors to those tasks that do not require much

---

27. See G. A. Gorry and M. S. Scott-Morton, 1971, "A Framework for Management Information Systems," *Sloan Management Review* (Fall), p. 61.

28. See M. J. Abdolmohammadi and A. Wright, 1987, "An Examination of the Effects of Experience and Task Complexity on Audit Judgments," pp. 1–13.

judgment (structured tasks).[29] Based on this line of previous research, we expect an inverse relationship between structure and knowledge base requirements for the auditing tasks. Table 3.2 presents this relationship. As presented, while only a naive level of knowledge may be sufficient to perform a structured task, a novice level of knowledge is needed for semistructured tasks. Expert knowledge is needed for unstructured tasks.

As explained in Chapter 6, we collected two measures of knowledge base for this study. One measure, years of audit experience, is a commonly used gauge of knowledge base. This study adds another metric, number of supervised instances, intended to capture the amount of practice required before an auditing task can be expected to be performed independently. We expect both these measures of knowledge base to be inversely correlated with the task structure measure. The less structured the task, the more years of experience and the practice at the task should be necessary. The data in this study will be used to test the following general hypotheses.

H_{3-1a} There is an inverse relationship between task structure and the years of general audit experience required to perform the task independently.

H_{3-1b} There is an inverse relationship between task structure and the number of supervised instances required to perform the task independently.

Table 3.2
Task Structure and Knowledge Base Relationship

	Task Structure		
	Structured	Semi-structured	Unstructured
Knowledge base	Low (Naive)	Medium (Novice)	High (Expert)

29. See D. Prawitt, 1995, "Staffing Assignments for Judgment-Oriented Audit Tasks: The Effects of Structured Audit Technology," *The Accounting Review* 70 (3), pp. 443–465.

In addition to the data collected in this study, we also use the data base in a previous study in which knowledge base was defined as the professional rank in one's accounting firm.[30] The formal hypothesis tested and reported on in Chapter 8 is as follows:

$H_{3\text{-}1c}$ There is an inverse relationship between task structure and professional rank.

Simon's model of the decision process also has implications for the type of decision aid used in practice. This issue is discussed in Chapter 4 where related hypotheses are also presented.

---

30. M. J. Abdolmohammadi, 1999, "A Comprehensive Taxonomy of Task Structure and Knowledge Base Demands in Auditing," pp. 51–92.

Chapter 4

Decision Aids in Auditing

The purpose of this chapter is to discuss decision aids, in particular, automation, decision support systems (DSS), and knowledge-based expert systems (KES). The first section of the chapter provides some background information on the use of decision aids in auditing. The second section provides definitions for each of the decision aids included in this study, as well as discussing the distinction between DSS and KES. The third section presents some of the advantages and disadvantages associated with decision aids. In the fourth section, the issue of development of decision aids in auditing is discussed, specifically how tasks or areas of the audit should be chosen for decision aid development. The fifth section provides a brief review of related literature. The final section consists of a conclusion to the chapter and states two research hypotheses for investigation.

BACKGROUND

Research indicates that accounting firms began using standardized tools and techniques, such as decision aids, and a top-down approach to the design and execution of audit engagements in the early 1980s.[1] The objective of using decision aids in auditing is to help auditors make better decisions by not falling prey to potential biases and omissions

---

1. Professors Barry Cushing and James Loebbecke made these observations in a study of the audit manuals of the then 14 largest accounting firms. See B. E. Cushing and J. K. Loebbecke, 1986, "Comparison of Audit Methodologies of Large Accounting Firms," *Studies in Accounting Research No. 26* (Sarasota, Fla.: American Accounting Association).

that can occur in unaided decision-making situations.[2] Auditors use many decision aids, such as the internal control questionnaire, routinely throughout an audit. The challenge is to identify those parts of the audit that would benefit from having a decision aid and to choose the best type of decision aid on a cost-benefit basis. Accordingly, academic researchers and professional accountants have developed a number of decision aids for some audit tasks.[3] As a result, all major accounting firms have had various computerized aids (automation, decision support systems, and knowledge based expert systems) for use in practice since the 1980s. For example, a study reported in 1991 that all the then Big Six accounting firms were either using expert systems and/or they had current projects to develop expert systems for future use.[4]

The determination of the benefits that can be derived from a particular decision aid requires an understanding of the auditor's decision-making process. In particular, one must understand the source of any inefficiency or ineffectiveness that a decision aid can help overcome in performing a particular task. The decision aid should be aimed specifically at helping the decision maker overcome these problems. Other ways to improve decision making should also be considered, such as training the auditor to make better unaided decisions and/or requiring the auditor to provide justification for his or her decision. Providing justification for a particular decision increases the auditor's attention to the situation and results in more effort being put into the decision and therefore results in a better decision.

---

2. In a review of the usefulness of decision aids to auditing practice, Duke University professor, Robert Ashton and KPMG Peat Marwick partner, John Willingham made this statement. They also provided a discussion of advantages and disadvantages of decision aids in auditing. See R. H. Ashton and J. J. Willingham, 1988, "Using and Evaluating Audit Decision Aids," in R. P. Srivastava and J. E. Rebele, (eds.), *Auditing Symposium IX: Proceedings of the 1988 Touche Ross/University of Kansas Symposium on Auditing Problems* (Lawrence, Kans.: University of Kansas Printing Service), pp. 1–25.

3. Recent reviews of this literature are provided by W. F. Messier Jr., 1995, "Research in and Development of Audit Decision Aids," in R. H. Ashton and A. H. Ashton (eds.), *Judgment and Decision Making Research in Accounting and Auditing* (New York: Cambridge University Press), pp. 207–228; and D. Brown and M. M. Eining, 1996, "The Role of Decision Aids in Accounting: A Synthesis of Prior Research," *Advances in Accounting Information Systems* 4, pp. 305–332.

4. See C. E. Brown, 1991, "Expert Systems in Public Accounting: Current Practice and Future Directions," *Expert Systems with Applications* 3, pp. 3–18.

Decision aids can exist at many levels of complexity. At one end of the spectrum are simple decision aids. For example, consider the case of two decision aids consisting of a list of potential errors cross-classified by transaction cycle and audit objective, and a mechanical-aggregation aid. A study reported that the mechanical-aggregation aid was more useful in improving judgments than the list aid, but both were beneficial to improving auditors' judgments.[5]

At the other end of the decision aid spectrum are the systems based on artificial intelligence. These systems attempt to capture human intelligence and program it into computers. Two artificial intelligence tools that have been particularly popular in business are knowledge based expert systems and neural networks.[6] Knowledge based expert systems are computerized systems which attempt to provide the knowledge base of an expert to assist auditors in the field. They represent the expert knowledge in a long chain of if-then rules (e.g., if the current ratio is low, then consider other liquidity ratios). While these systems can be updated and revised periodically for the changes in expertise, such changes are not automatic. In contrast, neural networks are mathematical models that are based on the human brain. They are learning systems and attempt to model expertise in a way that goes beyond expert systems by learning as they are used—they automatically update as the knowledge base develops.

Both expert systems and neural networks require powerful software shells to accommodate complex chains of inference. While this inference is based on deductive reasoning in expert systems, it is based on inductive reasoning in neural networks. Consequently, neural networks have been popular with researchers in dealing with tasks that continually change and have an element of uncertainty. An example of such tasks in an audit setting is the going concern judgment.[7] However, expert systems have been more popular with practicing auditors because of their deductive reasoning capabilities where a general model is applied to many particular tasks of similar nature. Also, expert systems provide an explanation of their recommendation for the

---

5. See S. Bonner, R. Libby and M. W. Nelson, 1996, "Using Decision Aids to Improve Auditors' Conditional Probability Judgments," *The Accounting Review* 71 (2), pp. 221–240.

6. For a recent descriptive paper on expert systems and neural networks in accounting and business, see A. A. Qureshi, J. K. Shim and J. G. Siegel, 1998, "Artificial Intelligence in Accounting and Business," *The National Public Accountant* 43 (7), pp. 13–16.

7. See M. J. Lenard , P. Alam, and G. R. Madey, 1995, "The Application of Neural Networks and a Qualitative Response Model to the Auditor's Going Concern Uncertainty Decision," *Decision Sciences* 26 (2), pp. 209–227.

auditors to understand the reasoning. Using inductive knowledge, neural networks rely on examples of action from which general conclusions are drawn, but no explanation is provided. Thus, neural networks are at a great disadvantage in comparison with expert systems for auditing where the auditors has to support his/her actions with specific explanations. Consequently, neural networks are rare in audit practice. We are aware of only one system that KPMG Peat Marwick developed for predicting commercial bank failures which was subsequently abandoned.[8] As a result we do not present a detailed discussion of neural networks in this book.

In addition to the two types of decision aids discussed above, there are automated processing and decision support systems. Automated processing consists of using a computer to process data in a deterministic way, providing a clear-cut response that could be used by the auditor to help make or support a decision. A decision support system is a computerized aid that provides information to the auditor to help make a decision.

Some experienced auditors have argued that the audit is becoming more structured overall due to the new auditing standards that have been issued in an attempt to reduce the expectations gap. The purpose of the standards is to provide more guidance to auditors in their approach to difficult and complex issues, such as deciding whether to issue a going concern opinion. There is a limit however, as to how automated the audit can become. Although these experienced auditors advocate the use of automation for highly structured tasks, they warn that the ever-changing, ever-complex audit environment requires actual auditors who learn from their experiences and who are adaptable.[9]

---

8. See T. Bell, G. S. Ribar and J. Verchio, 1990, "Neural Nets Versus Logistic Regression: A Comparison of Each Model's Ability to Predict Commercial Bank Failures," in R. P. Srivastava (ed.), *Auditing Symposium X: Proceedings of the 1990 Deloitte and Touche/ University of Kansas Symposium on Auditing Problems* (Lawrence, Kans.: University of Kansas Printing Service).

9. For example, see S. J. Aldersley, 1988, Discussant's Response to "Using and Evaluating Audit Decision Aids," in R. P. Srivastava and J. E. Rebele, (eds.), *Auditing Symposium IX: Proceedings of the 1988 Touche Ross/University of Kansas Symposium on Auditing Problems* (Lawrence, Kans.: University of Kansas Printing Service), pp. 26–31

DEFINITIONS

A major problem in studying decision aids is the definition used for various types. Although there are many definitions, we have adopted the more generally accepted ones as listed in Table 4.1.

Complete Automation

Complete automation refers to the development and use of computer programs that completely perform a task. These programs tackle routine tasks and perform such tasks at a high speed. Furthermore, these programs seldom commit any error unless there is

Table 4.1
Decision Aid Definitions Used in the Study

Decision Aid Type	Meaning
1. Complete automation	Some tasks such as footing, recalculation, and cross-checking may be done completely by a computer, based on some predetermined formula. This is referred to as complete automation.
2. Decision support systems (DSS)	A DSS is an interactive computer-based software that assists decision makers in making decisions. DSSs use certain statistical or mathematical models and data to make inferences for the use of the decision maker.
3. Knowledge-based expert systems (KES)	A KES is an interactive computer-based software that assists decision makers in using expert(s) decision rules to make their decisions. To create a KES, the decision rules of the expert(s) must be elicited and expressed in terms of a number of if-then rules. To employ a KES, the decision maker provides answers to questions posed by the system. The KES then presents a recommendation to the decision maker. The decision maker has the option of accepting or rejecting the recommendation developed by the KES.
4. Strictly human processing	Some tasks may not be suitable for automation, DSS, or KES. These tasks require strictly human processing. It should be noted that all decision aids have a human processing component to them.

Source: Adopted from M. J. Abdolmohammadi, 1987 "Decision Support and Expert Systems in Auditing: A Review and Research Directions," *Accounting and Business Research* (Spring), pp. 173–185.

an error in the program itself or a programming bug develops in its code. In such a situation, errors occur systematically and repeatedly. In contrast, when routine tasks are performed manually, errors occur randomly as a result of human fatigue, impatience, or boredom. Accounting examples of the tasks that can be automated are footing, recalculation, and cross-checking. Most bookkeeping activities are now typically performed by general ledger software packages.

Decision Support Systems

Tasks that cannot be programmed completely can nevertheless be partially programmed. Decision support systems, or DSSs, are appropriate when part of the task can be programmed to generate input into a person's decision-making process. A DSS is an interactive computer-based software that assists decision makers partially by addressing certain parts of a problem. These DSSs typically use certain statistical or mathematical models that process and analyze data for the decision maker. Easy-to-use statistical packages such as SAS or Minitab can be classified broadly as DSSs. Examples of auditing tasks that are typically performed using DSSs are statistical sampling and analytical review procedures.

Knowledge-based Expert Systems

There are many other computer decision aids that also assist decision makers. One is a knowledge-based expert system (KES). A KES is developed by the creation of a software incorporating the decision rules of one or more experts. These decision rules are elicited and expressed with a number of if-then rules in the software and are provided to decision makers for consultation. It is like having the opinion of an expert at your finger tips. To employ a KES, the decision maker provides answers to questions posed by the system. The KES then presents a recommendation to the decision maker. The decision maker has the option of accepting or rejecting the recommendation developed by the KES. An example of KES is ExperTAX, a tax-planning expert system developed in the 1980s by Coopers & Lybrand.

DSS versus KES

The difference between DSS and KES is that DSS is provided to assist the person who is very knowledgeable about a domain in making a decision. A KES is intended to replace an expert in providing assistance to a less knowledgeable decision maker in making a decision.[10]

The distinction between DSS and KES has important implications. DSS is meant to help decision makers, whereas the purpose of a KES is to replace an expert. Their different natures become more clear when one considers the components of each. An expert system includes "user interface, a knowledge base that includes facts and rules, and an inference engine that includes reasoning methods" while a DSS consists of "user interface, database, and model base."[11] The difference between these two descriptions provides some insight into how they might be used in an auditing firm and for what tasks. A DSS requires significant user input and user knowledge about the problem. The KES is meant to distribute expertise. The interface is established so that a nonexpert can provide information to the system and the system will perform like an expert, providing the user with a recommended solution. With a DSS, the user and the system work together to solve the problem, the user has more control over procedures and alternative strategies than in a KES. The KES basically makes the decisions about the strategy taken to solve the problem and executes it.

Strictly Human Processing

Some tasks may not be suitable for automation, DSS, or KES. These tasks require strictly human processing regardless of their degree of structure. For example, consider a decision situation facing a managerial accountant concerning the impact of technological advances on the useful life and salvage value of old, but expensive, computer equipment. While the manager will have to gather much information about the decision, perhaps from data bases, vendors, and engineers, the ultimate decision may be based on an unaided judgment using the available information. The variables may be so diverse and dynamic that their inclusion in a software package in a timely manner may be impossible. Thus, tasks of this nature require human processing and may not be automated at any level.

---

10. For more detailed information about the relationship between DSS and KES, one might refer to E. Turban's *Decision Support and Expert Systems*, (New York: Macmillan Publishing Co., 1990).

11. See I. Benbasat and B. R. Nault, 1988, "Empirical Research in Decision Support and Expert Systems: An Examination of Research to Date and Emerging Topics," in A. Bailey, (ed.), *Auditor Productivity in the Year 2000: 1987 Proceedings of the Arthur Young Professors' Roundtable*, p. 261.

ADVANTAGES AND DISADVANTAGES OF DECISION AIDS

Accounting firms are interested in the use of decision aids because decision aids are perceived to enhance efficiency and effectiveness. Based on a review of the literature related to DSS and KES we have identified various advantages and disadvantages of these decision aids which are discussed in the following paragraphs and are summarized in Table 4.2.

Table 4.2
Advantages and Disadvantages of DSS and KES

	DSS and KES	KES Only
Advantages	Provides problem structure: facilitates thought and results in greater consistency	Assists in staff training: provides explanations of decision processes and communicates relationships as well as facts
	Development effort can highlight specifics of decision process leading to improved decision making	Knowledge sharing, distributed expertise
	Improvement of communication	Can provide second professional opinion
	Ability to do "what-if" analyses	Higher consistency in decision making
		Ability to deal with large amounts of data and explore more alternatives
		Shorter decision time
Disadvantages	May prolong decision process	High cost of developing and maintaining system
	May reduce communication between individuals in organization	May inhibit development of expertise/professional judgment by users
		Could promote competition if others gain access to KES
		Potential legal liability both from using and not using available systems

Advantages

A major benefit of decision aids is that they provide a structure for the task. This is a benefit in an audit because it allows auditors to view the audit task in a systematic way which may prevent them from neglecting important aspects of the task. Thus, decision aids help auditors to facilitate their thoughts and to focus on relevant issues.[12] A consequence of providing structure to a task is that it will result in high levels of consistency between decision makers and between decision situations. For example, in a survey of auditors, consistency was viewed as a valuable benefit of having a KES.[13]

The process of developing a DSS or KES forces the documentation of the specific aspects of the decision process, which in itself may lead to improved decision making. This process also can provide improved communication by presenting common frameworks in which to discuss problems or decisions. "The ability to communicate relationships as well as facts" was a benefit cited by auditors in a survey of KES.[14] Related to this benefit is the fact that decision aids can be programmed to be capable of sensitivity or "what-if" analysis. For example, answers to questions asked by a KES can be varied to result in sensitivity analysis. This aspect of KES provides the user with more than one potential recommendation depending on changing conditions.

A KES has several other benefits from a practical perspective.[15] First, a KES can assist in staff training. A KES informs users of decision heuristics that are useful and can provide explanations as it goes through the decision process, allowing a novice to learn as he or she uses the system. KES can help auditors to improve their decision making ability more quickly by providing adequate explanation to accompany the KES's processing of a problem. The novice benefits from the processes that were derived from expert auditors and has the opportunity to benefit from that expertise without regard for the availability and willingness of the actual expert to provide such guidance. For example, in a study, the use of a KES for internal control

---

12. Facilitation of thoughts as an advantage of decision aids was suggested by D. R. Pieptea and E. Anderson, 1987, "Price and Value of Decision Support Systems," *MIS Quarterly* 11 (4), pp. 514–527.

13. See C. E. Brown and D. S. Murphy, 1990, "The Use of Auditing Expert Systems in Public Accounting," *Journal of Information Systems* 4 (3), pp. 63–72.

14. Ibid, p. 70.

15. These benefits were discussed in R. K. Elliott and J. A. Kielich (1985), "Expert Systems for Accountants," *Journal of Accountancy* (September), pp. 126–134.

evaluation improved auditors' judgments significantly over time compared to unaided groups, and compared to a group of auditors who used a simpler decision aid, an internal control questionnaire.[16]

Second, a KES allows for knowledge sharing resulting in expertise being more widely available throughout the organization. Given the high cost of experts to organizations, few firms can afford to have their most experienced auditors available for every engagement, yet the expertise and experience of those auditors are really needed to guide every audit.[17]

A third benefit of KES is "augmented professional judgment." A KES could provide a decision maker with an additional opinion to compare to his or her own while at the same time being able to deal effectively with large amounts of data.[18]

Finally, a KES helps to make decisions in a shorter decision time. A KES can focus the decision maker on only the relevant facts. Once questions have been answered by the user, the system processes the information very quickly. For example, in a study, students who used a KES to make internal control assessments spent less time to reach a conclusion than did students who did not have a decision aid.[19] Auditing firms that have implemented KES in the past generally cite increased auditor efficiency as a benefit of using such systems.[20]

While the perceived benefits of decision aids are many as summarized in this section, it may be difficult to *quantify* these benefits. For decision aids that apply to structured problems, it is easier to quantify the economic benefits they provide. It is for unstructured problems, however, that a decision aid may provide the greatest intangible benefits. In general, DSS has the advantage of being less expensive to develop than KES. This is because often DSS uses databases and computing resources that are common to those of transaction processing systems, which the organization has to provide

---

16. M. M. Eining and P. B. Dorr, 1991, "The Impact of Expert System Usage on Experiential Learning in an Auditing Setting," *Journal of Information Systems* (Spring), pp. 1–16.

17. This observation was made by L. E. Graham (1990), "A Technological Response to the Changing Audit Environment," *The Auditor's Report* (Summer), p. 15.

18. See C. E. Brown and D. S. Murphy, 1990, "The Use of Auditing Expert Systems in Public Accounting," p. 70.

19. See M. M. Eining and P. B. Dorr, 1991, "The Impact of Expert System Usage on Experiential Learning in an Auditing Setting," pp. 1–16.

20. See C. E. Brown and D. S. Murphy (1990), "The Use of Auditing Expert Systems in Public Accounting," pp. 63–72.

independently of the existence of the DSS.[21] As summarized above, KES has several advantages (e.g., expert knowledge sharing) not found in a DSS, however, KES also requires substantially more investment to develop than DSS.

Disadvantages

There are several disadvantages associated with decision aids as well. Some evidence suggests that having access to a decision aid may prolong the decision process since the decision maker has the opportunity to explore and consider more alternatives than an unaided decision maker.[22] The use of DSS and KES may reduce communication between the user and others in the organization because of the focus of the decision maker on the decision aid. A decision maker who relies heavily on the support of DSS and/or KES may do so to the exclusion of consulting colleagues whose input could be valuable to the decision process.

Most relevant to KES, is the cost of developing and maintaining the system. The cost and effort of soliciting information from experts to build the system, as well as the cost of updating and maintaining the system as conditions change, are substantial.

There is some evidence that use of an expert system by novices may actually inhibit the development of the novice's knowledge base. The concern is that eliminating the problem-solving process (i.e., replacing it with an expert system) does not allow the practice needed for a novice to gain the valuable elements of experience that lead to improved performance. For example, in a study, a researcher found that use of an expert system, versus a manual practice aid, inhibited the novices' ability to develop semantic memory (domain knowledge) and episodic memory (using episodes from experience to apply the domain knowledge).[23] Similarly, the use of KES may result in the deterioration of professional judgment. If auditors frequently defer to the conclusions offered by expert systems and do not use their own initiative to explore

---

21. See D. R. Pieptea and E. Anderson 1987, "Price and Value of Decision Support Systems," p. 521.

22. J. Mackay, S. Barr, and M. Kletke, 1992, "An Empirical Investigation of the Effects of Decision Aids on Problem-Solving Processes," *Decision Sciences* 23, pp. 648–672.

23. See D. Murphy, 1990, "Expert System Use and the Development of Expertise in Auditing: A Preliminary Investigation," *Journal of Information Systems* 4 (3), pp. 18–35.

other possibilities, they may miss opportunities to develop their professional judgment in specific audit areas.[24]

Another conceivable disadvantage is that once decision aids have been developed, they can be available outside the firm where they were first developed. For example, a disgruntled employee can provide the decision aid to competitors. Firms, other than public accounting firms, may then be in a position to offer services traditionally provided by public accounting firms.

Finally, there could be a potential legal liability arising from decision aids in general, and KES in particular. If an auditor relies on KES advice and the result is unfavorable, a lawsuit could be brought against the audit firm. On the other hand, if the auditor consults the expert system but does not follow its conclusion or does not even consult an available KES, the auditor may be held liable for an incorrect decision because he or she did not take advantage of the available technology.[25]

DEVELOPMENT AND MAINTENANCE OF DECISION AIDS

Rapid changes in information technology provide opportunities for development of new decision aids, as well as for maintaining (including upgrading) of current systems. An understanding of the status of decision aids developed in the past can provide information that might be useful to someone deciding on developing new decision aids. For example, the results of a survey about the current state of 97 early KESs (developed by 1987) developed for several domains, including auditing indicate that approximately one-half of the systems were abandoned by 1995.[26] About one-third of those that could still potentially be used were not being maintained, while the other two-thirds were still in use. Most respondents, even those who were no longer using the systems, spoke favorably of the results achieved by the systems. However, the most common reasons for not using the systems were that: (1) there weren't people in the organizations who dedicated themselves to maintaining the system and (2) users did not buy into the

---

24. See K. Yuthas and J. Dillard, 1996, "An Integrative Model of Audit Expert System Development," *Advances in Accounting Information Systems* 4, pp. 55–79.

25. For a detailed discussion of these issues see S. Sutton, R. Young, and P. McKenzie, 1994, "An Analysis of Potential Legal Liability Incurred through Audit Expert Systems," *Intelligent Systems in Accounting, Finance and Management* 4, pp. 191–204.

26. See G. Gill, 1995, "Early Expert Systems: Where Are They Now," *MIS Quarterly* 19 (1), pp. 51–81.

system because they had not been involved in developing it. The results of this survey would be very useful for anyone attempting to develop and maintain an expert system. In this section we present major issues to consider in developing decision aids in auditing.

Suitability of Tasks for Decision Aid Development

While there have been significant changes in the technology and design of decision aids in recent years, the manner in which tasks have been selected for decision aid development has remained adhoc in nature. The literature surrounding the issues of decision aid development in auditing has largely relied on the management science and information systems literatures that have assumed (1) that tasks vary in their degree of task structure and (2) that there is a contingency between task structure and decision aid type: automation for structured tasks, DSS for semistructured tasks, and KES for unstructured tasks.[27] As predicted, a study showed that task structure is a major factor in auditors' choices of applicable decision aids.[28] However, the data in a related study showed that only 13% of a comprehensive list of audit tasks indicated a contingency relationship between task structure and decision aid type.[29]

These results indicate the need for a careful investigation of the literature and provision of further data on factors that are important in identifying decision aids for various audit tasks. The research reported in the current book asks auditors which tasks are suitable for KES development, automated processing, DSS, or strictly human processing. Admittedly, not all auditors have the extensive background that may be required to provide accurate responses for all tasks. The auditors' agreement with potential DSS or KES applications, however, may be an initial step required in the long research and development process to result in effective decision aids.

---

27. M. J. Abdolmohammadi, 1987, "Decision Support and Expert Systems in Auditing: A Review and Research Directions," pp. 173–185.

28. See M. J. Abdolmohammadi, 1991a, "Factors Affecting Auditor's Perceptions of Applicable Decision Aids for Various Audit Tasks," *Contemporary Accounting Research* 7 (2), pp. 535–548 for a discussion of various factors affecting the choices of decision aids.

29. See M. J. Abdolmohammadi, 1991b, "A Test of the Relationship Between Task Structure and Decision Aid Type in Auditing" L. A. Ponemon and D. R. L.Gabhart (eds.), *Auditing: Advances in Applied Behavioral Research* (New York: Springer-Verlag Publishing), pp. 131–142, for the proportion of tasks selected for decision aids by auditors.

In a previous study, for 45 auditing tasks that auditors had indicated were suitable for expert systems development, the authors analyzed the nature of responses.[30] They found that the audit firm that would be classified as semistructured in its audit approach, was more likely to indicate suitability for expert systems for these tasks than auditors from the highly structured or highly unstructured firms.[31] The authors reason that perhaps a firm that is heading towards more structure in its audit approach would be open to including more tasks in the "expert systems" category. In the same study, auditors with more experience in electronic data processing (EDP) and high-technology audits were less likely to indicate tasks as suitable for expert systems development. This evidence indicates that having a better understanding of how expert systems are developed may lead someone to not consider them to be beneficial in as many situations as those who do not have that understanding.

Other authors have provided lists of evaluation criteria for subjecting tasks to expert system development. For example, applying a list of 14 evaluation criteria (e.g., task is knowledge intensive), a study reported that the 45 tasks selected for expert system development by auditors in a previous study, indeed received average and above average ratings for their suitability for KES development.[32]

Beyond having auditors provide an overall assessment of suitability of a task for decision aid development, a more comprehensive analysis has been proposed by several researchers. Most of the research has had as its focus the economic feasibility of developing an expert system for particular tasks. Technical considerations are paramount in these studies. A few others, however, have broadened the perspective and

---

30. See M. J. Abdolmohammadi and M. S. Bazaz, 1991, "Identification of Tasks for Expert Systems Development in Auditing," *Expert Systems with Applications* 3 (1), pp. 99–108.

31. Accounting firms were classified according to their audit methodology approach by Cushing and Loebbecke, 1986, "Comparison of Audit Methodologies of Large Accounting Firms;" and W. Kinney, 1986, "Audit Technology and Preference for Auditing Standards," *Journal of Accounting and Economics* 8 (1), pp. 73–89. While significant changes have occurred since these initial classifications of accounting firms, a recent study indicates that audit methodology classification is still a viable source of variation for some decisions, such as staff assignment. See D. Prawitt, 1995, "Staffing Assignments for Judgment-Oriented Audit Tasks: The Effects of Structured Audit Technology," *The Accounting Review* 70 (3), pp. 443–465.

32. I. Han And J. Choi, 1995, "Selection of Appropriate Tasks for Expert System Development in Auditing" (working paper).

included sociological considerations in making the KES development decisions. These two approaches are discussed in turn below.

Technological Perspective

Given a subset of tasks which are potential candidates for KES, the next step is to use some theoretically based strategy to evaluate the tasks on multiple dimensions to determine suitability for KES development. For example, a researcher compiled a series of checklists that include practical as well as technical aspects of implementing expert systems. In addition to questions about characteristics of the task, the researcher includes checklists to address: potential benefits of the system, management support of development and use of the system, quality of the system designer, and availability and characteristics of domain expert.[33] The author includes a section on user characteristics in his questionnaire. For example, one question relates to whether the system would displace any current workers. The author's emphasis, however, is on task characteristics and the payoff that is expected to result from implementing the system.

In another study, authors asked auditors to respond to questions about task characteristics for nine auditing tasks.[34] Twenty-nine statements were presented to practicing auditors to evaluate each of nine auditing tasks. Six of the tasks already have associated expert systems developed in at least one of the then Big Six auditing firms, two of the tasks have been the basis for development of prototype expert systems by academic researchers and one is an audit judgment task with no known associated expert system. Based on a factor analysis of the 29 evaluation statements, four factors emerged: task complexity, expertise requirements, task manageability, and task objectives. The results of this study show that two of the tasks deemed most suitable for KES development were indeed those for which the most KES systems already exist: determination of compliance with GAAP and audit work program development. [35]

---

33. See T. Beckman, 1991, "Selecting Expert Systems Application," *AI Expert* (February), pp. 42–48. See also G. Gill, 1995, "Early Expert Systems: Where are They Now," pp. 51–81.

34. See V. Karan, U. S. Murthy, and A. S. Vinze, 1995, "Assessing the Suitability of Judgmental Auditing Tasks for Expert Systems Development: An Empirical Approach," *Expert Systems with Applications* 9, pp. 441–455.

35. Publicly available knowledge about existing KES systems may not be complete. V. Karan, U. S. Murthy, and A. S. Vinze, 1995, "Assessing the Suitability of Judgmental Auditing Tasks for Expert Systems Development: An Empirical Approach," pp. 441–455, note that one Big Six firm, for example,

Sociological Emphasis

Although some "practical" considerations were included in the studies reported in the previous section, they do not focus on sociological considerations. A cadre of researchers would emphasize the nontechnical aspects of researching expert systems use and potential.[36] For example, these researchers emphasize the need to consider various stakeholders who will be affected by the implementation of an expert system. They also are concerned with the rights and well-being of the experts whose knowledge is used to develop a KES. They question the ethical implications of the firm abstracting an individual's expertise and essentially putting it into a computer where it can be used by nonexpert auditors regardless of whether or not the expert remains with the firm. These researchers advocate receiving input, on an equal basis, from all parties affected, to develop systems that have high probability of successful implementation and sustained use.

RESEARCH RELATED TO DECISION AIDS

Several review papers have appeared in journals in recent years. In one paper, the author provides a review of the research related to decision aids and progress made in auditing related to decision aids.[37] He presents a table that relates decision-making phases, type of task and type of decision aid. The decision-making phases used are: information acquisition, information evaluation, and action/choice. These phases parallel the three phases in Simon's model of the decision process as presented in Chapter 2: Intelligence, Design, and Choice. The author of the review paper describes a contingency relationship between the structure of the task and the type of decision aid which is consistent with the current study. He relates structured tasks to simple or deterministic decision aids, semi-structured tasks to decision support systems and unstructured tasks to expert systems. He also describes

---

does not disclose information about its use of KES while two others disclose information about existing and *planned* systems.

36. See for example, K. Yuthas and J. Dillard, 1996, "An Integrative Model of Audit Expert System Development," pp. 55–79 and S. Sutton, V. Arnold, and T. Arnold, 1995, "Toward an Understanding of the Philosophical Foundations for Ethical Development of Audit Expert Systems," *Research on Auditing Ethics* 1, pp. 61–74.

37. See W. F. Messier Jr., 1995, "Research in and Development of Audit Decision Aids," in R. H. Ashton and A. H. Ashton (eds.), *Judgment and Decision Making Research in Accounting and Auditing* (New York: Cambridge University Press), pp. 207–228.

several expert systems that have been developed within auditing firms. Each of the Big Six auditing firms report having at least one expert system. This number may be underreported since the firms may not want to disclose all information available about these systems for competitive reasons.

This author calls for more research on decision aids. For example, simple decision aids could be developed at fairly low cost for significant benefit.[38] Research should focus on identifying situations where these types of decision aids would be useful. Expert systems research should focus on how to transfer knowledge to the system to benefit auditors without expertise who will be using the expert system. The cost and benefit of using expert systems should be compared to alternatives. The effects of using expert systems on decision quality and on the development of expertise in those less experienced auditors who rely on the expert system should also be studied

In another paper, two authors review audit decision aid research and reveal many areas that are in need of further research.[39] Specifically, the authors cite lack of a "usable taxonomy of task types and their characteristics" as a hindrance to progress in auditing decision aid research. To generalize the findings of the research being done, one needs to know similar tasks for which the results may hold. The authors report that there are many instances of auditors circumventing or not placing reliance on available decision aids. Beyond research on task suitability for decision aid development, there needs to be extensive research aimed at increasing auditors' use of decision aids where their use would be beneficial, in other words, where their use would result in an increase in the efficiency and/or effectiveness of the audit.

TASK STRUCTURE AND SUITABILITY OF DECISION AIDS

Two researchers provide the basis for expecting that the placement of tasks along the structured-unstructured continuum implies the suitability of tasks for particular types of decision aids.[40] These researchers state that the use of terms "structured" and "unstructured"

---

38. See for example, S. Bonner, R. Libby and M. W. Nelson, 1996, "Using Decision Aids to Improve Auditors' Conditional Probability Judgments," pp. 221–240.

39. See D. Brown and M. M. Eining, 1996, "The Role of Decision Aids in Accounting: A Synthesis of Prior Research," pp. 305–332.

40. See P. G. W. Keen and M. S. Scott-Morton, 1978, *Decision Support Systems: An Organizational Perspective* (Reading, Mass: Addison-Wesley).

for programmed and nonprogrammed implies less dependence on the computer and more dependence on the basic character of the problem-solving activity. However, the authors also state that "In a very structured situation much if not all of the decision making process can be automated and (these systems) will be significantly different from those designed to assist managers in dealing with unstructured problems."[41] Other researchers view an efficient organization as automating as much as possible those tasks and parts of tasks that are highly structured, leaving managers time to use their judgment and expertise for performing tasks that cannot be automated.[42] This view seems to be shared by researchers in the auditing domain to motivate research and development of decision aids for auditors.[43]

The nature of tasks can change over time, causing reclassification and perhaps automation of tasks previously thought to be semistructured or unstructured. Classifying tasks for the purpose of developing a particular type of decision aid must be done with the input of those who normally perform the task. As some authors have argued, "we are interested in the manager's *perception* of what is structured and unstructured."[44]

Structured tasks can be given to a clerk (rather than a high level manager) or be performed using some automated process. Semistructured tasks seem suited for DSS since some part of the task can be automated but the remainder requires a manager's judgment and experience. Unstructured tasks may appear to be so, but after further detailed analysis, "deep structure" may be identified beneath the seemingly unstructured surface characteristics. Alternatively, parts of the task may be identified as being structured, placing the entire task in the semi-structured category.

Task structure has been shown to be a major factor in auditors' choices of applicable decision aids.[45] However, a close scrutiny of the management science and decision aid literature that have been relied upon in auditing studies, indicate that the assumption of the equivalence of structured/unstructured and programmability/

---

41. Ibid, p. 60.

42. See G. A. Gorry and M. S. Scott-Morton, 1971, "A Framework for Management Information Systems," *Sloan Management Review* (Fall), pp. 55–70.

43. See R. H. Ashton and J. J. Willingham, 1988, "Using and Evaluating Audit Decision Aids," pp. 1–25.

44. See P. G. W. Keen and M. S. Scott-Morton, 1978, *Decision Support Systems: An Organizational Perspective*, p. 96.

45. See M. J. Abdolmohammadi, 1991a, "Factors Affecting Auditor's Perceptions of Applicable Decision Aids for Various Audit Tasks," pp. 535–548.

nonprogrammability classifications may not map onto the nature of auditing tasks. Much of the information systems literature is based on these management tasks and the assumed relationship between task structure and decision aids.[46] Auditing tasks, however, are inherently different from most management tasks in that they relate to the collection and analysis of verification evidence on reported financial information as compared with operational, planning and control, and strategic tasks performed by management.

The adhoc developmental projects in auditing provide evidence that this contingency model has implicitly been used in the auditing domain. For example, the professional literature indicates that a large number of structured tasks have already been automated by major accounting firms in early 1980s.[47] Other researchers have reported decision support systems such as TICOM to assist auditors in designing, evaluating, and analyzing internal control systems, a semistructured task.[48] The EDP-Xpert system developed in the 1980s was designed for an unstructured task.[49]

However, a close examination of audit tasks for decision aid development brings under question the contingency relationship. Although many auditing tasks may appear to be structured, the entire task cannot be completed without the personal involvement of the auditor. For example, consider the task of inquiry from management as a preliminary evidence collection task. While many checklists (computerized or manual) are in use to guide the auditor in his/her inquiry, the act of personal inquiry is a strictly human processing task that is performed by the auditor and is not delegated to a computer regardless of its degree of structure. The result is that only a proportion of audit tasks may be considered to be programmable and only those can be subject to the relevance of the contingency model.

---

46. C. S. Sankar, 1990, "A Framework to Integrate Applications, Management, and Movement of Information," *Information Management Review* 5 (3), pp. 55–67, makes the argument that the framework suggested by Gorry and Scott-Morton, 1971, has been the dominant framework used in the management literature.

47. See C. E. Grease, 1984, "Accounting for Change," *World* 18, pp. 16–17.

48. See A. D. Bailey, G. L. Duke, J. Gerlach, C. Ko.; R. D. Meservy and A. B. Whinston, 1985, "TICOM and the Analysis of Internal Controls," *The Accounting Review* (April), pp. 186–201, for information on this decision support system.

49. See J. V. Hansen and W. F. Messier, Jr. (1986), "A Preliminary Test of EDP-Expert," *Auditing: A Journal of Practice and Theory* 6 (1), pp. 109–123 for information on this expert system.

In a study, authors performed an investigation of the relationship between task structure and decision aids. They investigated this issue by collecting data from 134 audit seniors on 30 risk-related audit tasks. They found that while some tasks are viewed as strictly subject to human processing, and thus nonprogrammable regardless of their level of task structure, others are viewed as programmable. The authors found a contingency relationship between task structure and decision aid type for these tasks.[50]

The current study results in an extensive listing of audit tasks, providing a taxonomy of tasks and their characteristics that is consistent with the direction suggested by these authors. It provides the data for an investigation of the relationships between task structure and decision aid type. Table 4.3 presents these relationships. Consistent with the prior research, the initial hypothesis recognizes that some tasks are considered "nonprogrammable" regardless of their level of structure.

While for programmable tasks some form of a decision aid will be applicable, nonprogrammable tasks are not subject to a primary decision aid and are processed strictly by people. Thus:

$H_{4\text{-}1}$ Regardless of their degree of structure, some tasks are perceived as programmable and others as nonprogrammable.

Table 4.3
Relationships among Task Programmability, Task Structure, and Decision Aids

	Programmable			Nonprogrammable
	Structured	Semistructured	Unstructured	
Decision aid:	Automation	Decision support systems (DSS)	Decision support and knowledge-based expert systems (DSS & KES)	Strictly human processing

Source: From: M. J. Abdolmohammadi and W. J. Read, 1996, "An Investigation of the Relationship between Task Structure and Task Programmability in Audit Risk Assessment," *Asia-Pacific Journal of Accounting* 3 (1), pp. 137–154.

---

50. M. J. Abdolmohammadi, and W. J. Read, 1996, "An Investigation of the Relationship between Task Structure and Task Programmability in Audit Risk Assessment," *Asia-Pacific Journal of Accounting* 3 (1), pp. 137–154.

For those tasks that are classified as programmable, there is a contingency between task structure and decision aid type where tasks can be classified as structured for which the primary decision aid would be automation or semistructured for which the primary decision aid would be a DSS or unstructured in which the primary decision aid would be a KES. Thus:

H_{4-2} For programmable tasks, task structure determines the perceived choice of the decision aid: automation for structured tasks, DSS for semi-structured tasks, and KES for unstructured tasks.

The comprehensive inventory of audit tasks and the method used to compile it is provided in Chapter 5. In Chapter 6, we present the method used to collect data for the investigation of these hypotheses and those stated in Chapter 3.

Chapter 5

A Comprehensive Inventory of Auditing Tasks

In this chapter, we first describe the method used to develop a comprehensive inventory of audit tasks. We then present the details of 433 specific auditing tasks that we identified. In the next chapter we discuss the design and administration of a complete questionnaire used to collect data on task structure, experience level, and decision aids for these tasks from a sample of highly experienced auditors. While the data collected should inform other researchers about task characteristics, the inventory itself provides useful documentation of an extensive number of audit tasks.

FRAMEWORK USED FOR ORGANIZING THE AUDIT TASK INVENTORY

The basis for the inventory of audit tasks used in this study was the inventory of audit tasks developed by Abdolmohammadi.[1] The framework of the original inventory was modeled after one presented by Felix and Kinney.[2] The current inventory consists of six phases: Orientation, Understanding the Control Structure, Tests of Controls, Substantive Tests, Forming Opinion, and Financial Statements Reporting. Each phase is defined in Table 5.1. For the first five phases,

---

1. See M. J. Abdolmohammadi, 1999, "A Comprehensive Taxonomy of Task Structure and Knowledge Base Demands in Auditing," *Behavioral Research in Accounting* 11, pp. 51–92 for details about the original inventory.

2. For background related to the model, see W. L. Felix Jr., and W. R. Kinney Jr., 1982, "Research in the Auditor's Opinion Formulation Process: State of the Art," *The Accounting Review* 57(2), pp. 245–271.

Table 5.1
Descriptions of the Six Phases of the Audit

Orientation Phase
Definition: Orientation may be broadly defined as the gathering of information about the client and the environment in which it operates. As such, the orientation process can be regarded as a prerequisite to the development of a planning scheme at a strategic level. In the orientation step, the auditor gains knowledge of the geographic, economic, and industrial setting of the client organization, the nature of the client's operations, the competence and ethics of managerial and financial personnel and the nature and characteristics of the accounting or financial reporting systems of the client.

Understanding the Control Structure Phase
Definition: This phase relates to an understanding of the client's control environment, the accounting system, and control procedures. This understanding is based on observation and inquiry, involving a walk-through of various types of individual transactions to establish that prescribed procedures are understood and applied. Basically, this is an assessment of the error-generation propensities of the various components of the client accounting system. Error-generation propensities are related to the auditor's assessment of the quality of the design of the internal accounting controls and the likely compliance of system operation with the design.

Tests of Control Phase
Definition: The purpose of tests of controls is to provide reasonable assurance that the accounting control procedures are being applied as prescribed. Such tests are necessary if the prescribed procedures are to be relied on in determining the nature, timing, or extent of substantive tests of particular classes of transactions or balances but are not necessary if the procedures are not to be relied on for that purpose.

Substantive Tests Phase
Definition: The purpose of substantive tests is to obtain evidence of the validity and propriety of the accounting treatment of transactions and balances or, conversely, of errors or irregularities therein. Substantive tests are applied when the auditor's purpose is to see whether the dollar amount of an account balance is materially misstated. Thus, substantive tests are used to obtain evidential matter.

Forming Opinion Phase
Definition: After a reevaluation process is carried out for all components of the financial statements, the evidence from all of the components is, according to current practice, aggregated subjectively. As a result of this subjective aggregation process, the auditor is in a position to express an opinion in the auditor's report on the financial statements taken as a whole. An audit report formally communicates the auditor's conclusion on the presentations of financial statements and concisely states the basis for that conclusion.

Financial Statements Reporting Phase
Definition: This phase relates to an overall review of financial statements and related notes by the auditor. Although the auditor issues the audit report, management is responsible for the financial statements including related notes and supplementary data, whether contained in a document prepared by the client or submitted by the auditor.

the definitions were adapted from Felix and Kinney[3] and for the sixth phase, the definition was developed by one of the authors.

DEVELOPMENT OF THE LIST OF AUDITING TASKS

To develop the current inventory of audit tasks, each task in the original inventory was reviewed to determine whether it was still valid. Changes in terminology were made to individual tasks where necessary to be consistent with Statements on Auditing Standards in effect at the time. After updating the original task inventory for changes in auditing standards, Canadian authoritative auditing literature was reviewed for revisions that would make the task inventory appropriate for both U.S. and Canadian auditors.[4] Only one task was reworded to be more general. Task FO-269 includes reference to the OSC (Canada's securities regulatory authority) in addition to referring to the SEC (Securities and Exchange Commission). Otherwise every task was expected to be equally applicable to auditors, whether from the United States or Canada.

Abdolmohammadi's original inventory of tasks consisted of 332 auditing tasks and drew on several audit manuals and an auditing text. Several additional sources were used to supplement the original inventory, providing in total 433 auditing tasks in the current inventory. The CICA (Canadian Institute of Chartered Accountants) Handbook,[5] Professional Engagement Manual,[6] "Bridging the GAAP,"[7] an audit manual from an anonymous auditing firm and an auditing text[8] were consulted.

The CICA Handbook includes generally accepted accounting principles (GAAP) and generally accepted auditing standards for Canadian chartered accountants. The Professional Engagement

---

3. Ibid., p. 247.
4. We had intended to include both U.S. and Canadian auditors in this study but found it unfeasible to secure participation from Canadian auditors. We therefore include only U.S. auditors in the results with one exception. There is one participant from a Canadian office of one of the Big Six public accounting firms.
5. Canadian Institute of Chartered Accountants, 1994, *CICA Handbook, Volume I and II* (Toronto: The Canadian Institute of Chartered Accountants).
6. R. Goodall and A. Skinner, 1994, *Professional Engagement Manual* (Toronto: The Canadian Institute of Chartered Accountants).
7. Coopers and Lybrand, 1991, *Bridging the GAAP: Accounting in Canada and the United States, 1991-92 Edition* (Canada: Coopers and Lybrand).
8. A. A. Arens and J. K. Loebbecke, 1994, *Auditing: An Integrated Approach* (Upper Saddle River, N.J.: Prentice-Hall).

Manual was also published by the CICA. Whereas the CICA Handbook provides official pronouncements, the Professional Engagement Manual provides guidelines for performing an audit. The manual is intended to be used by firms as the basis for their own audit manuals. The Professional Engagement Manual includes several sample checklists and forms for use by auditors. The Coopers and Lybrand publication, "Bridging the GAAP" summarizes significant differences between U.S. and Canadian GAAP. Careful review of these three sources yielded additional tasks that applied to both U.S. and Canadian audits. Table 5.2 compares the task inventory from Abdolmohammadi's original inventory to the current task inventory. In total, 247 tasks were exactly the same in both inventories. Fourteen tasks from Abdolmohammadi's inventory were eliminated. Seventy-one other tasks were similar across both inventories but had slightly different wording. The majority of the wording changes were made to clarify or enhance the task description. Some wording changes were made to align the description of the task with Statements on Auditing Standards which came into effect subsequent to Abdolmohammadi's inventory. A total of 115 auditing tasks were added in the inventory in an attempt to make it as comprehensive as possible. Because of the similarity between Canadian and American auditing standards, we did not find it necessary to add any tasks to accommodate possible use of the inventory by Canadian

Table 5.2
Comparison of Task Inventory in 1988 Study to Current Task Inventory

Phase of Audit	Number of Tasks				
	Total 1988 Study	Total 1996 Study	Exactly the Same	Some Difference	Added to Enhance Inventory
Orientation	45	58	35	10	13
Understanding the Control Structure	41	48	35	5	8
Tests of Controls	34	38	17	11	10
Substantive Tests	171	244	128	36	80
Forming Opinion	23	27	15	8	4
Financial Statements Reporting	18	18	17	1	0
Totals	332	433	247	71	115

auditors. We found however, that consulting the Canadian auditing resources was very useful in improving the comprehensiveness of the inventory.

After speaking with a few Canadian auditors and two Canadian Accounting professors, and reviewing the Coopers and Lybrand publication and a Canadian auditing text,[9] it became apparent that there are not many surface differences between audit tasks performed in Canada and those performed in the United States. In the introduction to "Bridging the GAAP," the authors state, "Financial statement presentation and disclosure, accounting principles and their methods of application are very similar in Canada and the United States."[10]

DESCRIPTION OF THE COMPREHENSIVE INVENTORY OF TASKS

The method described above resulted in a comprehensive listing of 433 audit tasks. The total task inventory is organized into six general audit phases and 39 subphases. Definitions of the six major phases were provided in Table 5.1. Each of the major phases was broken down into several subphases with detailed tasks within each subphase. The appendix to this chapter includes the detailed audit tasks organized by phase and subphase. The first column indicates the task's number in the current study (1996 study). The second column refers to the task number of the comparable task in Abdolmohammadi's inventory[11] (1988 study). A brief explanation of the contents of each phase follows.

Orientation

The purpose of the Orientation phase is for the auditor(s) to obtain information about the client, its operations, management, accounting systems and the company's environment. Therefore, the Orientation phase section of the audit task inventory consists of four subsections: Understanding the Client's Business (14 tasks),

---

9. W. B. Meigs, O. R. Whittington, R. F. Meigs, and W. P. Lam, 1987, *Principles of Auditing,* 3d Canadian ed. (Homewood, Ill.: Irwin).

10. Coopers and Lybrand, 1991, *Bridging the GAAP,* p. 4.

11. See the Appendix of M. J. Abdolmohammadi, 1999, "A Comprehensive Taxonomy of Task Structure and Knowledge Base Demands in Auditing," pp. 51–92 for a detailed listing of tasks in the original inventory.

Engagement Risk Assessment (23 tasks), Inherent Risk Assessment (14 tasks), and General Considerations (7 tasks) for a total of 58 tasks. The end result of this phase of the audit should be a tentative audit strategy. The detailed auditing tasks for the Orientation phase are listed in the appendix.

Primary to developing a tentative audit strategy is knowing the nature of the business(es) the client is in and obtaining an understanding of how the company produces its product(s) and/or performs services. To determine a general level of audit intensity, auditors attempt to determine the level of engagement risk and inherent risk for the various accounts to be audited. To assess engagement risk one must consider the potential for management fraud as well as the overall probability that the audit firm would issue an unqualified opinion in error. Many of the tasks in this phase therefore require the auditor to consider the management, outside influences that might motivate management fraud or misstatements, and the potential for accounting or auditing problems to occur due to the nature of transactions.

The preliminary assessment of inherent risk for each account consists of evaluating how susceptible the account may be to misstatement. Under general considerations, the tasks include assessing the potential that an outsider might question complete compliance with generally accepted auditing standards (GAAS). The auditor(s) must also consider the high-risk areas of the audit, the potential use of client staff and a preliminary determination of materiality. The Orientation phase as a whole is a very critical information gathering phase of the audit. The preliminary assessment of the scope of the audit will be made in this phase.

Understanding the Control Structure

The second major phase of the audit is Understanding the Control Structure phase. The tasks in this phase are separated into 10 subsections: General Considerations (7 tasks), Accounting Systems and Internal Control (9 tasks), Special Internal Control Factors (4 tasks), Preventive Controls (4 tasks), Detective Controls (3 tasks), Control Environment (6 tasks), Competence of Personnel (3 tasks), EDP Control Environment (8 tasks), Internal Audit Function (3 tasks), and Management Override (1 task) for a total of 48 tasks. These tasks are presented in the appendix.

This phase requires the auditor to gain an understanding of the client's control environment, accounting controls, and internal controls in general. The auditor achieves this understanding by talking to key personnel in the client firm with knowledge of the control systems. Tasks include evaluating policies and procedures within the accounting system in place as well as performing walk-through tests on a few transactions to ensure that existing policies and procedures are being followed. Some tasks relate to whether the employees' duties are designed to prevent and detect errors. The auditor must also evaluate the personnel policies and recent history to ascertain whether current personnel pose a risk to internal control.

The quality of the control environment is assessed to help the auditor determine the confidence that should be placed in the control systems and the likelihood that employees will be encouraged to comply with the systems. After investigating the control structure, the auditors should be prepared to decide how much they will rely on the client's control systems and internal auditing function when planning detailed testing. The preliminary assessment of control risk results from information gained in this phase. If control risk is assessed at the maximum level indicating that controls should not be relied on, then testing of controls will not take place. However, if the auditor decides that there is less than maximum risk, he or she determines the cost of testing controls and decides whether the benefit of reduced substantive testing is worth the cost of testing controls.

Tests of Controls

The third phase of the audit is the Tests of Controls Phase. After the auditor gains a sufficient understanding of the control structure of the client company, and the controls that are in place, the auditor would have decided how much reliance would be placed on the control system as opposed to more extensive substantive testing. The controls that will be relied on are tested to assure the auditor that they are effective in preventing and detecting errors and irregularities. This phase consists of five subsections: Nature, Timing and Extent of Tests (15 tasks), EDP Issues (2 tasks), Audit Sampling for Tests of Controls (7 tasks), Control Deviations (3 tasks), and Evaluation of Results of Tests of Controls (11 tasks) for a total of 38 tasks. These tasks are presented in the appendix.

This phase differs from the previous phase in its approach to the control system. To gain an understanding of the control structure, one studies the system purported to be in place to determine whether it appears to be adequate. In the testing phase, one determines whether that system is being adhered to by employees and then whether the system is effective.

For testing, initially the auditor attempts to determine whether there is adequate separation of duties and whether other general accounting controls are being followed. For example, the auditor determines the level of adherence to procedures for safeguarding access to and use of assets and records.

Then the auditor determines the adequate sample size and selects samples as test data to run through the controls. If there are deviations from the way controls are intended to work, they will be evaluated as to cause and then effect on planned reliance. The results of the tests of controls are evaluated to determine the level of control risk for the audit. The acceptable level of detection risk is also determined in preparation for the next phase of the audits which is substantive testing.

Substantive Tests

The fourth phase of the audit is the Substantive Tests Phase. The purpose of this phase is to perform tests of accounting data that will provide direct evidence about the validity of account balances. This section consists of 11 subsections: General Procedures (4 tasks), Analytical Review Procedures (3 tasks) and nine sub-sections of substantive testing for individual accounts and transaction cycles, Cash (20 tasks), Revenue and Receipt Cycle (31 tasks), Purchasing and Disbursements Cycle (39 tasks), Inventory (37 tasks), Fixed Assets (30 tasks), Payroll and Related Costs (16 tasks), Investments (25 tasks), Indebtedness (26 tasks), and Ownership Equity (13 tasks) for a total of 244 tasks. Detailed task descriptions are listed in the appendix to this chapter.

Under General Procedures, the auditor considers the risk of misstatement in each area as well as acceptable detection risk to determine that planned procedures will result in detecting material misstatements with an acceptably low level of detection risk. Analytical review procedures are used in the initial planning phase of substantive testing as well as during the testing phase to assist in providing direct evidence in various areas and after substantive testing is completed and adjustments are made to determine the overall reasonableness of the financial information.

The tasks listed in each account and/or transaction cycle subsection are the specific substantive tests that would be performed by the auditor. For example, in the Cash subsection, two tasks are "the footing of cash receipts journal and cash disbursement journal and tracing to general ledger postings and bank statements" and "the counting or confirming of cash on hand and verification of reconciliation (e.g., petty cash, undeposited receipts, etc.)."

Forming Opinion

The fifth phase of the audit, Forming Opinion phase consists of evaluating the results of testing as well as other information to determine the type of audit opinion that should be issued. This phase consists of six subsections: General Considerations (6 tasks), Accounting Considerations (10 tasks), Adequacy of Disclosures in Financial Statements (4 tasks), Uncertainties (3 tasks), Other Information (2 tasks), and Type and Wording of the Audit Opinion (2 tasks) for a total of 27 tasks. These tasks are listed in the appendix to this chapter. In general, the auditor assesses whether the financial statements have been prepared in accordance with GAAP and SEC regulations and considers whether GAAS was followed. The auditor also considers whether uncorrected misstatements are material, whether they might be indicative of further undetected misstatements and whether they materially affect the assessed level of inherent and control risk.

In determining the appropriate audit opinion, the auditor must also consider the adequacy of disclosure in the financial statements, whether the client should be requested to add disclosure items and whether there are any material uncertainties that would influence the wording in the audit opinion or the type of audit opinion issued.

Financial Statements Reporting

The final phase of the audit is the Financial Statements Reporting phase. Although the financial statements are the responsibility of the management of the client firm, the auditor will review the financial statements and related notes in detail. This phase consists of three subsections: Financial Statements (7 tasks), Consolidated Statements (6 tasks), and Footnotes to the Financial Statements (5 tasks) for a total of 18 tasks. These tasks are listed in the appendix to this chapter. The auditor may make suggestions to the client for changes in the presentation of the financial statements and/or to the footnotes. The auditor's detailed review described in this section complements the considerations made about the financial statements and notes that were described in the Forming Opinion phase.

CONTRIBUTION OF THE COMPREHENSIVE TASK INVENTORY

The level of detail at which the 433 auditing tasks are specified should prove very useful to auditing researchers, practitioners, educators, and students. Although some of the large professional service firms have changed their overall audit approaches to focus on business processes and/or risk, the specific detailed tasks performed should not change substantially.

Auditing researchers can refer to the comprehensive task inventory to find in one place the various tasks that are performed in each stage of the audit. They may want to know, for example, that one task is performed in Understanding the Control Structure phase that is essentially similar to another task in Substantive Testing. Audit professionals may find the inventory useful to guide training programs. Training directors may refer to the inventory to make sure they incorporate the necessary auditing tasks for particular phases of the audit. Audit educators and students may use the inventory to supplement a textbook or other materials in an Auditing class. The inventory provides valuable information that might otherwise be provided in an engagement manual or electronic database at an auditing firm but not usually available at a college or university. Even without the results of the study (reported in Chapters 7 and 8), the detailed task inventory has many potential uses for various constituencies.

APPENDIX

Orientation Phase: Comprehensive Listing of Audit Tasks

1996 Study	1988 Study	Understanding the Client's Business
OR 1	—	The setting up of a permanent file to capture relevant and significant information of a continuing nature (first year engagement)
OR 2	—	The updating of a permanent file as necessitated by major changes in client's circumstances (continuing clients)
OR 3	OR 3	The assessment of client's business and organization (ownership and management characteristics; organizational structure; attorneys, bankers, consultants, and underwriters)
OR 4	—	The assessment of the effects of external variables (significant industry trends; primary competitors; effects of general economic and political conditions on operations, financing or investment activities)
OR 5	—	The evaluation of key financial management characteristics (general planning, budgets, financial statements, managerial and internal reports and documents, liquidity, ability to generate working capital)
OR 6	OR 6	The evaluation of key operating factors (products, methods of production and peculiar characteristics). (See industry audit guide or similar industry information and watch the company make the product.)
OR 7	OR 7	The review of the correspondence files, permanent files, and the work papers of last year
OR 8	—	The preparation of the memorandum for the interim audit file giving a brief description of all client accounting ledgers, journals and records
OR 9	—	The examination of client monthly or annual financial statements (including those of subsidiaries and affiliates) to identify trends, audit risks and as a basis for determining the planning materiality
OR 10	—	The participation in meetings with client's audit committee
OR 11	OR 9	The communication with a predecessor auditor for a new engagement
OR 12	OR 10	The tour of client's office and facilities
OR 13	OR 11	The identification of client's short- and long-term objectives (e.g., pretax earnings, company's market share, etc.)
OR 14	OR 12	The study and evaluation of client's plans for achieving short- and long-term objectives (e.g., disposition of unprofitable product lines or subsidiaries, acquisition of additional product lines or companies)

Orientation Phase: Comprehensive Listing of Audit Tasks (Cont'd)

1996 Study	1988 Study	Engagement Risk Assessment
OR 15	OR 13	The assessment of management experience and knowledge
OR 16	OR 14	The assessment of management turnover during the audit period
OR 17	OR 15	The assessment of management aggressiveness in committing the entity to high risk ventures or projects
OR 18	OR 19	The assessment of the degree of emphasis on meeting earnings projections
OR 19	OR 16	The assessment of the degree to which the accounting function is decentralized
OR 20	—	The determination of adequacy of number of accounting personnel as well as their experience and ability to carry out tasks properly
OR 21	OR 17	The assessment of the profitability of the entity relative to its industry
OR 22	OR 18	The assessment of the sensitivity of operating results to inflation and changes in interest rates
OR 23	OR 20	The assessment of the rate of change in entity's industry
OR 24	OR 21	The assessment of the centralization of operations
OR 25	OR 22	The examination of allegations of improper or criminal behavior against the entity or its management
OR 26	OR 23	The assessment of the degree of regulation of the entity
OR 27	OR 24	The determination of the ownership of the entity
OR 28	OR 25	The assessment of the expectation of change in ownership or organization structure in the next year
OR 29	—	The determination of the outside debt (degree to which client is leveraged)
OR 30	OR 27	The assessment of the management attitude about financial reporting
OR 31	OR 28	The identification of contentious accounting issues
OR 32	OR 29	The determination of the frequency and significance of hard-to-audit transactions
OR 33	—	The performance of analytical review of interim financial statements to identify potential accounting or auditing problems affecting current year
OR 34	—	The assessment of credit and contract terms, warranty plans, right of return and guarantees of customer obligations
OR 35	—	The evaluation of projected income error discovered in prior year's audit
OR 36	OR 31	The determination of the period of relationship with client
OR 37	—	The aggregation of all factors identified above to assess engagement risk

Orientation Phase: Comprehensive Listing of Audit Tasks (Cont'd)

1996 Study	1988 Study	**Inherent Risk Assessment**
OR 38	OR 33	The determination of unusual accounting policies and practices (consult the number and significance of audit adjustments and waived audit differences in prior year's audit)
OR 39	OR 34	The evaluation of the complexity of underlying calculations or principles
OR 40	—	The assessment of the susceptibility of the asset under audit to material fraud or misappropriation (e.g., evaluation of cash management practices: electronic funds transfer, interbank transfer, overnight investments of excess cash)
OR 41	—	The assessment of problems relating to realization of assets, contingent liabilities or other unusual uncertainties
OR 42	OR 36	The assessment of the experience and competence of accounting personnel responsible for the account
OR 43	—	The assessment of the degree of judgment required in the timing of revenue recognition
OR 44	—	The assessment of significant problems relating to accounting estimates or measurements of unusual significance resulting from the nature of the industry or relative importance in the financial statements
OR 45	OR 37	The assessment of the difficulty in judging the balance of the account
OR 46	OR 38	The determination of the mix and size of items comprising the account
OR 47	OR 39	The assessment of the degree to which circumstances (e.g., the financial condition of the company) may motivate management to misstate the account
OR 48	OR 41	The assessment of the volume and complexity of transactions flow and control over these flows
OR 49	OR 42	The assessment of the susceptibility to management override of existing controls
OR 50	—	The evaluation of extent of system computerization and application risks associated with processing transactions (risks and controls vary from one application system to another)
OR 51	—	The aggregation of all factors identified above to assess inherent risk for each account
		General Considerations
OR 52	—	The assessment of the likelihood that the compliance of the examination with generally accepted auditing standards may be questioned (consider independence, previous auditor's scope limitations, reliance on another firm, affiliated companies, related parties)

Orientation Phase: Comprehensive Listing of Audit Tasks (Cont'd)

1996 Study	1988 Study	General Considerations (Cont'd)
OR 53	OR 43	The identification of critical audit areas (areas difficult to audit, judgmental areas, high inherent risk areas)
OR 54	OR 44	The coordination of the audit with client's staff (schedules to be prepared by the client, arrangements for availability and retention of client records, arrangements for inventory observation)
OR 55	OR 45	The scheduling of audit staff and consideration of other audit logistics (budgets; specialists, if any; timing of the review of the audit by the in-charge accountant, manager or/and partner)
OR 56	—	The preliminary determination of materiality
OR 57	—	The development of a tentative audit strategy
OR 58	—	For subsidiary and affiliated companies, the determination of appropriate procedures if other auditing firms audited these companies

Understanding the Control Structure Phase: Comprehensive Listing of Audit Tasks

1996 Study	1988 Study	General Considerations
CS 146	CS 1	The preliminary evaluation of internal controls (client accounting policies and procedures; general condition under which accounting data are produced, processed, reviewed, and accumulated within the organization) including EDP operations
CS 147	CS 2	The review of correspondence files, prior year's work papers, permanent files, and prior years' financial statements and audit reports
CS 148	CS 3	The inquiry of personnel familiar with control environment and observation of the control environment and flow of transactions through the accounting system
CS 149	CS 4	The completion of a generalized questionnaire, checklist, or narrative memorandum that organizes and summarizes the information obtained by applying the procedures for preliminary evaluation
CS 150	—	The preliminary assessment of control risk supported by understanding gained
CS 151	—	The determination of whether control risk could be reduced to below maximum with sufficient evidence from tests of controls, and the cost and efficiency of obtaining such evidence
CS 152	—	The determination of cost of testing controls for which risk is preliminarily assessed at below maximum and the accumulation of sufficient audit evidence to support the assessment

Accounting Systems and Internal Control

CS 153	—	The study and evaluation of policy and procedures manuals relating to the conduct of business
CS 154	CS 31	The evaluation of policies and procedures to safeguard records and assets (e.g., recovery procedures, and detection of unauthorized access to assets and records)
CS 155	—	The evaluation of policies and procedures for authorization and approval (general and specific) of transactions and activities
CS 156	CS 8	The evaluation of policies and procedures to prevent or detect errors and irregularities
CS 157	CS 9	The evaluation of the policies and procedures to secure the accuracy and completeness of the accounting records

Understanding the Control Structure Phase: Comprehensive Listing of Audit Tasks (Cont'd)

1996 Study	1988 Study	Accounting Systems and Internal Control (Cont'd)
CS 158	CS 10	The evaluation of the policies and procedures for the timely preparation of reliable financial information
CS 159	CS 11	The determination of the controls that could be relied upon should compliance tests indicate low error rates
CS 160	CS 12	The documentation of the system only to the extent needed to gain an understanding and develop an audit program which concentrates on substantive testing
CS 161	—	The performance of simple walk through tests on a few transactions to ensure that the accounting and internal control procedures described are in fact carried out by accounting personnel
		Special Internal Control Factors
CS 162	CS 13	The determination of the existence and adequacy of boundary controls (use and control of prenumbered shipping documents, EDP control components: access, system development and program change)
CS 163	CS 14	The determination of the existence and adequacy of processing controls (e.g., review account distribution by responsible official, variance analyses)
CS 164	CS 15	The determination of the existence and adequacy of safeguarding controls
CS 165	CS 16	The identification and proper classification of population and accuracy controls in examining boundary and processing controls
		Preventive Controls
CS 166	CS 17	The evaluation of the division of duties of client staff
CS 167	CS 18	The determination of the degree to which duties of client staff are documented
CS 168	CS 19	The determination of the degree of reperformance of tasks by client staff
CS 169	CS 20	The examination of the use of batch totals by client
		Detective Controls
CS 170	—	The determination of the reconciliations prepared by the client (e.g., reconciling accounting records and detailed source documents)
CS 171	CS 22	The assessment of the degree of client's reviews of procedures and accounting data

Understanding the Control Structure Phase: Comprehensive Listing of Audit Tasks (Cont'd)

1996 Study	1988 Study	
		Detective Controls (Cont'd)
CS 172	CS 23	The assessment of the degree of comparisons made by a client staff not involved in the activity being controlled
		Control Environment
CS 173	—	The evaluation of control consciousness to establish the degree to which the client management has recognized the need for effective controls (management's philosophy, operating style, functioning of the board of directors and audit committee)
CS 174	—	The inquiry of management (through questionnaires and/or interviews) to understand the financial reporting risk assessment process of the client
CS 175	CS 25	The assessment of the clarity of definitions of responsibilities
CS 176	CS 26	The assessment of adequacy of management involvement in designing and approving accounting system procedures and controls
CS 177	CS 27	The examination of the client's responsiveness to identified control problems
CS 178	—	The consideration of external influences that affect an entity's operations and practices (e.g., examinations by regulatory agencies)
		Competence of Personnel
CS 179	CS 28	The evaluation of the relevant experience of personnel
CS 180	CS 29	The determination of the turnover of personnel
CS 181	CS 30	The evaluation of the client's procedures related to replacement, training, supervision and evaluation of personnel
		EDP Control Environment
CS 182	—	The evaluation of segregation of duties between electronic data processing (EDP) department and related user departments and within EDP department
CS 183	CS 33	The evaluation of sufficiency of policies and procedures pertaining to access to computer, terminals, magnetic storage media, and documentation

Understanding the Control Structure Phase: Comprehensive Listing of Audit Tasks (Cont'd)

1996 Study	1988 Study	**EDP Control Environment (Cont'd)**
CS 184	—	The evaluation of the sufficiency of safeguards that contribute to the continuity of processing (e.g., offsite back-up of data and computer programs and recovery procedures in case of theft, loss or intentional or accidental destruction of data or computer programs)
CS 185	CS 34	The evaluation of development controls concerning the design and testing of new systems
CS 186	—	The evaluation of controls pertaining to changes to existing systems
CS 187	CS 35	The evaluation of the controls entirely dependent on manual procedures
CS 188	CS 36	The evaluation of the controls dependent upon a combination of manual and computerized procedures
CS 189	CS 37	The evaluation of the existence and adequacy of EDP application controls: input, file, processing, and output controls
		Internal Audit Function
CS 190	CS 38	The evaluation of the qualifications and performance of internal audit personnel
CS 191	CS 39	The evaluation of objectivity and unbiasedness of internal audit personnel
CS 192	CS 40	The evaluation of adequacy of documentation of work performed by internal audit personnel
		Management Override
CS 193	CS 41	The assessment of significant management override (circumstances motivating override, e.g., income based bonus plans or market pressures to meet forecast results)

Tests of Controls Phase: Comprehensive Listing of Audit Tasks

1996 Study	1988 Study	Nature, Timing, and Extent of the Tests
TC 290	—	The estimation of the degree to which the client segregates incompatible functions of its staff (e.g., separation of authorization of transactions, recording of transactions and custody of assets)
TC 291	TC 15	The evaluation of the degree of employees' understanding of the duties of others
TC 292	—	The determination of the level of adherence to authorization and approval (general and specific) policies and procedures for transactions and activities
TC 293	TC 3	The determination of recording accuracy of transactions (accurate classification, correct amount, proper period, and adequate detail)
TC 294	—	The determination of the level of adherence to procedures for safeguarding access to and use of assets and records
TC 295	—	The determination of the level of adherence to procedures for reconciling accounting records and detailed source documents (including procedures to record adjustments)
TC 296	—	The determination of the extent of client's review and reconciliation procedures (clerical checks, reconciliations, management review of computer-generated reports)
TC 297	TC 6	If manual accounting system, the action of obtaining evidence in the form of signatures, initials, audit stamps, and the like to determine the degree to which the procedures were performed, and by whom
TC 298	—	The determination of the degree to which the client segregates incompatible functions within the data processing department
TC 299	TC 8	The determination of the degree of segregation between data processing and user department personnel performing review procedures
TC 300	—	The determination of the level of adherence to control procedures for access to data and computer programs
TC 301	—	The determination of the nature (i.e., inquiry, observation, inspection, reperformance), extent and amount of tests of transactions or account balances involved
TC 302	—	The documentation of tests of controls including the specific transactions examined and the specific tests carried out on those transactions
TC 303	—	The evaluation of the results of the tests of controls

Tests of Controls Phase: Comprehensive Listing of Audit Tasks (Cont'd)

1996 Study	1988 Study	Nature, Timing, and Extent of the Tests (Cont'd)
TC 304	TC 14	The evaluation of the propriety of operations in the entire period covered by the financial statements
		EDP Issues
TC 305	TC 17	If computer assisted audit techniques are feasible, the preparation of test data to be processed using client's programs, and the comparison of obtained results with anticipated results
TC 306	TC 18	If computer assisted audit techniques are not feasible, the consideration of a manual performance while ensuring cost-effectiveness
		Audit Sampling for Tests of Controls
TC 307	—	The definition of the population from which the sample is to be drawn, and ensuring that it is appropriate for the specific audit objective
TC 308	TC 20	The determination of the maximum rate of deviations from a prescribed control procedure that will be acceptable, without altering planned reliance
TC 309	TC 21	The definition of error or deviations in relation to the tests' objectives
TC 310	TC 22	The definition of the sampling item and of sample size in relation to the control procedure to be tested
TC 311	TC 23	The determination of the manner in which the documents are filed and cross-referenced
TC 312	TC 24	The selection of the sampling method (random selection, stratified random sampling, sampling with probability proportional to size, systematic sampling) to be used
TC 313	TC 25	The evaluation of the limitations that hinder the application of planned audit procedures
		Control Deviations
TC 314	—	The investigation of the cause of control deviations
TC 315	TC 26	The evaluation of the audit significance of cause of the deviations
TC 316	TC 28	The assessment of the effect of deviations on planned reliance
		Evaluation of Results of Tests of Controls
TC 317	—	Based on the results of tests of controls, the evaluation of the adequacy of internal controls, and determination of the degree of reliance that is appropriate

Tests of Controls Phase: Comprehensive Listing of Audit Tasks (Cont'd)

1996 Study	1988 Study	Evaluation of Results of Tests of Controls (Cont'd)
TC 318	TC 30	If reliance on a particular internal control is not appropriate, the ascertaining as to whether there is another control which would satisfy the purpose
TC 319	—	The investigation of internal control weaknesses including, for example, comparing documents with their supporting evidence and comparing actual with budgeted figures and investigation of the differences
TC 320	—	The evaluation of the effect of weaknesses on potential errors (e.g., identify types of errors and materiality)
TC 321	—	If an internal accounting control objective is not met, the evaluation of the audit risks of there being material error or fraud in the financial statements and the determination of what effect this will have on the auditor's opinion
TC 322	—	Where the results of tests of controls indicate that internal accounting control procedures are not performed, the modification of the system documentation to describe the system as it actually is functioning
TC 323	—	The documentation in the working papers of the conclusions on potential misstatements as a result of internal control weaknesses discovered
TC 324	—	The communication of material weaknesses to the client on a timely basis
TC 325	TC 34	The projection of sample results to the population
TC 326	—	Based on the tests of controls performed and control weaknesses identified, the assessment of level of control risk and acceptable level of detection risk
TC 327	—	Documentation of the bases for conclusions about the assessed level of control risk (unless assessed at the maximum level)

Substantive Tests Phase: Comprehensive Listing of Audit Tasks—General and Analytical Review Procedures

1996 Study	1988 Study	General Procedures
ST 59	ST 1	The assessment of the risk of material misstatement associated with a given specific account area and a given audit objective
ST 60	—	The determination of the quality and type of audit evidence required to limit the detection risk to an acceptable level
ST 61	ST 4	The evaluation of the effect of immaterial misstatements in "high-profile" areas (e.g., related parties)
ST 62	—	The modification of audit procedures to ensure that any material errors have a reasonable chance of being detected
		Analytical Review Procedures (ARP)
ST 63	ST 5	The use of ARP in the initial planning stages to assist in determining the nature, extent and timing of other auditing procedures
ST 64	ST 6	The use of ARP during the conduct of examination in conjunction with other procedures applied by the auditor to individual elements of financial information
ST 65	ST 7	The use of ARP at or near the conclusion of the examination as an overall review of the financial information

Substantive Tests Phase: Comprehensive Listing of Audit Tasks — Cash

1996 Study	1988 Study	
ST 66	ST 25	The reviewing of balance sheet classification of cash
ST 67	ST 8	The selection of a sample of remittance advices and tracing to accounting records (accounts receivable detail, bank statements, recorded cash receipts)
ST 68	ST 10	The footing of cash receipts journal and cash disbursement journal and tracing to general ledger postings and bank statements
ST 69	—	The inquiry and observation of bank reconciliations prepared by client
ST 70	ST 11	The inspection of client reconciliations and reperformance of one or a few reconciliations
ST 71	—	The task of establishing whether all bank accounts are included (consider prior year working papers, accounts authorized in the minutes); confirm accounts closed since the previous audit
ST 72	ST 20	The receipt of bank confirmation letters and confirmation of bank balance
ST 73	ST 21	The agreeing of bank reconciliations to confirmations
ST 74	—	The agreeing of bank reconciliation to general ledger
ST 75	ST 22	The verification of the propriety of reconciling items
ST 76	ST 12	The consideration of reasonableness of reconciling items and explanations of such items
ST 77	ST 13	For the sample of canceled checks, the inspection of supporting documents for cancellation, check number, and endorsement
ST 78	ST 15	For the sample of canceled checks, the comparison of check number, amount, payee, and date with cash disbursement record.
ST 79	ST 16	The consideration of whether canceled checks cleared the bank within a reasonable period of recording and were treated properly in bank reconciliation
ST 80	ST 17	The agreeing of supporting schedules to trial balance and subsidiary records
ST 81	ST 18	The verification of mathematical accuracy of all relevant supporting schedules
ST 82	ST 23	The verification of cut-off for payments, receipts and transfers
ST 83	—	The counting or confirming of cash on hand and verification of reconciliation (e.g., petty cash, undeposited receipts, etc.)

Substantive Tests Phase: Comprehensive Listing of Audit Tasks— Cash (Cont'd)

1996 Study	1988 Study	
ST 84	—	The documentation of transactions and ending balances with intergroup or other related parties
ST 85	ST 26	The review of classification of accounts (current/noncurrent, credit balances, trade, intercompany, employees)

**Substantive Tests Phase: Comprehensive Listing of Audit Tasks—
Revenue and Receipt Cycle**

1996 Study	1988 Study	
ST 86	ST 46	The review of classification of accounts (current/noncurrent, credit balances, trade, intercompany, employees)
ST 87	ST 47	The review of revenue recognition policies for propriety and consistency
ST 88	ST 27	The comparative studies of sales, bad debts, cash receipts, warranties, returns, etc. (by product line and/or compared to budgets)
ST 89	ST 28	The review of aging analysis
ST 90	ST 29	The preparation of various ratio analyses for sales, cost of sales, and interest income
ST 91	ST 30	The verification of cut-off of sales, cash receipts, returns, and allowances
ST 92	ST 9	The observation of mailing of monthly statements, examining customer correspondence and complaints, and investigating noncash credits to accounts receivable
ST 93	ST 31	The confirmation of recorded receivables (amount, date, terms, interest rate, etc.)
ST 94	—	The confirmation of recorded sales transactions by customer (including tracing to purchase orders)
ST 95	ST 33	The review of sales contracts for terms, prices
ST 96	—	The agreement of selling price on selected sales invoices to authorized price list
ST 97	ST 34	The vouching of aging details to supporting documents, discussion of collectibility of receivables with responsible official and review of correspondence
ST 98	ST 35	The vouching of recorded receivables to supporting documentation
ST 99	—	The reconciliation of cash receipts to bank statement (proof of cash)
ST 100	ST 37	The verification of computation of interest income including premiums and discounts
ST 101	ST 38	The vouching of subsequent write-offs of bad debts and other credits to receivables in the subsequent period
ST 102	—	The scanning of sales and cash receipts journals for the year for large and unusual items and ascertaining the propriety of such items
ST 103	—	The checking of extensions and additions of selected sales invoices and credit notes
ST 104	—	The examination of selected credit notes for proper authorization and the agreement of selected credit notes to sales journal

**Substantive Tests Phase: Comprehensive Listing of Audit Tasks—
Revenue and Receipt Cycle (Cont'd)**

1996 Study	1988 Study	
ST 105	—	The agreement of selected sales invoices and credit notes to accounts receivable ledgers
ST 106	—	The checking of selected sales invoices and credit notes to ensure that the numerical sequence of prenumbered sales invoices and credit notes has been properly accounted for and that unused canceled copies are on file
ST 107	ST 39	The vouching of recorded receivables to subsequent cash receipts
ST 108	—	The vouching of sales from shipping records to related sales invoices and agreeing the amounts to the sales journal (including prices and other data)
ST 109	—	The tracing of sales from sales journal to shipping records
ST 110	—	For selected period, the agreement of sales journal to the general ledger
ST 111	ST 44	The analysis, review, and vouching of returns and allowances to supporting documentation
ST 112	ST 45	The analysis, review, and vouching of write-offs of uncollectible receivables to supporting documentation
ST 113	—	Documentation of the adequacy of the allowance for doubtful accounts.
ST 114	—	The documentation of transactions and ending balances with intergroup or related parties
ST 115	—	The investigation of material credit balances in accounts receivable; consider confirmation and reclassification to accounts payable
ST 116	ST 48	The vouching and review of disclosures (related parties, segment, significant customer, imputed interest income, economic dependency)

**Substantive Tests Phase: Comprehensive Listing of Audit Tasks—
Purchasing and Disbursements Cycle**

1996 Study	1988 Study	
ST 194	ST 66	The review of description and classification of accounts (current/noncurrent, intercompany)
ST 195	ST 67	The review of relevant accounting principles for propriety and consistency
ST 196	ST 49	The comparison of payables, purchases, and payments to budgets and prior periods
ST 197	—	The review of purchase general ledger accounts for large or unusual items
ST 198	—	The review of purchase journal for large or unusual items and ascertaining the propriety of such items
ST 199	—	The footing of the purchase journal for selected period
ST 200	—	The agreeing of purchase journal to general ledger
ST 201	ST 50	The comparison of accrual balances and related expenses to prior years
ST 202	ST 51	The computation of various ratios for purchases, payables, etc.
ST 203	—	The verification and documentation of cut-off for purchases, payments, claims, etc.
ST 204	—	The request for confirmation of suppliers' statements and preparation of a summary of confirmation results
ST 205	—	The ensuring that related costs of freight, brokerage, customs duties, and sales taxes for domestic and foreign purchasing transactions are recorded immediately
ST 206	—	The vouching of open claims to supporting documentation (invoices, receiving reports, shipping reports, vendor credit memos, correspondences)
ST 207	ST 55	The review of purchase contracts and creditors' terms of supply
ST 208	ST 56	The verification of computation of period accruals
ST 209	ST 57	The tracing of unmatched receiving reports to accounts payable provision
ST 210	ST 58	The vouching of unmatched invoices to accounts payable provision
ST 211	—	The verification of accounts payable by agreeing to suppliers' statements
ST 212	—	The selection of check copies from cash disbursements journal and agreeing them to accounts payable ledger
ST 213	—	The verifying of payment of selected invoices by examination of paid checks

**Substantive Tests Phase: Comprehensive Listing of Audit Tasks—
Purchasing and Disbursements Cycle (Cont'd)**

1996 Study	1988 Study	
ST 214	—	The review of selected check copies from cash disbursements journal for proper account distribution
ST 215	—	The review of liabilities recorded after period end, and review of the subsequent cash payments (vouching of subsequent disbursements to recorded receipt of goods and accounts payable balances)
ST 216	—	The obtaining of written confirmation from client's lawyers regarding outstanding litigation
ST 217	ST 61	The review of subsequent claims for credit from suppliers
ST 218	—	The scanning of cash disbursements journal for the year for large and unusual items and ascertaining the propriety of such items
ST 219	ST 62	The tracing of purchases from receiving reports to purchase journal (voucher register) including quantities, prices and other relevant data
ST 220	—	The verification that allowable discounts on selected purchase invoices were taken
ST 221	—	The verification of selected purchase invoices for proper account distribution
ST 222	—	The agreeing of prices charged on selected purchase invoices to purchase orders or other authority for the acquisition of goods and services
ST 223	—	The examination of selected purchase invoices for cancellation of supporting documents to prevent their reuse
ST 224	—	The verification of arithmetic on selected purchase invoices
ST 225	ST 63	The vouching of purchases and other disbursements from purchase journal to supporting documents including quantities, prices and other relevant data
ST 226	—	The examination of selected purchase invoices for evidence of proper approval of the expenditure
ST 227	—	The tracing of selected acquisitions under operating leases to general ledger, agreement of details to supporting documentation, and ascertainment that leases are properly classified as operating leases (inspect leased assets, confirm details with lessors)
ST 228	ST 64	The vouching of bank statement payments to canceled checks, cash book entry, and supporting documentation

**Substantive Tests Phase: Comprehensive Listing of Audit Tasks—
Purchasing and Disbursements Cycle (Cont'd)**

1996 Study	1988 Study	
ST 229	—	The discussion of the possible existence of commitments, contingencies or other significant subsequent events with client management
ST 230	—	The investigation of material debit balances in accounts payable and the consideration of reclassification to accounts receivable
ST 231	—	The review of insurance coverage to ensure adequate protection against normal risk
ST 232	—	The vouching and review of disclosures (related parties, segments, significant dependencies, subsequent events, commitments, etc.)

Substantive Tests Phase: Comprehensive Listing of Audit Tasks—Inventory

1996 Study	1988 Study	
ST 328	ST 95	The review of categorization of inventories
ST 329	ST 96	The review of relevant accounting principles for propriety and consistency
ST 330	—	The comparison of cost of sales and gross profit percentages by product line to prior period and to budget and obtaining explanation for large variations
ST 331	—	The comparative analysis of inventories by location as compared to prior periods
ST 332	ST 71	The computation of various inventory ratios
ST 333	ST 98	The performance of detailed analysis of various inventory ratios
ST 334	ST 72	The selection of a sample of vouchers and inspection for existence of supporting documents, agreement of details, clerical accuracy of vendor's invoice, and indication of approval
ST 335	ST 75	For the sample of vouchers selected, the review for correct classification and accounting period and indication of review and approval
ST 336	ST 73	The review of reports of unmatched items and inquiry about disposition
ST 337	ST 74	The selection of a sample of receiving reports and tracing to purchases journal or voucher register
ST 338	ST 76	The footing of voucher register and tracing to general ledger and inspection of supervisory review and approval of summarization and posting
ST 339	ST 77	The footing of purchases journal and tracing to accounts payable subsidiary ledger and inspection of supervisory review and approval of summarization and posting
ST 340	ST 78	The inspection of reconciliation and reperformance of one or a few reconciliations
ST 341	—	The review of client's inventory count instructions to ascertain that instructions provide for an accurate physical inventory count
ST 342	—	The inspection of inventories or testing of perpetual records
ST 343	ST 81	The identification of all inventory locations, considering locations owned and leased, outside contractors, etc.

Substantive Tests Phase: Comprehensive Listing of Audit Tasks—Inventory (Cont'd)

1996 Study	1988 Study	
ST 344	—	The performance of test counts for a sample of inventory throughout each inventory location observed and noting damaged, obsolete, and slow-moving items
ST 345	—	The evaluation of replacement cost, net realizable value or net realizable value less normal profit margin, as appropriate, of damaged, obsolete, and slow-moving items noted at physical inventory inspection
ST 346	—	The agreeing of quantities and amounts to physical inventory listing. The tracing of adjustments to general ledger and investigation of large or unusual items
ST 347	ST 87	The agreeing of quantities to test counts or auditor controlled count records
ST 348	—	The checking of clerical accuracy (additions and extensions of inventory listing)
ST 349	—	The agreeing of the pricing of major inventory categories by reference to: 1) supplier's invoices, 2) details of carrier's invoices, 3) payroll records for labor rates, and 4) subsequent sales invoices, price lists and customer contracts for net realizable or market values
ST 350	ST 80	The investigation of reasons for differences between perpetual and physical inventories
ST 351	ST 82	The confirmation of physical quantities held by third parties
ST 352	ST 83	The determination that cut-off is proper (purchases, shipments, intercompany, stage of production)
ST 353	ST 84	The vouching of material, labor, and overhead components
ST 354	ST 85	The analysis of variances from standard costs
ST 355	—	If standard costs are used, the ensuring that the disposition of variance accounts is appropriate
ST 356	ST 86	The verification of elimination of intercompany profits
ST 357	—	The documentation of transactions and ending balances with intergroup or related parties
ST 358	ST 89	The review of purchase commitments for losses and determination that disclosure is appropriate
ST 359	ST 91	The evaluation of whether selling prices according to contracts or invoices support value and recognized losses
ST 360	ST 92	The review of sales activity by product
ST 361	ST 93	The vouching of purchases of inventory to and from perpetual records

Substantive Tests Phase: Comprehensive Listing of Audit Tasks—Inventory (Cont'd)

1996 Study	1988 Study	
ST 362	ST 94	The vouching of sales to and from perpetual records
ST 363	—	The vouching and review of disclosures (valuation, method of determination, effect of change in valuation, unusual market write-downs, losses on purchase commitments)
ST 364	—	The review for consignment sales, pledging or assignment of inventories, customer and vendor goods on site

**Substantive Tests Phase: Comprehensive Listing of Audit Tasks—
Fixed Assets**

1996 Study	1988 Study	
ST 233	—	The review of classification and description of fixed assets
ST 234	ST 119	The review of relevant accounting principles for propriety and consistency
ST 235	ST 100	The comparative analysis of depreciation expense including tax basis depreciation
ST 236	ST 101	The comparative analysis of repairs and maintenance expense
ST 237	ST 102	The agreeing of beginning balances in fixed assets accounts to prior year working papers
ST 238	ST 103	The inspection of assets and tracing to records
ST 239	ST 104	The tracing of records to physical assets
ST 240	—	The examination of condition of assets to determine useful life (note any excess, unusable, or idle facilities)
ST 241	—	The review of tax bills, vehicle licenses and the making of other inquiries to verify that client has title to fixed assets
ST 242	ST 107	The review of propriety of asset valuation (land and buildings)
ST 243	—	The review for potential writedown of capital assets
ST 244	—	In the case of uncertainty as to the recoverability of the carrying value of capital assets, the determination that the write-down is appropriately determined
ST 245	—	The determination as to whether any liens and restrictions on ownership exist
ST 246	—	The ensuring of proper disclosure when adjustments are made to book values as a result of appraisals
ST 247	ST 108	The confirmation of assets held by third parties
ST 248	ST 109	The recomputation of depreciation (amortization) — book and tax basis
ST 249	ST 110	The review of propriety of cost of internally manufactured assets
ST 250	ST 113	The recomputation of capitalized interest
ST 251	ST 115	The examination of labor costs capitalized
ST 252	ST 111	The vouching of additions to supporting documents
ST 253	—	The physical examination of additions
ST 254	—	The vouching of disposals to supporting documents and recomputing gain or loss on disposals; the investigation of large or unusual items and the tracing of gains and losses to entries in general ledger

**Substantive Tests Phase: Comprehensive Listing of Audit Tasks—
Fixed Assets (Cont'd)**

1996 Study	1988 Study	
ST 255	—	The examination of leasing contracts; the testing of mathematical accuracy of capitalized lease amounts and confirmation of details with lessor
ST 256	—	The determination of the appropriateness of treatment of leases as capital leases
ST 257	ST 116	The examination of loan agreements
ST 258	—	The ensuring that the cost of capital assets acquired for research purposes are properly accounted for
ST 259	ST 117	The vouching of purchases and other disbursements for detecting fixed assets erroneously classified in some other expense or asset account
ST 260	—	The consideration of writing off assets fully depreciated, abandoned, destroyed, or otherwise put out of service
ST 261	—	The documentation of transactions and ending balances with intergroup or related parties
ST 262	—	The vouching and review of disclosures (e.g., capital leases, appraisal particulars, write-down of capital assets, and pledged assets)

**Substantive Tests Phase: Comprehensive Listing of Audit Tasks—
Payroll and Related Costs**

1996 Study	1988 Study	
ST 117	—	The act of having a responsible client's official review payroll details with you, examining personnel records for authorization of employment, current compensation basis and rate
ST 118	ST 130	The reviewing of relevant accounting principles for propriety and consistency
ST 119	ST 121	The comparison of payroll and related costs to expected values (budgets, prior years, union contracts, industry comparisons, etc.)
ST 120	—	The comparing of the number of employees by department with prior periods and obtaining plausible explanations of changes in number
ST 121	ST 122	The analysis of portion of payroll charged to assets versus expenses
ST 122	ST 123	The verification of payroll accrual based on ultimate amounts paid
ST 123	ST 124	The verification of calculations of accruals for payroll and related costs (profit sharing, vacation, holidays, bonuses, etc.)
ST 124	—	The reviewing of employee deduction accounts to ensure proper clearance each month
ST 125	—	The examination of paid payroll checks of selected employees and agreement of check number, date, payee, and amount with data in the payroll journal
ST 126	ST 125	The review and testing of compensation plans requiring actuarial computations including data submitted and assumptions made
ST 127	—	The verification of payroll deductions of selected employees
ST 128	ST 126	The vouching of subsequent remittance of amounts withheld
ST 129	—	For selected period, the addition of the payroll journal and agreement of payroll journal to the general ledger.

**Substantive Tests Phase: Comprehensive Listing of Audit Tasks—
Payroll and Related Costs (Cont'd)**

1996 Study	1988 Study	
ST 130	—	The vouching of payroll disbursements to supporting documentation including personnel records, timecards, or other support of hours worked, ascertaining that payroll is charged to appropriate account
ST 131	—	The attendance at payroll payout on a surprise basis, ensuring that employees sign to evidence receipt and that unclaimed wages are recorded
ST 132	ST 131	The reviewing of disclosure of pensions and other benefit plans

Substantive Tests Phase: Comprehensive Listing of Audit Tasks—Investments

1996 Study	1988 Study	
ST 365	ST 145	The review of relevant accounting principles for propriety and consistency
ST 366	ST 146	The review of description and classification of accounts
ST 367	ST 148	The review of minutes and management representations
ST 368	ST 132	The comparative review of income earned or receivable
ST 369	ST 133	The consideration of overall increase or decrease in portfolio value
ST 370	ST 134	The agreeing of beginning balances of investments to prior year working papers
ST 371	—	The inspection of securities on hand and evidence of title for securities held, ensuring that investment certificates on hand are maintained in vaults or safe deposit boxes
ST 372	ST 136	The confirmation of investments held by third parties
ST 373	—	The ensuring that long-term investments are written down where loss in value is not temporary
ST 374	ST 137	The testing of market price computation to published information
ST 375	—	The obtaining of market or current values, as of year-end date, of investments and comparing to book value
ST 376	—	The checking of material changes between year-end and date of auditor's report
ST 377	—	The verification that investments are reported at proper carrying value
ST 378	—	The inspection of latest financial statements of investees, examining the opinion of independent auditors and testing the accuracy of purchase accounting adjustments (amortization)
ST 379	ST 139	The review of investments for income receivable
ST 380	ST 140	The recomputation of profit taken on equity basis from audited financial statements
ST 381	ST 141	The vouching of purchases of investments to supporting documentation
ST 382	ST 142	The vouching of sales of investments to supporting documentation and recomputation of gain or loss on disposal
ST 383	ST 143	The vouching of income details to published information or other supporting data

Substantive Tests Phase: Comprehensive Listing of Audit Tasks—Investments (Cont'd)

1996 Study	1988 Study	
ST 384	—	The review of cash receipts subsequent to period end for unrecorded dividends or interest
ST 385	—	The recomputation of amortization of premium or discount
ST 386	ST 150	The inquiry about related parties
ST 387	—	The documentation of transactions and ending balances with intergroups and other related parties
ST 388	—	The act of obtaining reconciliation of investment listing to general ledger. Investigate larger or unusual reconciling items
ST 389	ST 147	The vouching and review of disclosures

Substantive Tests Phase: Comprehensive Listing of Audit Tasks—Indebtedness

1996 Study	1988 Study	
ST 390	ST 160	The review of relevant accounting principles for propriety and consistency
ST 391	ST 151	The comparative analysis of indebtedness to industry and prior years
ST 392	ST 152	The comparative analysis of effective interest rates including relationship to relevant external factors
ST 393	ST 153	The agreeing of beginning balances in schedules to prior year working papers
ST 394	ST 154	The confirmation of amount, terms and security of indebtedness with knowledgeable parties (holder, bank, trustee, etc.)
ST 395	—	The agreeing of overdrafts to cash section of working papers
ST 396	—	The agreement of proceeds of any bond issue to cash receipts journal and to terms of issue
ST 397	—	The verification that any bond issue is authorized in the company's minutes
ST 398	ST 158	The tracing of additional indebtedness to bank statement
ST 399	—	The examination of trust deeds or mortgage deeds for new debt issues; the obtaining of copies for permanent file
ST 400	—	The examination of evidence (e.g., canceled checks) of recorded principal and interest payments
ST 401	—	The examination of canceled notes for debt retired during period
ST 402	—	The ensuring that the security for a note payable or bank loan repaid during the year has been released
ST 403	—	The ensuring that all lease obligations are properly classified either as capital or operating
ST 404	—	The documentation of contingencies
ST 405	—	The verification of accrued liabilities by examining supporting documentation
ST 406	—	The consideration of whether adequate provision for accruals has been made
ST 407	—	The agreement of deferred income accounts to appropriate documentation
ST 408	—	The documentation of analytical review procedures performed
ST 409	ST 156	The determination that imputed premium or discount is properly accounted for

**Substantive Tests Phase: Comprehensive Listing of Audit Tasks—
Indebtedness (Cont'd)**

1996 Study	1988 Study	
ST 410	ST 157	The verification of computation of interest expense and accruals and amortization of premium or discount
ST 411	—	The ensuring that cut-off procedures are documented
ST 412	—	The documentation of transactions and ending balances with intergroups and other related parties
ST 413	—	The checking of interaccount, intergroup transfers for a period before and after year end
ST 414	ST 162	The determination of compliance with loan agreement and confirmation of waivers or determination of the impact of violations
ST 415	—	The vouching and review of disclosure (e.g., interest rates, maturity dates, lease obligations and sinking funds)

**Substantive Tests Phase: Comprehensive Listing of Audit Tasks—
Ownership Equity**

1996 Study	1988 Study	
ST 133	ST 169	The review of relevant accounting principles for propriety and consistency
ST 134	ST 163	The agreeing of beginning balances in equity schedules to prior year working paper
ST 135	—	The updating of permanent file for each class of capital stock, warrants or options
ST 136	—	The confirmation with registrar and transfer agent of the capital stock authorized, issued and outstanding, unbilled fees, dividends paid or payable, share options exercised during year and share options outstanding at year end
ST 137	—	If client keeps its own share records: 1) the examination of canceled certificates and 2) the agreement of ledger and share certificate stubs to client accounting records
ST 138	ST 165	The inspection of and accounting for unissued, canceled and treasury stock certificates
ST 139	ST 166	The verification of computation and disclosure of restrictions of retained earnings and dividends in arrears
ST 140	ST 167	The vouching of capital transactions during period including transactions related to issuance, retirement, treasury stock and changes in retained earnings
ST 141	ST 171	The tracing of transactions to minutes and contractual agreements, reviewing for proper authorization, amount, etc.
ST 142	—	The obtaining of analysis of accounts for each class of capital stock. The checking and agreeing to general ledger
ST 143	ST 168	The determination that dividends declared and/or paid are properly accounted for
ST 144	—	The documentation of transactions and ending balances with intergroup and other related parties
ST 145	—	The vouching and review of disclosures (e.g., authorized capital, issued capital, commitments such as options and rights, capital stock transactions during the year)

Forming Opinion Phase: Comprehensive Listing of Audit Tasks

1996 Study	1988 Study	**General Considerations**
FO 263	FO 2	The determination as to whether the financial statements comply with relevant requirements and have been prepared using generally accepted accounting principles, which have been properly applied, producing results that are consistent with the auditor's knowledge of the client's business
FO 264	FO 3	The determination that there is disclosure of all material matters relevant to an adequate understanding of the financial statements
FO 265	FO 5	The determination as to whether the accounting policies are consistently applied
FO 266	—	The determination as to whether the audit was conducted in accordance with required auditing standards
FO 267	FO 1	The assessment of the adequacy and appropriateness of the scope of the audit
FO 268	—	The assessment of the degree of scope limitations imposed by external circumstances (e.g., inability to observe the physical inventory count due to a late engagement), and if material, consideration of the issuance of an opinion other than an unqualified opinion
		Accounting Considerations
FO 269	—	The determination that the accounting policies selected and applied conform with the requirements of GAAP and applicable regulatory securities commission (e.g., SEC or OSC) or otherwise have general acceptance
FO 270	FO 9	The determination that the client's accounting policies are appropriate in the circumstances
FO 271	FO 10	The determination that transactions are recorded in accordance with their substance, rather than their form
FO 272	FO 11	The determination that information presented in the financial statements is classified and summarized in a reasonable manner

Forming Opinion Phase: Comprehensive Listing of Audit Tasks (Cont'd)

1996 Study	1988 Study	Accounting Considerations (Cont'd)
FO 273	—	The determination of the nature and cause of uncorrected misstatements (arithmetical error, disagreement as to valuation or inappropriate use of an accounting principle)
FO 274	FO 12	The aggregation of the effects of errors and departures in a way that allows consideration of their materiality in relation to individual amounts as well as to the overall financial statements
FO 275	—	The determination of the extent to which existence of uncorrected misstatements indicates possibility of further misstatements
FO 276	—	As a result of the analysis of uncorrected misstatements, the determination as to whether the assessed levels of inherent and control risk are still valid
FO 277	—	If there is a change in accounting principles or accounting entity, preparation of the comment in the audit report as to the inconsistency
FO 278	—	The evaluation of appropriateness of accounting treatment for the change in accounting principle or accounting entity; the consideration of whether an explanatory or reservation paragraph should be added to the audit report or whether an opinion other than an unqualified opinion should be issued
		Adequacy of Disclosures in Financial Statements
FO 279	FO 13	The consideration as to whether a particular matter should be disclosed in light of circumstances and facts
FO 280	FO 14	The consideration of the adequacy of disclosure of material uncertainties or contingencies (e.g., outcome of litigation, valuation or realization of non-current assets, settlement of tax liabilities)
FO 281	—	The task of requesting the client to include in the notes to the financial statements all disclosures required by GAAP
FO 282	—	If the client has not observed GAAP in the presentation of the financial statements due to the inadequacy of disclosures, the consideration of expressing an opinion other than an unqualified opinion

Forming Opinion Phase: Comprehensive Listing of Audit Tasks (Cont'd)

1996 Study	1988 Study	Uncertainties
FO 283	—	The determination as to whether the financial statements are affected by any material uncertainties
FO 284	—	If the outcome of material uncertainties is not susceptible to reasonable estimation, the consideration of expressing an opinion other than an unqualified opinion
FO 285	FO 17	If material uncertainties exist, the consideration as to whether the financial statement items affected have been stated in conformity with GAAP in all material respects other than those contingent on the outcome of the uncertainties
		Other Information
FO 286	FO 20	The reading of other information accompanying the financial statements to ensure that it is not materially inconsistent with the financial statements
FO 287	FO 21	If other information in documents containing audited financial statements includes material inconsistencies, the determination as to whether financial statements or the other information need revision, and the advising of the client accordingly
		Type and Wording of the Audit Opinion
FO 288	FO 22	For unqualified report with modified wording, the decision on appropriate modification to the standard audit report
FO 289	FO 23	For other than unqualified reports, the decision on the type of opinion (qualified, adverse, disclaimer) and wording of the audit report

Financial Statements Reporting Phase: Comprehensive Listing of Audit Tasks

1996 Study	1988 Study	Financial Statements
FR 416	FR 1	The task of ensuring that all information necessary for a fair presentation is included in the basic financial statements
FR 417	FR 2	The task of ensuring that other reports issued in connection with the same engagement are consistent with the basic presentations of the first report
FR 418	FR 3	The determination as to whether the classification, grouping, and description of accounts are sufficiently complete to achieve clarity of presentation
FR 419	FR 4	The consideration of the existence of certain regulatory agencies' rules as to disclosures and financial statement presentation of specific items
FR 420	FR 5	The consideration of the desirability of including the details of major categories, such as property, plant and equipment, or long-term debt in a footnote and showing only the totals or net amounts on the face of the balance sheet
FR 421	FR 6	The completion of the financial statement disclosure checklists when appropriate
FR 422	FR 7	The establishment as to whether the method of accounting differs between the books and financial statements, and if the effect is pervasive, the disclosing of the nature of difference in a note to the financial statements (e.g., cash basis vs. accrual basis; completed contract method vs. percentage-of-completion method)
		Consolidated Statements
FR 423	FR 8	For consolidated statements, the decision as to the most meaningful financial presentation in the circumstances
FR 424	FR 9	The determination of proper inclusion of all subsidiaries
FR 425	FR 10	The decision on what is the most suitable format for the presentation of information relating to foreign subsidiaries (the consideration of local conditions, etc.)
FR 426	FR 11	If a domestic or foreign subsidiary is not consolidated, the adjustment of the investment in the subsidiary for the consolidated group's share of accumulated undistributed earnings and losses since acquisition

Financial Statements Reporting Phase: Comprehensive Listing of Audit Tasks (Cont'd)

1996 Study	1988 Study	Consolidated Statements (Cont'd)
FR 427	—	For subsidiaries whose principal business activity is leasing property or facilities to other members of an affiliated group, ensuring that the proper consolidation method is used
FR 428	FR 13	The decision on disclosure of consolidation policies in the footnotes or in the headings of the financial statements
		Footnotes to Financial Statements
FR 429	FR 14	The evaluation of the propriety of each footnote (information that is merely interesting, but not important, should be omitted)
FR 430	FR 15	The determination that footnotes are stated in nontechnical language and that the wording is clear and concise
FR 431	FR 16	The consideration of the use of parenthetical comments directly on the face of the statements in lieu of a footnote
FR 432	FR 17	If matters considered essential to a fair presentation are omitted, the determination that such matters are covered in the auditor's report
FR 433	FR 18	The identification of any subsequent event that may have taken place, and the decision as to the appropriate course of action to take (e.g., disclosure or adjustment with or without disclosure)

Chapter 6

Research Method

In the previous chapter we described the process used to develop a comprehensive inventory of 433 auditing tasks. In this chapter we describe how we used the resulting inventory to conduct a study in 1996 to provide data related to the hypotheses stated in Chapters 3 and 4. To test the hypotheses we administered a questionnaire that asked that each participating auditor determine for each auditing task: the level of structure of the task, the years of experience and the number of supervised instances required to perform the task independently, as well as the type of decision aid most suitable for the task. For data collection purposes, the comprehensive inventory was broken down into three sections so each auditor could evaluate only one-third (either 144 or 145) of the tasks. First we describe the experimental materials, then we explain how the task instrument was divided into three versions for the purpose of data collection. The final section includes information about how the materials were administered and reports demographic data on the auditors who participated in the study. Data collected in a similar study in 1988 were also used to test the hypotheses in Chapters 3 and 4. Results from both studies are reported in Chapter 7 (for task-level analysis) and Chapter 8 (for audit phase and aggregate level analysis).

DESCRIPTION OF THE EXPERIMENTAL MATERIALS

Demographic Questions and Overview Section

Each participating auditor received a booklet of approximately 15 pages, which constituted the research instrument for this study. The booklet included a few pages of preliminary information and questions (see the appendix to this chapter) which appeared before the listing of audit tasks. The first page of the booklet described the instrument and asked for demographic information. The auditors were asked to indicate their years of audit experience, rank, and specialty. Four questions related to the structure of the participant's audit firm and then two questions addressed the individual's use of and knowledge about computerized audit techniques and decision aids.

For a project of this magnitude, it was important that all terms used be clearly defined. Accordingly, the next two and one-half pages of the booklet consisted of an overview of the project. The overview section included a table based on Simon's model of the decision process. The table provided a framework for the definition of task structure using nontechnical terms. Each of the three levels of task structure: structured, semistructured and unstructured, were described using three dimensions representing decision aspects. The three dimensions are the nature of the problem, the nature of the alternative courses of action, and the requirements of the final choice. These three dimensions mirror the three decision-making phases described by Simon: Intelligence, Design and Choice.[1]

The nature of the problem is represented on a continuum from well defined to ill defined. The alternative courses of action may be limited and well specified at one end of the continuum to infinite and unspecified at the other end. The final choice may require little judgment or, at the other end of the continuum, judgment and insight. Considering the decision aspects in this way should help the auditor determine whether a specific auditing task should be considered structured or unstructured. Each of the three levels of task structure was described with reference to the table. A structured task would be one with a well-defined problem, limited and well-specified alternative courses of action with the final choice requiring little judgment. An unstructured task would consist of an ill-defined problem with few or no guidelines, infinite and unspecified alternative courses of action, and would require judgment and insight to make the final choice among alternative courses of action. A semistructured task would have characteristics somewhere in between the two extremes. Nonauditing examples of a structured and an unstructured task were given.

---

1. H. Simon, 1960, *The New Science of Management* (New York: Harper and Row).

The knowledge base measures were then explained to the participating auditors in the overview section. Two measures of knowledge base were used in the 1996 study: the years of general audit experience and the number of supervised instances required to perform the task independently. The decision aid section of the overview described each type of decision aid: complete automation, decision support systems, and knowledge-based expert systems. Complete automation refers to performing the task on a computer using a predetermined formula. A decision support system is described as an interactive computer-based software package that uses a statistical or mathematical model and data to make inferences for the use of the decision maker. A knowledge-based expert system attempts to replicate the decision rules of one or more experts. The user provides answers to questions asked by the interactive software. The input is subjected to the simulated reasoning process of the expert and a recommendation results that the user may or may not adopt. The fourth category under the decision aid item on the questionnaire was called human processing. The overview section explained that for this option we were interested in tasks that would not be appropriate for any of the decision aids listed, but would require strictly human processing to complete the task. Auditors were instructed to consider which level would be appropriate for each task without regard to the cost of actually developing such a decision aid for the task.

Description of Requested Responses

At the end of the overview section, instructions were provided to guide participating auditors in their completion of the questionnaire to follow. For the questionnaire section, each participating auditor was given a listing of about one-third of all the auditing tasks studied, organized by phase of the audit. Objectives related to determining the composition of each of the three versions are explained in a subsequent section of this chapter. For each auditing task the auditor was asked to indicate the level of structure of the task, the knowledge base requirement and the type of decision aid for which the task is best suited.

For the level of structure of the task, auditors were asked to first consider whether the task was structured, semistructured or unstructured and then to check a box along the scale provided. The scale selected for eliciting this information was a Likert scale[2] that ranged from 1 to 9, where 1 to 3 represented structured, 4 to 6 represented semistructured, and 7 to 9 represented unstructured. For each task, the auditor was asked to indicate the appropriate knowledge base required to perform the task along two dimensions. First, the auditor was requested to write the number of the years of audit experience that he or she thought was necessary before one could be asked to perform the task independently. Second, the auditor was to indicate the number of supervised instances of performing the task before the auditor should be able to perform the task independently. The last question for each task related to an appropriate decision aid. The auditor was to indicate, by checking a box, whether the task was most suited for automation, decision support system, expert system, or strictly human processing.

KNOWLEDGE BASE VARIABLES USED

To capture the knowledge base requirement for each task, two measures of audit experience were used. One measure that is fairly common in this type of research is the number of years of audit experience required before a person can be expected to perform the task independently. The generally accepted auditing standards require that auditing tasks be properly supervised. The level of supervision required depends on the task itself and the skills and knowledge of the auditor. For each task there should be a point (e.g., a certain number of years of experience) at which one would be expected to perform the task without supervision. To elicit the perception of what this point would be, the number of years of general audit experience was chosen rather than the auditor's rank since the auditors being surveyed would be from several different firms. There may be differences between firms in the rate at which they promote auditors to different ranks as well as differences in the specific terms used to identify various levels of rank within the firm (e.g., heavy senior, supervising senior, and supervisor). The years of general audit experience are thought to be more amenable to combining data from different firms.

In addition to this typical measure of audit experience, a complementary measure of audit experience was developed. Auditors

---

2. The literature indicates that optimal scale for survey responses ranges between 5 and 9. See E. P. Cox III, 1980, "The Optimal Number of Response Alternatives for a Scale: A Review," *Journal of Marketing Research* 17 (November), p. 413.

were asked to identify the number of supervised instances of the task required before someone could be expected to perform the task independently. This measure of audit experience relates to the amount of *practice* required for a task. The purpose of this measure is to learn more about what type of experience or preparation is required for task competence. For example, a task may require several instances of supervised performance of the task but not many years of general audit experience. This type of task is one that requires practice but perhaps not much sophistication. Another task may require several years of general audit experience but not many or not any supervised instances of the task. This would be a task that requires much judgment and audit sophistication or maturity. Comparing the number of years and the number of supervised instances will allow a more comprehensive analysis of each task than has been achieved before.

DESIGN OF TASK VERSIONS

The 433 tasks identified in Chapter 5 were divided into three groups (two each with 144 tasks and one with 145 tasks). In allocating the tasks to the groups, an attempt was made to put tasks of varying complexity levels in each group. We did not balance the complexity level between versions on a task-by-task basis but referred to the results from the previous study[3] to make sure that each version had a variety of tasks with respect to the rank of auditor expected to perform the task. Subcategories of tasks were kept together so the auditor would not infer that some tasks not there were included in other tasks. For example, the substantive tests phase of the task inventory was distributed among the three versions. Each group of auditors then would have exposure to some substantive test tasks. However, all the substantive tests related to an account or cycle (e.g. cash, revenues and receipts cycle) were kept together and assigned to one group of participating auditors.

Table 6.1 illustrates how the tasks were broken down between the three versions of the research instrument. The design was determined by adhering to three objectives. The first objective was to assign an equal number of tasks to each version. The second objective

---

3. M. J. Abdolmohammadi, 1999, "A Comprehensive Taxonomy of Task Structure and Knowledge Base Demands in Auditing," *Behavioral Research in Accounting* 11, pp. 51–92.

Table 6.1
Description of Three Versions of Task Inventory

VERSION 1

Title of Phase or Section	Task Numbers	Number of Tasks in Section
Orientation		
Understanding the Client's Business	OR-1 - OR-14	14
Engagement Risk Assessment	OR-15 - OR-37	23
Inherent Risk Assessment	OR-38 - OR-51	14
General Considerations	OR-52 - OR-58	7
Substantive Tests (ST)		
General Procedures	ST-59 - ST-62	4
Analytical Review Procedures	ST-63 - ST-65	3
ST for Cash	ST-66 - ST-85,	20
ST for Revenue and Receipt Cycle	ST-86 - ST-116	31
ST for Payroll and Related Costs	ST-117 - ST-132	16
ST for Ownership Equity	ST-133 - ST-145	13
Total number of tasks in Version 1		145

VERSION 2

Understanding the Control Structure		
General Considerations	CS-146 - CS-152	7
Accounting Systems and Internal Control	CS-153 - CS-161	9
Special Internal Control Factors	CS-162 - CS-165	4
Preventive Controls	CS-166 - CS-169	4
Detective Controls	CS-170 - CS-172	3
Control Environment	CS-173 - CS-178	6
Competence of Personnel	CS-179 - CS-181	3
EDP Control Environment	CS-182 - CS-189	8
Internal Audit Function	CS-190 - CS-192	3
Management Override	CS-193	1
Substantive Tests		
ST for Purchasing and Disbursements Cycle	ST-194 - ST-232	39
ST for Fixed Assets	ST-233 - ST-262	30
Forming Opinion		
General Considerations	FO-263 - FO-268	6
Accounting Considerations	FO-269 - FO-278	10
Adequacy of Disclosures in Financial Statements	FO-279 - FO-282	4
Uncertainties	FO-283 - FO-285	3
Other Information	FO-286 - FO-287	2
Type and Wording of the Audit Opinion	FO-288 - FO-289	2
Total Number of Tasks in Version 2		144

Table 6.1 (continued)
Description of Three Versions of Task Inventory

VERSION 3

Title of Phase or Section	Task Numbers	Number of Tasks in Section
Tests of Controls		
Nature, Timing and Extent of the Tests	TC-290 - TC-304	15
EDP Issues	TC-305 - TC-306	2
Audit Sampling for Tests of Controls	TC-307 - TC-313	7
Control Deviations	TC-314 - TC-316	3
Evaluation of Results of Tests of Controls	TC-317 - TC-327	11
Substantive Tests		
ST for Inventory	ST-328 - ST-364	37
ST for Investments	ST-365 - ST-389	25
ST for Indebtedness	ST-390 - ST-415	26
Financial Statements Reporting		
Financial Statements	FR-416 - FR-422	7
Consolidated Statements	FR-423 - FR-428	6
Footnotes to Financial Statements	FR-429 - FR-433	5
Total Number of Tasks for Version 3		144
Total Number of Tasks in Complete Inventory		433

was to ensure that subcategories of tasks were kept together. The third objective was to make sure that each group of auditors (each group receiving one of the three versions of the research instrument) would receive tasks of varying complexity so that responses within a version of the research instrument would be varied with respect to audit experience and level of task structure. As an example of the variety desired, Version 2 of the task instrument includes substantive tests for purchasing and disbursements (expected to be suited for a less experienced auditor) as well as tasks related to forming an opinion (expected to be suited for a more experienced auditor).

ADMINISTRATION OF THE QUESTIONNAIRE AND PARTICIPANTS

Knowledge of, and experience with, all audit tasks was necessary for the assessment of the task structure, knowledge base, and decision aids for all phases of the audit. Consequently, we limited the participation in the study to managers and partners in accounting firms. We contacted partners in eight offices of Big Six accounting firms in Boston, Hartford, New York, and Philadelphia as well as the Boston office of a regional firm. All but the New York and Philadelphia offices agreed to participate. Each contact partner was sent 10 packets, each with a cover letter and the task instrument. Task instruments were distributed in such a way that the three versions were distributed approximately equally among firms. The contact partner was provided with a sample interoffice memorandum to facilitate distribution to participants. The contact partner was requested to collect the completed questionnaires and send them to the authors by a deadline. Based on the previous study[4] it was expected that each subject would have to spend approximately one and one-half hours to complete the task instrument. A total of 41 responses were received from the first mailing, for a response rate of 51.25%. Two follow-up letters with additional packages were sent, but only two additional responses were received from this process resulting in a total of 43 responses from American firms. The respondents represent five of the Big Six firms and one large regional accounting firm.

A similar process was used to collect data from several offices of Big Six firms as well as several offices of Certified General Accountants Association (CGA) firms in Canada. Unfortunately, despite repeated follow-ups, only one response was received from a Big Six office and four responses were received from the CGA firm offices. We included the response from the Big Six office in our analysis, but dropped the four responses from the CGA firms. This decision was based on the fact that, while the Big Six office's audit approach corresponded very closely to the US practice, there were significant practice and organizational differences between the CGA firms and the Big Six firms. The 44 subjects, as described in Table 6.2 were randomly assigned to the three versions of the task instrument. The result was three groups of approximately equal size, each completing one version of the task instrument.

Table 6.2 presents the demographic information related to the participants and their accounting firms. In Panel A, we present the participating auditors' experience in years and their professional rank. Panel B provides a summary of the specialty areas of these auditors. Factors related to the audit methods of their firms are provided in Panel C.

---

4. Ibid.

Table 6.2
Characteristics of Participants in the 1996 Study

Panel A: Experience and Professional Rank

Attribute	*Version 1* *N 15*	*Version 2* *N 15*	*Version 3* *N 14*	*Total* *N 44*
Years of Experience:				
Mean	10.23	9.37	8.79	9.48
Standard deviation	6.09	4.81	3.91	4.96
Range	5–24	4–22	5–19	4–24
Professional Rank:				
Manager	12	12	11	35
Partner	3	2	3	8
Total	15	14*	14	43*

* Does not include one missing datum.

Panel B: Specialty

Specialty	Frequency			
	Version 1	Version 2	Version 3	Total
• High Technology (including software, telecommunication, computer auditing)	5	6	3	14
• Business assurance, consulting, tax, and various auditing	6	6	1	13
• Financial Services (including banking, investment, and insurance)	4	7	1	12
• Manufacturing	2	2	5	9
• Other (Construction, health-care, Media, Non-profit, Real Estate, Retail, Small-business, Utilities)	4	4	7	15
Total	21	25	17	63**

** The total number of specialties (63) is greater than the number of auditors (44) due to possession of multiple specialties by some auditors.

Table 6.2 (continued)
Characteristics of Participants in the 1996 Study

Panel C: Audit Method of the Firm

Audit Method Attribute Scale: (3 = extensive, 2 = moderate, 1 = minimal)	Version 1	Version 2	Version 3	Total
a. Policies, practices, and positional responsibilities are formalized.	3	3	3	3
b. To assist in performing audit tasks, detailed procedures are developed and used.	3	3	3	3
c. Logical sequence of procedures, decisions, and documentation steps are available.	3	3	3	3
d. In conduct of audits, computerized and/or manual decision aids are used.	2	2	3	2
e. Extent to which you personally have used computerized applications such as automation, decision support systems and expert systems in your audit	2	2	2	2
f. Level of your personal knowledge of computerized audit techniques is	2	2	2	2

On average, the auditors possessed 9.48 years of experience with a standard deviation of 4.96 years. Their experience ranged from 4 to 24 years and while eight were partners, 35 were managers.[5] While a slight decreasing trend in the mean experience levels was observed from Version 1 to Version 3, the standard deviations were also showing a slight decreasing trend. The distribution of participants by

5. One supervisor and two senior managers are grouped with managers. One subject did not reveal his or her rank.

rank resulted in approximately equal numbers of managers and partners per version.

Panel B presents the major specialty areas of the auditors. Overall, high technology was the most frequently listed area of specialty (14). This was followed by the traditional lines of business assurance, consulting, tax, and audit services (13). Financial services was next with 12 listings followed by manufacturing with nine listings. All other areas of specialty were grouped as "Other" with 15 listings. These areas included Construction, Health Care, Media, Nonprofit, Real Estate, Retail, Small Business, and Utilities. The total number of specialty listings was 63, which is greater than the total number of participants (44). This was due to the fact that some respondents reported multiple areas of specialty.

An interesting observation is a difference between Version 3 auditors and other auditors in the number of listings of various areas of specialty. Namely, Version 3 respondents had fewer listings in areas of high technology, traditional lines, and financial services, but more listings for manufacturing and other areas than Versions 1 and 2 subjects. We cannot directly compare the responses of these groups due to the different tasks used in each version.

The audit method attributes listed in Panel C indicate that while respondents reported extensive ratings for the first three attributes, the last three attributes received a moderate rating. The auditors in the three versions are remarkably similar in their responses here. The only exception is that Version 3 participants indicated that they used computerized and/or manual decision aids extensively in the conduct of audits (attributed), while those in the other versions rated this attribute as moderate. We conclude that there were not significant differences in audit methods (along the measured dimensions) between the firms represented in our sample.

APPENDIX
Task Instrument Instructions

AUDIT TASK STRUCTURE, EXPERIENCE REQUIREMENT AND DECISION AIDS

This booklet contains the research instrument. On this page, you are requested to respond to certain demographic questions about yourself and your firm for data analysis purposes. **Please do not identify your name anywhere on this research instrument to assure confidentiality.** The following three pages provide an overview of the project as well as definitions of key terms and instructions for completing the audit task questionnaire. Beginning on page 5 you will find the detailed audit tasks for your consideration.

Demographic information

1.   Years of audit experience: ____& Rank: _____

2.   Specialty: _____

3.   Please mark one box for each of the following statements relating to the audit function of your firm:

		Extensively	moderately	minimally
a.	Policies, practices, and positional responsibilities are formalized:	☐	☐	☐
b.	To assist in performing audit tasks, detailed procedures are developed and used:	☐	☐	☐
c.	Logical sequence of procedures, decisions, and documentation steps are available:	☐	☐	☐
d.	In conduct of audits, computerized and/or manual decision aids are used:	☐	☐	☐
e.	Extent to which you personally have used computerized applications such as automation, decision support systems and expert systems in your audits:	☐	☐	☐
f.	Level of your personal knowledge of computerized minimal audit techniques is:	☐	☐	☐

OVERVIEW OF THE PROJECT AND KEY TERMS

The purpose of this project is to learn more about the nature of various audit tasks. Specifically, we are investigating the degree of structure of each audit task, the audit experience required to perform the task independently, and the type of decision aid applicable to perform the task. We have compiled a comprehensive inventory of audit tasks and have listed about a third of them for your evaluation (two other groups of participants will evaluate the remaining two thirds of the tasks). This section provides you with an overview of the key terms.

A Model of Task Structure

One widely recognized model of task structure uses three dimensions for classification of the task along a continuum from structured to unstructured. The three dimensions and their relationship with task structure are depicted in the following chart. This is followed by definitions in narrative form.

Decision Aspect	Task Structure Continuum Structured----------Semistructured----------Unstructured		
The Problem is:	Well defined ---------------------		Ill defined with few or no guidelines
Alternative Courses of Action are:	Limited & well specified ---------------------		Infinite & unspecified
Final Choice requires:	Little judgment---------------------		Judgment & insight

From this chart we derive the definitions of structured, semistructured and unstructured tasks as follows:

Structured Tasks. These are tasks in which the problem is well-defined; the alternatives are well-specified; there is a developed, recognized approach to evaluate alternatives; and the final decision requires limited judgment.

Unstructured Tasks. These are tasks in which the nature of the problem can be ambiguous; there is a large number of alternatives; the evaluation of alternatives is not specified and it involves a high degree of judgment; and the final decision requires a high degree of judgment and insight.

Semistructured Tasks. The chart describes the endpoints of the structured/unstructured continuum. There are several possible combinations and variations of the three decision aspects that could be used to describe a semistructured task. One example is a task where the problem is reasonably defined, the alternative courses of action are many and there is a need for some judgment to choose a course of action. Another example is a task where the problem is ill-defined and few or no guidelines are available and the alternative courses of action are numerous, but little judgment or insight is needed to choose a course of action.

Nonauditing Examples. An example of a nonauditing structured task is to determine the economic order quantity (EOQ) for inventory. The nature of this problem is to determine the amount of inventory to order at one time so that the annual inventory cost is minimized. The alternatives are to order frequently in small quantities or to order less frequently in large quantities. The final choice requires little insight or judgment once the EOQ formula is applied. An example of a nonauditing unstructured task is that of determining a 5 to 10 year business plan for a large corporation.

For each task in the attached listing, you will be asked to indicate where you think the particular task falls on the scale from structured to unstructured (as described in the chart above).

Appropriate Experience Level

Within the audit, a certain level of experience and knowledge is required to perform a particular task. In the questionnaire that follows you are asked to indicate two measures of auditing experience that you believe are necessary for an auditor to perform each task independently. The first measure is general auditing experience measured in number of years. The second measure is the number of instances of supervised task performance required before an auditor is qualified to perform the task independently.

What we are after is the experience level (both in terms of general audit experience and the specific instances of supervised experiences with the task) at which the auditor is qualified to perform each task independently. It is important to note that we recognize that some data gathering could be delegated to less experienced auditors for each task and the normal review process is performed by more experienced auditors.

Appropriate Decision Aid

While some tasks could be completely automated, other tasks may require strict human processing. In the middle of this continuum are tasks that may be accomplished by human judgment with support from some computer programs called decision support or expert systems. For the purpose of this study, the intended definitions of these terms are given below.

Complete Automation. Some audit tasks may be done completely by a computer based on some predetermined formula. This is referred to as complete automation.

Decision Support Systems. A Decision Support System is an interactive computer-based software package that assists decision-makers in making decisions. Decision Support Systems use certain models (e.g. statistical or mathematical models) and data to make inferences for the use of the decision-maker.

Knowledge-based Expert Systems. A Knowledge-based Expert System is an interactive computer-based software package that assists decision-makers in using one or multiple experts' decision rules to make their decisions. To create a Knowledge-based Expert System, the decision rules of the expert(s) must be elicited and expressed in terms of a number of IF-THEN rules. To employ a Knowledge-based Expert System, the decision maker provides answers to questions posed by the system and the expert system presents a recommendation to the decision-maker based on his or her input. The decision-maker has the option of accepting or rejecting the recommendation presented by the expert system.

Strictly Human Processing. Some audit tasks may not be suitable for automation, decision support system or expert system and may require strictly human processing. We recognize that even tasks that are subject to some form of decision aid may have human processing components to them. For this category, however, we are interested in identifying tasks that are strictly subject to human processing.

It is important to note that we are interested in knowing what decision aids could be used as a primary aid to complete the task without regard to cost or other considerations of the decision aid development.

INSTRUCTIONS

Beginning on the next page you will find a list of detailed audit tasks for your consideration. Please proceed to:

* Evaluate each audit task for its **level of structure** by marking the appropriate box;
* Write down **years of audit experience** and **the number of instances of supervised experience with the task** before an auditor is qualified to perform the task independently;
* Indicate the **applicable decision aid** for each task by marking the appropriate box.

Thank you once again for your participation. As a token of our appreciation, we will be happy to send you a copy of the detailed results upon completion. Please attach a business card to the completed questionnaire if you would like to receive a copy.

Chapter 7

Task-Level Results

In this chapter we present descriptive data at the task level on each of the three dimensions being studied: task structure, experience level, and applicable decision aid. Along each of the three dimensions we report appropriate descriptive statistics for each task in the inventory compiled in 1996. If the same task was also evaluated in the 1988 study[1] the appropriate descriptive statistic from that study is provided for comparison purposes.[2] For each task, the order of the tasks within subphase is based on the structure ratings in the 1996 study. The most structured task is presented first and the least structured task is presented last with all others in ascending order from most to least structured. The 1988 data are not necessarily presented in order of the level of structuredness, since the 1988 tasks are presented in association with the equivalent task from the 1996 inventory. The order of task presentation in the experience and decision aid tables matches the order in the structure tables.

The first set of tables in the appendix to this chapter (Table 7.1 to 7.16) report on evaluations of task structure. The second set of tables (Table 7.17 to 7.32) report on evaluations related to years of experience, number of supervised instances and professional rank deemed necessary to perform each task. The final set of tables (Table 7.33 to 7.48) report on the appropriate level of decision aid for each

---

1. See M. J. Abdolmohammadi, 1999, "A Comprehensive Taxonomy of Task Structure and Knowledge Base Demands in Auditing," *Behavioral Research in Accounting* 11, pp. 51–92.

2. For comparison purposes, we only included the task from the 1988 study if it was worded exactly the same as the task in the 1996 inventory.

task. A discussion of the results at the individual task level is presented below in the same order that the data tables appear. In Chapter 8, we report the results on an aggregate basis at the audit phase level and in total for the audit. The implications of the results for the research hypotheses are also discussed in Chapter 8. Concluding remarks for both individual tasks and in the aggregate are presented in Chapter 9.

TASK STRUCTURE

The first set of tables in the appendix to this chapter presents the structure data for all tasks in the 1996 inventory and comparable tasks in the 1988 task inventory. Within each audit phase or subphase (for the Substantive Tests phase) the mean structure rating and coefficient of variation is provided for each task in order from most to least structured task. The task structure was rated on a scale of 1 (most structured) to 9 (least structured). The mean structure ratings for equivalent tasks (in both the 1996 and 1988 studies) are compared using a two-sample t test. The t value and p value are presented in the tables. Negative t values indicate that the structure evaluation from the 1996 study was lower (the task was considered to be more structured) than the structure evaluation of the same task in the 1988 study. Significant differences[3] in structure ratings are highlighted.

Orientation

Table 7.1 presents the individual task-level structure data for the Orientation (OR) phase for both the 1996 and the 1988 studies. This phase had 58 specific tasks in the 1996 study and 45 tasks in the 1988 study. Thirty-five of these tasks were exactly the same across both studies and therefore were compared in terms of their task structure. The mean structure ratings range from 3.00 for task number OR 27, to 7.20 for task number OR 12 in the 1996 data. The mean structure ratings for selected tasks from the 1988 study range from 2.90 (for the task equivalent to OR 27) to 7.50 (for the task equivalent to OR 25). The coefficient of variation in the 1996 data ranges from a low of .23 for OR 13 (ranked 56.5), OR 32 (ranked 52), and OR 39 (ranked 33) to .76 for the 5.5th ranked OR 7. The coefficient of variation for comparable tasks in the 1988 data ranges from a low of .19 for the

---

3. A significant difference is defined as one with an associated p value that is less than or equal to .05.

task equivalent to OR 47 to .74 for the task equivalent to OR 36. In comparing the two sets of data only one of these tasks (OR 12) is considered to be significantly more unstructured in the current study (7.20) than in the 1988 study (5.33) with a t statistic of 2.46 and a p value of .02. These results indicate that the task structure ratings for the Orientation phase are stable over the study period.

Control Structure

Table 7.2 presents the individual task-level structure data for the Control Structure (CS) phase for both the 1996 and the 1988 studies. This phase had 48 specific tasks in the 1996 study and 41 tasks in the 1988 study. Thirty-five of these tasks were exactly the same across both studies and therefore were compared in terms of their task structure. The mean structure ratings for the 1996 data range from 2.40 for task number CS 169, to 6.67 for task number CS 152. The mean structure ratings for selected tasks from the 1988 study range from 2.67 (for the task equivalent to CS 169) to 6.16 (for the task equivalent to CS 193). The coefficient of variation in the 1996 data ranges from a low of .25 for CS 152 (ranked 48th in structure) to .56 for the 12th ranked CS 180. The coefficient of variation for comparable tasks in the 1988 data ranges from a low of .27 for the task equivalent to CS 193 to .71 for the task equivalent to CS 169. In comparing the two sets of data only one of the Control Structure tasks (CS 179) is considered to be significantly more unstructured in the current study (6.60) than in the 1988 study (5.22) with a t statistic of 2.72 and a p value of .01. These results indicate that the task structure ratings for the Control Structure phase are stable over the study period.

Tests of Controls

Table 7.3 presents the individual task-level structure data for the Tests of Controls phase for both the 1996 and the 1988 studies. This phase had 38 specific tasks in the 1996 study and 34 tasks in the 1988 study. Seventeen of these tasks were exactly the same across both studies and therefore were compared in terms of their task structure. The mean structure ratings for the 1996 data range from 2.36 for task number TC 293, to 6.14 for task number TC 291. The mean structure ratings for selected tasks from the 1988 study range from 2.37 (for the task equivalent to TC 297) to 5.86 (for the tasks equivalent to TC 304 and TC 313). The coefficient of variation in the 1996 data ranges from a low of .23 for TC 291 (ranked 38th in structure) to .59 for the 5th ranked TC 292. The coefficient of variation for comparable tasks in the 1988 data ranges from a low of .25 for the task equivalent to TC 291 to .68 for the task equivalent to TC 325. In comparing the two sets of data only one of the Tests of Controls tasks (TC 305) is considered to be significantly more structured in the current study (3.43) than in the 1988 study (4.47) with a t statistic of −2.45 and a p value of .02. For comparable tasks over the eight-year period then, the task structure ratings for the Test of Controls phase remained stable.

Substantive Tests

Tables 7.4 through 7.13 present the individual task-level structure data for the Substantive Test (ST) phase for both the 1996 and the 1988 studies. This phase had 244 specific tasks in the 1996 study and 171 tasks in the 1988 study. One hundred and twenty-eight of these tasks were exactly the same across both studies and therefore were compared in terms of their task structure. Because of the large number of tasks, this phase of the audit was further divided into subphases for data reporting purposes. Table 7.14 summarizes the task structure data for the entire Substantive Tests phase by subphase. The summary table provides the overall mean task structure rating, coefficient of variation, and low and high mean structure rating for each subphase for the two studies.

The mean structure ratings for the 1996 data range from 1.47 for task number ST 199 in the Purchasing and Disbursements Cycle subphase, to 6.20 for task number ST 244 in the Fixed Assets subphase. The mean structure ratings for selected tasks from the 1988 study range from 1.20 (for the task equivalent to ST 73 in the Cash subphase) to 6.18 (for the task equivalent to ST 61 in the General and Analytical Review subphase). The coefficient of variation in the 1996 data ranges from a low of .21 for ST 377 to .79 for ST 371. Both tasks are in the Investments subphase of Substantive Tests. The coefficient of variation for comparable tasks in the 1988 data ranges from a low of .25 for the task equivalent to ST 61 in the General and Analytical Review subphase to .63 for the tasks equivalent to ST 92 in the Revenue and Receipt Cycle subphase and ST 239 in the Fixed Asset subphase.

In comparing the two sets of data there are 18 tasks throughout the Substantive Tests phase with significant differences in perceived task structure between the two periods: 1 in General and Analytical Review Procedures, 1 in Cash, 2 in Revenue and Receipt Cycle, 2 in Purchasing and Disbursements Cycle, 2 in Inventory, 3 in Fixed

Assets, 2 in Payroll, and 5 in Investments. Three of the 18 tasks were considered to be more structured in the 1996 study than in the 1988 study: 1 in General and Analytical Review, 1 in Revenue and Receipts Cycle, and 1 in Inventory. The other 15 tasks were considered to be less structured by participants in the 1996 study than by those evaluating the tasks in the 1988 study. Overall, these tasks are approximately 15% of the comparison tasks in the Substantive Tests phase.

Forming Opinion

Table 7.15 presents the individual task-level structure data for the Forming Opinion phase for both the 1996 and the 1988 studies. This phase had 27 specific tasks in the 1996 study and 23 tasks in the 1988 study. Fifteen of these tasks were exactly the same across both studies and therefore were compared in terms of their task structure. The mean structure ratings for the 1996 data range from 4.07 for task number FO 265, to 6.73 for task number FO 284. The mean structure ratings for selected tasks from the 1988 study range from 5.47 (for the task equivalent to FO 265) to 6.96 (for the task equivalent to FO 280). The coefficient of variation in the 1996 data ranges from a low of .30 for FO 284 (ranked 27th in structure) to .59 for the 3rd ranked FO 281. The coefficient of variation for comparable tasks in the 1988 data ranges from a low of .20 for the task equivalent to FO 280 to .37 for the task equivalent to FO 274. In comparing the two sets of data, four of the Forming Opinion tasks were considered to be significantly more structured in the current study than in the 1988 study. They were: FO 265 (t statistic of -2.65, p value of .01), FO 274 (t statistic of -2.56, p value of .02), FO 288 (t statistic of -2.96, p value of .01), and FO263 (t statistic of -2.46, p value of .02). These differences are indicated in approximately 25% of the comparable tasks and there is a pattern (all are more structured in 1996 compared to the 1988 data). Thus, it may be concluded that tasks in the Forming Opinion phase have become more structured, perhaps due to the use of more decision aids. Further discussion of the connection with decision aid suitability is presented later in this chapter.

Financial Reporting

Table 7.16 presents the individual task-level structure data for the Financial Reporting phase for both the 1996 and the 1988 studies. This phase had 18 specific tasks in both the 1996 study and the 1988 study. Seventeen of these tasks were exactly the same across both studies and therefore were compared in terms of their task structure. The mean structure ratings for the 1996 data range from 2.58 for task number FR 421, to 5.75 for task number FR 431. The mean structure ratings for selected tasks from the 1988 study range from 3.71 (for the task equivalent to FR 421) to 6.71 (for the task equivalent to FR 432). The coefficient of variation in the 1996 data ranges from a low of .26 for FR 429 (ranked 15th in structure) to .65 for the 5th ranked FR 416. The coefficient of variation for comparable tasks in the 1988 data ranges from a low of .22 for the task equivalent to FR 432 to .50 for the task equivalent to FR 426. In comparing the two sets of data, eight of the Financial Reporting tasks were considered to be significantly more structured in the current study than in the 1988 study. They were: FR 421 (t statistic of -2.46, p value of .02), FR 419 (t statistic of -3.51, p value of less than .01), FR 424 (t statistic of -2.81, p value of .01), FR 417 (t statistic of -3.32, p value of less than .01), FR 416 (t statistic of -2.86, p value of .01), FR 418 (t statistic of -2.85, p value of .01), FR 425 (t statistic of -2.17, p value of .05), and FR 432 (t statistic of -3.19, p value of .01). The differences are indicated in approximately 50% of the comparable tasks and a pattern emerges (all tasks are more structured in 1996 compared to the 1988 data). Thus, it may be concluded that as in the Forming Opinion phase, tasks in the Financial Reporting phase may have become more structured, perhaps due to the use of more decision aids. Further discussion of the connection with decision aid suitability is presented later in this chapter.

Summary of Task Level Structure Ratings

As reported above there were relatively few significant differences between the two periods in terms of the structure level of the individual tasks. In each of the first three phases of the audit, Orientation, Control Structure, and Test of Controls, there was only one task for which the structure assessments were significantly different. This small number of significant differences in these phases may even be the result of chance. Within the Substantive Tests phase there were 18 tasks in total whose structure ratings were significantly different from 1988 to 1996. Because 15 of these tasks were considered to be less structured in 1996 than in 1988, one may conclude that in the Substantive Tests phases there has been some tendency toward less structure in some of the tasks. This seems to especially be the case in the Investments subphase where there were 5 tasks out of the 15 tasks that were compared which were judged to be less structured in 1996. These tasks were:

ST 368 — The comparative review of income earned or receivable
ST 369 — The consideration of overall increase or decrease in portfolio value
ST 379 — The review of investments for income receivable
ST 381 — The vouching of purchases of investments to supporting documentation
ST 383 — The vouching of income details to published information or other supporting data

This trend may be reflective of the more complex investment environment in 1996 compared to 1988.

In both the Forming Opinion and Financial Statements Reporting phases the differences between the two studies were toward more structure over time. Four tasks in Forming Opinion were considered more structured in 1996 than in 1988, they were:

FO 263 — The determination as to whether the financial statements comply with relevant requirements and have been prepared using generally accepted accounting principles, which have been properly applied, producing results that are consistent with the auditor's knowledge of the client's business
FO 265 — The determination as to whether the accounting policies are consistently applied
FO 274 — The aggregation of the effects of errors and departures in a way that allows consideration of their materiality in relation to individual amounts as well as to the overall financial statements
FO 288 — For unqualified report with modified wording, the decision on appropriate modification to the standard audit report

Within the Financial Statements Reporting phase eight tasks were considered to be more structured in 1996 than in 1988. Five of these related to the completeness and appropriateness of presentation and disclosure in the financial statements and notes to the statements. Two tasks related to the inclusion of subsidiaries and presentation of foreign subsidiaries. The eighth task was "If matters considered essential to a fair presentation are omitted, the determination that such matters are covered in the auditor's report." Based on the number of tasks in the last two phases that are perceived to be more structured than before it appears that audit firms have focused on the areas of financial statement preparation and opinion formation to provide more structure to auditors performing these tasks. Some insight may be gained when the same tasks are viewed with respect to required experience levels and suitability for decision aids over the same period.

EXPERIENCE REQUIREMENTS

Tables 7.17 through 7.32 in the appendix present data for all tasks with respect to the mean years of experience and the mean supervised instances required to perform the task independently from the 1996 study and the median professional rank required before performing the task independently from the 1988 study. Contrary to task structure assessments, there was no attempt to compare directly the experience requirements for individual tasks across the two studies since the response mode differed by study. Some observations may be made, however, with respect to the consistency (or lack thereof) between the number of years of experience required and the professional rank. The experience requirements for individual tasks may also be discussed in relation to the structure rating of the task. Each phase of the audit will be discussed in turn below. As was explained earlier in the chapter, the order of the tasks is determined by the structure rating of the task in the 1996 study, therefore, within each phase or subphase the tasks are ordered from most to least structured.

Orientation

Experience data for tasks in the Orientation phase are presented in Table 7.17 in the Appendix. Generally the means of experience and supervised instances show an increasing trend as the mean task structure rating increases (i.e., as the tasks become less structured). For the most structured task in the phase, OR 27, the required years of experience are 2.73 and the number of supervised instances is 2.64. From the 1988 study, this task is expected to require someone of the senior rank to perform it independently. The least-structured task, OR 12, indicates a requirement of 1.64 years, 2.00 supervised instances and a rank of senior to perform it independently. In general, however, as there is less structure associated with the task there is a higher experience requirement to perform it. As can be seen from Table 7.17 (and especially for the least structured task, OR 12) the experience requirements do not monotonically increase with the decrease in structure.

The coefficients of variation for mean years of experience range from .21 for OR 10 to .91 for OR 12 and for supervised instances from .49 for OR 25 and OR 32 to 1.32 for OR 36. The coefficients of variation for supervised instances are generally greater than those for years of experience indicating a higher level of variation in subjects' responses with respect to the supervised instances.

In comparing the experience requirements indicated in the 1988 study with those in the 1996 study we find that they are generally consistent with each other. For those tasks indicating that a senior should perform them, the required years of experience ranged from 1.64 to 4.53. For the one task that indicates a staff should perform it, the years of experience required are 2.40. For the eight tasks which require manager level, the mean years of experience required ranges from 3.67 to 5.13.

Control Structure

Experience data for tasks in the Control Structure phase are presented in Table 7.18 in the Appendix. As with the Orientation phase, the means of experience and supervised instances show a general increasing trend as the mean task structure rating increases (i.e., as the tasks become less structured). For the most structured task in the phase, CS 169, the required years of experience are 1.37 and the number of supervised instances is 1.87. From the 1988 study, this task is expected to require someone of the assistant staff rank to perform it independently. The least structured task, CS 152, indicates a requirement of 4.03 years of experience and 4.86 supervised instances to perform it independently. All tasks but one have the required rank of staff or senior from the 1988 study. In general then as there is less structure associated with the task there is a higher experience requirement to perform it, but the experience requirements do not monotonically increase with the decrease in structure.

The coefficients of variation for mean years of experience range from .28 for CS 160 to .68 for CS 149 and CS 162 and for supervised instances from .44 for CS 146 to .77 for CS 180. The coefficients of variation for supervised instances are generally greater than those for years of experience but the difference in dispersion between the two types of experience evaluations is not as pronounced as it was in the Orientation phase.

In comparing the experience requirements indicated in the 1988 study with those in the 1996 study we find that they are generally consistent with each other. For the one task that indicates an assistant staff should perform it, the years of experience required are 1.37. For those tasks indicating that a staff person should perform them, the required years of experience ranged from 1.70 to 2.43. For the tasks which require senior level, the mean years of experience required ranges from 2.20 to 4.37.

Tests of Controls

Experience data for tasks in the Tests of Controls phase are presented in Table 7.19 in the Appendix. As with the Orientation and Control Structure phases, the means of experience and supervised instances show a general increasing trend as the mean task structure rating increases (i.e., as the tasks become less structured) with the notable exception of the least structured task. For the most structured task in the phase, TC 293, the required years of experience are 1.25 and the number of supervised instances is 2.19. From the 1988 study, this task is expected to require someone of the assistant staff rank to perform it independently. The next to least structured task, TC 321, indicates a requirement of 4.04 years of experience and 8.19 supervised instances to perform it independently. Assessments for the least structured task, however, indicate a requirement of 2.32 years and 3.32 supervised instances with a rank of senior. All tasks but four have the required rank of senior from the 1988 study.

The coefficients of variation for mean years of experience range from .33 for TC 323 to .64 for TC 293 and for supervised instances from .38 for TC 300 to 1.28 for TC 324. Similar to the Orientation phase, the coefficients of variation for supervised instances are generally greater than those for years of experience.

In comparing the experience requirements indicated in the 1988 study with those in the 1996 study we find that they are generally consistent with each other. For those tasks indicating that an assistant staff person should perform them, the required years of experience ranged from .96 to 1.42. For the one task that indicates a staff person should perform it, the years of experience required are 2.19. For the tasks which require senior level, the mean years of experience required ranges from 2.11 to 3.29.

Substantive Tests

The experience data for tasks in specific subphases of the Substantive Tests phase are presented in Tables 7.20 to 7.29 in the Appendix to this chapter. Table 7.30 provides a summary of the experience data for the Substantive Tests phase. As with the Orientation, Control Structure, and Test of Control phases, the means for years of experience and supervised instances show a general increasing trend as the mean task structure rating increases (i.e., as the tasks become less structured) within each of the subphases of Substantive Tests. For the most structured task in each of the subphases except for General and Analytical Review, the required years of experience range from .90 in Purchasing and Disbursements Cycle and Fixed Assets to 1.14 in the Revenue and Receipt Cycle subphase. The number of supervised instances for the most structured tasks in each subphase (excluding General and Analytical Review) ranges from 1.21 for Payroll to 2.00 for Investments. Most of the tasks in the Substantive Tests phase require assistant staff or staff rank for performing the task. Senior rank is required for many of the less structured tasks. The least structured tasks in each subphase (excluding General and Analytical Review) require mean years of experience ranging from 2.00 years for the Cash subphase to 3.70 years for the Fixed Assets subphase. The number of supervised instances for the least structured tasks in each subphase (excluding General and Analytical Review) ranges from 2.23 for Cash to 4.18 for Inventory and Indebtedness subphases.

The General and Analytical Review Procedures subphase generally requires more experience to perform tasks independently than the other subphases in Substantive Tests. Mean years of experience range from 3.40 for the most structured task in the subphase to 4.07 for the least structured task and supervised experiences range from 3.08 to 5.00 for the most and least structured tasks in the subphase, respectively. The rank of senior is required for most tasks in the General and Analytical Review Procedures subphase.

The coefficients of variation for mean years of experience range from .22 for ST 89 in the Revenue and Receipts subphase to .75 for ST 214 in the Purchasing and Disbursements Cycle and ST 400 in the Indebtedness subphase and for supervised instances from .35 for ST 328 in the Inventory subphase to 1.14 for ST 126 in the Payroll subphase. Similar to the previous phases, the coefficients of variation for supervised instances are generally greater than those for years of experience.

In comparing the experience requirements indicated in the 1988 study with those in the 1996 study we find that they are generally consistent with each other. For those tasks indicating that an assistant staff person should perform them, the required years of experience ranged from .90 to 2.14. For tasks that indicate a staff person should perform them, the years of experience range from 1.53 to 3.07. For the tasks which require senior level, the mean years of experience required ranges from 1.88 to 3.67.

Forming Opinion

Experience data for the Forming Opinion phase are presented in Table 7.31 in the Appendix to the chapter. As with all previous phases, the means for years of experience show a general increasing trend as the mean task structure rating increases (i.e., as the tasks become less structured). The mean years of experience do not monotonically increase as the tasks become less structured. Supervised instances show an even less consistent pattern of increasing instances as the task becomes less structured. For the most structured task in the phase, FO 265, the required years of experience are 4.37 and the number of supervised instances is 5.07. From the 1988 study, this task is expected to require someone of the manager rank to perform it independently. The least structured task, FO 284, indicates a requirement of 7.10 years of experience and 5.47 supervised instances to perform it independently. All but two of the tasks have the required rank of manager from the 1988 study. One task indicates a senior rank and another indicates partner rank.

The coefficients of variation for mean years of experience range from .22 for FO 276 to .49 for FO 288 and for supervised instances from .33 for FO 287 to .83 for FO 268. Once again, the coefficients of variation for supervised instances are generally greater than those for years of experience.

In comparing the experience requirements indicated in the 1988 study with those in the 1996 study we find that they are generally consistent with each other. For the task indicating that a senior auditor should perform it, the required years of experience are 4.23. For the tasks indicating that a manager should perform them, the required years of experience ranged from 4.37 to 6.63 and for the task requiring a partner, the years of experience indicated are 6.90.

Financial Reporting

Experience data for the Financial Reporting phase are presented in Table 7.32 in the Appendix. As with most all of the previous phases, the means for years of experience and supervised instances show a general increasing trend as the mean task structure rating increases (i.e., as the tasks become less structured). Neither the mean years of experience nor the mean supervised instances monotonically increase with structure. For the most structured task in the phase, FR 421, the required years of experience are 3.17 and the number of supervised instances is 4.50. From the 1988 study, this task is expected to require someone of the senior rank to perform it independently. The least structured task, FR 431, indicates a requirement of 4.13 years of experience and 5.75 supervised instances to perform it independently. All but three of the tasks have the required rank of manager from the 1988 study. The remaining three tasks indicate a senior rank.

The coefficients of variation for mean years of experience range from .23 for FR 432 to .39 for FR 424 and for supervised instances from .56 for FR 421 to 1.01 for FR 428. Again, the coefficients of variation for supervised instances are generally greater than those for years of experience.

In comparing the experience requirements indicated in the 1988 study with those in the 1996 study we find that they are generally consistent with each other. For the tasks indicating that a senior auditor should perform them, the required years of experience range from 3.17 to 3.58. For the tasks indicating that a manager should perform them, the required years of experience ranged from 3.08 to 4.67.

DECISION AIDS

The decision aid data are presented in Tables 7.33 through 7.48 in the Appendix to the chapter. For each task in the 1996 task inventory, and for comparable tasks from the 1988 study, the percentage of responses falling into each of the decision aid categories (automation, decision support systems, knowledge expert systems, and strictly human processing) is reported. The median decision aid response is also reported. The discussion of results by phase focuses on those tasks for which the median decision aid was different between the two studies.

Orientation

Decision aid data for the Orientation phase are presented in Table 7.33. In the 1996 study, 81% of all tasks in the Orientation phase of the audit have a median response of HP (human processing). Of the 35 tasks that are comparable across studies, 89% have median assessments of HP in the 1996 study and 91% have median assessments of HP in the 1988 study. The assessments for two of the tasks, OR 21 and OR 46, shifted closer to HP, while the assessments for two other tasks, OR 48 and OR 23, shifted closer to the automation end of the spectrum in 1996 as compared with 1988.

Control Structure

Decision aid data for the Control Structure phase are presented in Table 7.34. In the 1996 study, 75% of all tasks in the Control Structure phase of the audit have a median response of HP. Of the 35 tasks that are comparable across studies, 71% have median assessments of HP in the 1996 study and 100% have median assessments of HP in the 1988 study. The assessments for 10 of the comparable tasks shifted closer to the automation end of the spectrum, most with larger percentages in the DSS category in 1996 than in 1988.

Tests of Controls

Decision aid data for the Tests of Controls phase are presented in Table 7.35. In the 1996 study, 71% of all tasks in the Test of Controls phase of the audit have a median response of HP. Of the 17 tasks that are comparable across studies, 59% have median assessments of HP in the 1996 study and 82% have median assessments of HP in the 1988 study. For the five comparable tasks that have different medians in the 1996 study the percentages of automation responses are larger than in the 1988 study. For example, for TC 325 and TC 310, 62% and 29% of the responses indicated AU (automation) in 1996 compared to 29% in 1988 for TC 325 and no responses for AU in 1988 for TC 310.

Substantive Tests

Decision aid data for the Substantive Tests phase are presented in Tables 7.36 to 7.46 in the Appendix. In the 1996 study, 86% of all tasks in the Substantive Tests phase of the audit have a median response of HP. Of the 128 tasks that are comparable across studies, 85% have median assessments of HP in the 1996 study and 80% have median assessments of HP in the 1988 study. Across comparable tasks there was a slight shift toward more tasks being considered suitable only for human processing, most notably in the Inventory subphase.

Forming Opinion

Decision aid data for the Forming Opinion phase are presented in Table 7.47. In the 1996 study, 100% of all tasks in the Forming Opinion phase of the audit have a median response of HP. Of the 15 tasks that are comparable across studies, 100% have median assessments of HP in the 1988 study also.

Financial Reporting

Decision aid data for the Financial Reporting phase are presented in Table 7.48. In the 1996 study, 89% of all tasks in the Financial Reporting phase of the audit have a median response of HP. The remaining 11% of tasks has a median response other than HP (consisting of two tasks, each with a median halfway between KES and HP). Of the 17 tasks that are comparable across studies, 94% have median assessments of HP with the remaining 6% having a median between KES and HP in the 1996 study and 100% have median assessments of HP in the 1988 study.

PATTERNS ACROSS TASK CHARACTERISTICS

For each task for which there is a significant difference in task structure rating from 1988 to 1996 we looked at the experience requirements and the percentage of responses in the decision aid categories for the two periods. In the Orientation and Control Structure phases there was one task in each phase (OR 12 and CS 179) with a significant difference in structure rating from 1988 to 1996. There was no practical difference in experience required from one period to the other, nor was there a difference in the percentage of responses indicating that HP was required for either task. In the Test of Controls phase, one task (TC 305) was judged to be more structured in 1996 than in 1988. The experience requirement did not change. However, consistent with the structure assessment, the percentage of responses indicating HP decreased from 37% in 1988 to 7% in 1996, while AU increased to 43% from 33% and DSS increased to 36% from 20% in the 1988 study.

In the Substantive Tests phase there were 18 tasks with significant differences in task structure assessments from 1988 to 1996. Because of the different response modes used for experience requirements across the two studies, it was difficult to objectively compare the assessed experience requirements over time. There did not seem to be major differences, however. With respect to suitability for decision aids there were some notable changes over time for some of the tasks with significant differences in task structure. These are highlighted below.

In the Revenue and Receipt Cycle subphase, ST 100 was considered to be less structured in 1996 than in 1988. Accordingly, the percentage of responses in the HP category increased from 27% in 1988 to 67% in 1996, while the percentage of responses in the AU category decreased from 63% in 1988 to 20% in 1996. In the Purchasing and Disbursements Cycle, ST 219 was considered to be less structured in 1996 than in 1988. The percentage of responses in the HP category for this task decreased from 94% in the 1988 to 46% in 1996 while the percentage of responses in the AU category increased from 6% in 1988 to 40% in the 1996. In this case, the shift in decision aid assessments seems counter to the change in perceived structure of the task. In the Inventory subphase, ST 360 was considered less structured in 1996 than in 1988. The percentage of responses for 1988 in the AU and HP categories, respectively, for ST360 were 35% and 45%, while in 1996, the corresponding percentages were 8% and 75%. In the Investments subphase, task ST 368 which was considered to be less structured in 1996 than in 1988 had a median response of HP in 1996 but a median response of DSS in 1988, indicating a shift in decision aid applicability consistent with the changed assessment of task structure.

In the Forming Opinion phase, four tasks were considered to be more structured in 1996 than in 1988. For all four, the percentage of responses in the HP category decreased over the period but the median response remained HP. A similar pattern occurred with the eight tasks in the Financial Reporting phase that were judged as being more structured in the 1996 study than in the 1988 study. For seven of these tasks, although the percentage of responses in the HP category decreased, six still maintained a median response of HP and one, FR 419, had a median between KES and HP in 1996.

These observations support the idea that the more structured the task the more likely it is that it will be evaluated as being suitable for decision aid development. Where there were practical changes in percentages in decision aid response categories, they were generally consistent with this notion; tasks that were considered more structured in 1996 compared to 1988 were also considered by a higher percentage of respondents to be more amenable to decision aid development in the 1996 study.

SUMMARY OF TASK LEVEL RESULTS

The preceding discussion of results and tables for 433 audit tasks from a 1996 study and 247 comparable tasks from a similar study in 1988 provide a wealth of information for auditing researchers, practitioners and students. Task-specific results revealed three general observations. First, in general, as the task structure rating increases, the coefficient of variation decreases indicating that there is more consensus among auditors for less structured tasks than for more structured tasks. Second, there were very few significant differences in assessed task structure from 1988 to 1996. Notable differences were in the Investments subphase of substantive tests where the tasks were judged to be less structured in 1996 and the Forming Opinion and Financial Reporting phases where some tasks were considered to be more structured in 1996 than in 1988. Third, the significant differences in task structure over time were generally consistent with changing perceptions about decision aid applicability for those tasks. The aggregate data reported on in Chapter 8 provides some indication of overall trends over the eight-year period and the relationship between the task characteristics. A discussion of the conclusions and implications for both the task-level data and aggregate data is provided in Chapter 9.

APPENDIX

Table 7.1
Orientation Phase: Task Structure

	1996 Study		1988 Study		Two-Sample t Tests	
Task	Mean	Coefficient of Variation	Mean	Coefficient of Variation	t statistic	p value
OR 27	3.00	.62	2.90	.64	.19	.85
OR 29	3.07	.61				
OR 55	3.33	.63	4.08	.49	−1.23	.23
OR 56	3.40	.62				
OR 54	3.67	.60	3.45	.48	.35	.73
OR 7	3.67	.76	4.06	.58	−.50	.62
OR 36	3.73	.74	3.68	.74	.06	.95
OR 21	4.07	.53	3.45	.57	.99	.33
OR 35	4.07	.47				
OR 40	4.20	.49				
OR 46	4.20	.50	3.47	.60	1.18	.25
OR 33	4.27	.45				
OR 8	4.33	.44				
OR 38	4.47	.47	5.10	.43	−1.01	.32
OR 9	4.47	.40				
OR 48	4.53	.54	5.18	.36	−.95	.35
OR 2	4.60	.40				
OR 26	4.60	.44	4.63	.43	−.04	.97
OR 34	4.60	.49				
OR 1	4.67	.43				
OR 50	4.71	.39				
OR 19	4.93	.43	4.17	.47	1.24	.23
OR 24	4.93	.38	4.52	.43	.74	.47
OR 16	5.00	.57	5.06	.47	−.08	.94
OR 52	5.07	.46				
OR 49	5.07	.38	6.10	.26	−1.82	.09
OR 5	5.13	.40				
OR 53	5.13	.41	6.02	.26	−1.51	.15
OR 57	5.13	.37				
OR 37	5.20	.26				
OR 43	5.20	.36				
OR 51	5.20	.33				
OR 39	5.27	.23	5.49	.34	−.54	.59
OR 20	5.40	.36				
OR 22	5.47	.44	5.33	.36	.20	.85

Table 7.1 (continued)
Orientation Phase: Task Structure

	1996 Study		1988 Study		Two-Sample t Tests	
Task	Mean	Coefficient of Variation	Mean	Coefficient of Variation	t statistic	p value
OR 3	5.47	.36	5.96	.34	−.83	.41
OR 58	5.47	.33				
OR 15	5.53	.45	6.54	.28	−1.46	.16
OR 45	5.60	.32	5.45	.29	.29	.77
OR 23	5.67	.38	6.40	.30	−1.20	.24
OR 31	5.67	.40	6.40	.26	−1.16	.26
OR 41	5.67	.32				
OR 42	5.67	.28	6.00	.29	−.70	.49
OR 30	5.71	.34	6.86	.24	−2.01	.06
OR 4	5.80	.39				
OR 44	5.87	.36				
OR 11	5.93	.39	5.92	.35	.01	.99
OR 18	5.93	.32	6.50	.25	−1.04	.31
OR 28	5.93	.40	6.81	.25	−1.33	.20
OR 6	6.13	.24	6.12	.27	.02	.98
OR 10	6.20	.35				
OR 32	6.20	.23	6.50	.28	−.67	.51
OR 47	6.20	.31	6.94	.19	−1.41	.18
OR 14	6.40	.25	6.71	.27	−.65	.52
OR 17	6.47	.33	7.25	.20	−1.33	.20
OR 13	6.53	.23	5.82	.35	1.48	.15
OR 25	6.53	.31	7.50	.23	−1.67	.11
OR 12	7.20	.34	5.33	.54	2.46	.02

Table 7.2
Control Structure Phase: Task Structure

	1996 Study		1988 Study		Two-Sample t Tests	
Task	Mean	Coefficient of Variation	Mean	Coefficient of Variation	t statistic	p value
CS 169	2.40	.44	2.67	.71	−.71	.48
CS 170	2.53	.33				
CS 167	3.07	.44	3.45	.60	−.84	.41
CS 149	3.27	.55	3.08	.52	.36	.72
CS 161	3.27	.39				
CS 162	3.40	.38	3.53	.56	−.30	.77
CS 164	3.53	.28	3.80	.49	−.71	.48
CS 168	3.53	.41	3.12	.58	.90	.37
CS 163	3.60	.31	3.86	.48	−.65	.52
CS 165	3.79	.30	3.94	.45	−.39	.70
CS 182	3.80	.42				
CS 180	3.87	.56	3.53	.51	.55	.59
CS 184	3.87	.42				
CS 148	3.93	.37	4.06	.41	−.29	.77
CS 183	4.07	.47	4.25	.38	−.34	.74
CS 147	4.20	.48	4.17	.51	.06	.96
CS 171	4.20	.34	3.69	.48	1.14	.27
CS 166	4.27	.34	4.02	.46	.54	.59
CS 185	4.40	.42	5.00	.32	−1.13	.27
CS 186	4.47	.36				
CS 189	4.47	.34	4.48	.37	−.03	.98
CS 155	4.50	.40				
CS 160	4.53	.37	3.82	.48	1.41	.17
CS 172	4.53	.36	3.98	.44	1.12	.27
CS 158	4.60	.36	4.37	.42	.47	.64
CS 146	4.87	.35	4.60	.31	.54	.59
CS 154	4.87	.35	4.18	.43	1.35	.19
CS 157	5.00	.32	4.45	.40	1.13	.27
CS 174	5.07	.38				
CS 192	5.07	.38	4.76	.33	.62	.54
CS 188	5.13	.34	4.81	.35	.66	.51
CS 156	5.20	.33	4.80	.37	.78	.44
CS 159	5.33	.35	4.53	.38	1.47	.16
CS 187	5.33	.34	4.69	.38	1.26	.22
CS 181	5.47	.39	4.90	.43	.91	.37
CS 175	5.53	.33	4.92	.35	1.16	.26
CS 176	5.53	.33	5.31	.34	.43	.67
CS 153	5.67	.34				

Table 7.2 (continued)
Control Structure Phase: Task Structure

	1996 Study		1988 Study		Two-Sample t Tests	
Task	Mean	Coefficient of Variation	Mean	Coefficient of Variation	t statistic	p value
CS 178	5.67	.33				
CS 190	5.80	.36	4.88	.37	1.57	.13
CS 177	6.00	.27	5.37	.35	1.29	.21
CS 191	6.00	.36	5.39	.33	1.04	.31
CS 173	6.20	.31				
CS 193	6.33	.31	6.16	.27	.34	.74
CS 150	6.47	.30				
CS 151	6.60	.33				
CS 179	6.60	.26	5.22	.32	2.72	.01
CS 152	6.67	.25				

Table 7.3
Tests of Controls Phase: Task Structure

	1996 Study		1988 Study		Two-Sample t Tests	
Task	Mean	Coefficient of Variation	Mean	Coefficient of Variation	t statistic	p value
TC 293	2.36	.49	2.73	.45	−1.07	.30
TC 297	2.50	.58	2.37	.52	.31	.76
TC 325	2.54	.55	2.90	.68	−.75	.46
TC 295	2.64	.38				
TC 292	2.71	.59				
TC 296	2.79	.49				
TC 311	3.23	.54	2.94	.63	.53	.60
TC 290	3.36	.38				
TC 300	3.36	.50				
TC 310	3.36	.45	3.90	.45	−1.14	.27
TC 294	3.43	.42				
TC 305	3.43	.36	4.47	.43	-2.45	.02
TC 307	3.71	.52				
TC 309	3.79	.52	4.23	.40	−.76	.45
TC 299	3.86	.44	4.39	.32	−1.07	.30
TC 298	4.00	.44				
TC 308	4.07	.48	4.12	.48	−.09	.93
TC 302	4.29	.35				
TC 303	4.43	.40				
TC 319	4.46	.38				
TC 301	4.64	.30				
TC 327	4.69	.48				
TC 323	4.77	.38				
TC 322	4.92	.47				
TC 312	5.00	.48	4.58	.39	.59	.56
TC 324	5.00	.56				
TC 326	5.08	.49				
TC 317	5.15	.37				
TC 306	5.21	.38	5.10	.30	.19	.85
TC 320	5.46	.43				
TC 315	5.58	.35	5.24	.36	.54	.60
TC 316	5.58	.35	5.00	.42	.90	.38
TC 318	5.62	.42	5.46	.26	.23	.82
TC 304	5.67	.44	5.86	.29	−.25	.81
TC 314	5.75	.30				
TC 313	5.85	.44	5.86	.26	−.01	.99
TC 321	6.00	.38				
TC 291	6.14	.23	5.73	.25	.95	.35

Table 7.4
Substantive Tests Phase: Task Structure—General and Analytical Review Procedures

	1996 Study		1988 Study		Two-Sample t Tests	
Task	Mean	Coefficient of Variation	Mean	Coefficient of Variation	t statistic	p value
ST 65	4.07	.43	4.76	.39	−1.31	.20
ST 64	4.40	.41	4.35	.36	.10	.92
ST 63	4.47	.40	4.90	.39	−.80	.43
ST 59	4.60	.37	5.41	.32	−1.62	.12
ST 61	4.79	.39	6.18	.25	−2.58	.02
ST 60	4.80	.39				
ST 62	5.80	.26				

Table 7.5
Substantive Tests Phase: Task Structure—Cash

	1996 Study		1988 Study		Two-Sample t Tests	
Task	Mean	Coefficient of Variation	Mean	Coefficient of Variation	t statistic	p value
ST 68	1.60	.57	1.35	.44	1.01	.33
ST 72	1.60	.62	1.39	.44	.79	.44
ST 73	1.60	.62	1.20	.42	1.50	.15
ST 74	1.60	.62				
ST 80	1.60	.57	1.41	.43	.77	.45
ST 81	1.80	.60	1.33	.47	1.61	.13
ST 83	1.93	.50				
ST 78	2.07	.53	1.53	.52	1.75	.10
ST 66	2.13	.46	2.71	.50	−1.81	.08
ST 69	2.14	.51				
ST 77	2.20	.52	1.78	.49	1.32	.20
ST 82	2.20	.49	2.33	.48	−.39	.70
ST 71	2.40	.41				
ST 75	2.53	.44	2.59	.51	−.17	.87
ST 79	2.53	.42	2.02	.40	1.72	.10
ST 67	2.60	.46	2.10	.50	1.46	.16
ST 70	2.60	.41	1.86	.48	2.47	.02
ST 84	3.07	.48				
ST 76	3.13	.47	3.63	.46	−1.12	.27
ST 85	3.20	.58	3.53	.41	−.63	.54

Table 7.6
Substantive Tests Phase: Task Structure—Revenue and Receipt Cycle

	1996 Study		1988 Study		Two-Sample t Tests	
Task	Mean	Coefficient of Variation	Mean	Coefficient of Variation	t statistic	p value
ST 103	1.73	.55				
ST 109	2.00	.50				
ST 110	2.00	.50				
ST 93	2.07	.43	2.08	.54	−.05	.96
ST 107	2.07	.56	1.76	.51	.95	.35
ST 108	2.07	.50				
ST 96	2.13	.66				
ST 106	2.13	.50				
ST 105	2.27	.49				
ST 94	2.33	.35				
ST 98	2.40	.41	2.16	.50	.80	.43
ST 99	2.40	.61				
ST 101	2.67	.46	2.20	.49	1.31	.21
ST 86	2.73	.47	3.51	.43	−1.97	.06
ST 104	2.80	.54				
ST 92	2.87	.41	2.46	.63	1.08	.29
ST 90	2.93	.46	2.79	.58	.34	.74
ST 91	3.07	.58	2.94	.54	.25	.81
ST 97	3.13	.50	4.40	.42	−2.62	.01
ST 111	3.20	.62	2.73	.51	.85	.41
ST 112	3.20	.52	2.98	.49	.46	.65
ST 89	3.27	.47	3.78	.46	−1.09	.29
ST 114	3.27	.42				
ST 100	3.33	.43	2.10	.54	3.02	.01
ST 115	3.73	.48				
ST 88	3.80	.47	4.20	.30	−.82	.42
ST 102	4.00	.52				
ST 95	4.07	.55	3.47	.40	.98	.34
ST 116	4.33	.53	4.82	.38	−.75	.46
ST 87	4.47	.36	4.94	.34	−.99	.33
ST 113	4.73	.43				

Table 7.7
Substantive Tests Phase: Task Structure—Purchasing and Disbursements Cycle

	1996 Study		1988 Study		Two-Sample t Tests	
Task	Mean	Coefficient of Variation	Mean	Coefficient of Variation	t statistic	p value
ST 199	1.47	.51				
ST 200	1.53	.48				
ST 224	1.73	.71				
ST 228	2.13	.46	1.88	.49	.89	.38
ST 202	2.20	.46	2.33	.60	−.39	.70
ST 204	2.27	.39				
ST 216	2.27	.39				
ST 223	2.33	.53				
ST 225	2.33	.50	1.94	.47	1.19	.25
ST 226	2.33	.58				
ST 206	2.40	.44				
ST 209	2.40	.38	2.14	.56	.89	.38
ST 210	2.40	.38	2.14	.53	.90	.38
ST 213	2.47	.59				
ST 211	2.53	.59				
ST 219	2.60	.41	1.82	.51	2.59	.02
ST 222	2.60	.50				
ST 212	2.73	.56				
ST 220	2.73	.47				
ST 208	2.87	.45	2.53	.54	.86	.40
ST 201	2.93	.42	3.10	.52	−.43	.67
ST 205	2.93	.30				
ST 203	3.00	.40				
ST 214	3.00	.45				
ST 227	3.00	.25				
ST 215	3.07	.44				
ST 221	3.07	.45				
ST 194	3.13	.51	3.78	.40	−1.38	.18
ST 217	3.20	.38	2.82	.44	1.07	.30
ST 196	3.53	.49	3.41	.61	.23	.82
ST 197	3.53	.51				
ST 198	3.87	.46				
ST 230	4.07	.47				
ST 195	4.20	.33	4.71	.35	−1.21	.24
ST 218	4.40	.38				
ST 207	4.53	.39	3.31	.47	2.42	.03
ST 231	5.07	.36				
ST 232	5.27	.38				
ST 229	5.73	.33				

Table 7.8
Substantive Tests Phase: Task Structure—Inventory

	1996 Study		1988 Study		Two-Sample t Tests	
Task	Mean	Coefficient of Variation	Mean	Coefficient of Variation	t statistic	p value
ST 348	1.58	.33				
ST 332	2.08	.54	2.29	.56	−.58	.57
ST 347	2.17	.27	1.98	.58	.80	.43
ST 338	2.23	.58	1.96	.54	.69	.50
ST 339	2.23	.58	1.96	.51	.70	.49
ST 361	2.50	.32	2.06	.54	1.56	.13
ST 362	2.50	.32	2.00	.56	1.78	.09
ST 351	2.58	.48	2.18	.54	1.01	.33
ST 334	2.62	.40	2.35	.44	.83	.42
ST 340	2.62	.51	2.59	.52	.06	.96
ST 335	2.77	.51	2.69	.49	.17	.87
ST 346	2.83	.42				
ST 337	2.85	.47	2.57	.50	.66	.52
ST 349	2.92	.49				
ST 328	3.08	.54	4.08	.35	−2.00	.06
ST 352	3.08	.43	3.14	.42	-.14	.89
ST 331	3.39	.43				
ST 330	3.46	.40				
ST 353	3.67	.37	2.80	.51	1.96	.07
ST 356	3.67	.42	4.13	.31	−.94	.36
ST 336	3.69	.49	3.08	.44	1.14	.27
ST 342	3.69	.47				
ST 357	3.75	.30				
ST 329	3.85	.38	5.00	.29	−2.53	.02
ST 343	3.85	.50	3.65	.47	.33	.74
ST 344	3.85	.46				
ST 354	4.25	.29	4.43	.30	−.45	.66
ST 333	4.31	.44	4.33	.38	−.03	.97
ST 350	4.33	.37	4.13	.39	.40	.69
ST 355	4.33	.39				
ST 359	4.33	.30	4.84	.33	−1.15	.27
ST 360	4.50	.31	3.39	.54	2.33	.03
ST 358	4.67	.33	4.69	.33	−.05	.96
ST 345	4.85	.46				
ST 364	4.92	.31				
ST 341	5.08	.33				
ST 363	5.08	.32				

Table 7.9
Substantive Tests Phase: Task Structure—Fixed Assets

	1996 Study		1988 Study		Two-Sample t Tests	
Task	Mean	Coefficient of Variation	Mean	Coefficient of Variation	t statistic	p value
ST 237	1.60	.52	1.29	.55	1.30	.21
ST 248	1.73	.41	1.42	.56	1.47	.15
ST 252	2.00	.42	1.71	.54	1.12	.27
ST 247	2.07	.53	1.88	.52	.60	.56
ST 253	2.07	.59				
ST 238	2.20	.39	1.88	.49	1.25	.23
ST 239	2.20	.39	1.86	.63	1.23	.23
ST 250	2.60	.43	2.41	.55	.56	.58
ST 254	3.13	.52				
ST 235	3.27	.39	2.57	.57	1.77	.09
ST 236	3.27	.36	2.43	.52	2.39	.03
ST 255	3.33	.49				
ST 233	3.40	.38				
ST 241	3.53	.41				
ST 259	3.60	.36	2.57	.57	2.61	.02
ST 234	3.73	.33	4.04	.35	−.82	.42
ST 245	3.73	.33				
ST 258	3.87	.35				
ST 251	4.00	.41	4.10	.41	−.21	.84
ST 256	4.07	.39				
ST 262	4.20	.39				
ST 261	4.27	.41				
ST 246	4.40	.50				
ST 257	4.73	.36	4.00	.45	1.43	.16
ST 260	4.93	.41				
ST 240	5.00	.31				
ST 249	5.00	.32	4.22	.36	1.66	.11
ST 243	5.27	.42				
ST 242	5.40	.42	4.02	.45	2.16	.04
ST 244	6.20	.31				

Table 7.10
Substantive Tests Phase: Task Structure—Payroll and Related Costs

	1996 Study		1988 Study		Two-Sample t Tests	
Task	Mean	Coefficient of Variation	Mean	Coefficient of Variation	t statistic	p value
ST 129	1.87	.53				
ST 125	2.07	.62				
ST 130	2.20	.46				
ST 128	2.60	.48	1.84	.54	2.18	.04
ST 127	2.73	.43				
ST 122	3.00	.38	2.22	.57	2.26	.03
ST 124	3.00	.45				
ST 123	3.20	.41	2.76	.48	1.14	.26
ST 131	3.40	.71				
ST 117	3.53	.55				
ST 119	3.73	.34	3.22	.49	1.27	.21
ST 120	3.73	.34				
ST 121	4.07	.38	3.78	.40	.64	.53
ST 118	4.20	.31	4.08	.37	.29	.77
ST 132	4.60	.37	4.67	.33	−.15	.88
ST 126	5.00	.36	4.43	.32	1.12	.28

Table 7.11
Substantive Tests Phase: Task Structure—Investments

Task	1996 Study		1988 Study		Two-Sample t Tests	
	Mean	Coefficient of Variation	Mean	Coefficient of Variation	t statistic	p value
ST 370	1.58	.50	1.39	.58	.76	.46
ST 372	1.92	.35	1.59	.53	1.43	.17
ST 374	2.42	.65	1.71	.50	1.50	.16
ST 375	2.42	.65				
ST 381	2.42	.37	1.69	.51	2.51	.02
ST 382	2.50	.36	1.98	.54	1.72	.10
ST 371	2.67	.79				
ST 383	2.75	.38	1.80	.47	2.91	.01
ST 385	2.75	.31				
ST 384	2.83	.33				
ST 380	2.92	.31	3.45	.47	−1.53	.14
ST 379	3.17	.30	2.47	.54	2.10	.05
ST 388	3.17	.35				
ST 366	3.58	.50	3.94	.35	−.64	.53
ST 365	3.75	.50	4.21	.33	−.80	.44
ST 368	3.75	.38	2.78	.49	2.15	.05
ST 387	3.92	.38				
ST 377	4.00	.21				
ST 386	4.08	.42	4.45	.40	−.65	.53
ST 367	4.25	.40	4.77	.37	−.93	.37
ST 369	4.33	.30	3.20	.39	2.71	.02
ST 376	4.33	.36				
ST 378	4.67	.23				
ST 389	4.75	.47	3.96	.38	1.17	.26
ST 373	5.08	.36				

Table 7.12
Substantive Tests Phase: Task Structure—Indebtedness

	1996 Study		1988 Study		Two-Sample *t* Tests	
Task	Mean	Coefficient of Variation	Mean	Coefficient of Variation	*t* statistic	*p* value
ST 393	1.67	.59	1.27	.54	1.32	.21
ST 394	1.83	.39	1.69	.53	.60	.56
ST 395	2.08	.56				
ST 400	2.08	.48				
ST 396	2.17	.43				
ST 401	2.25	.43				
ST 398	2.50	.53	1.90	.57	1.47	.16
ST 397	2.75	.44				
ST 402	2.75	.52				
ST 410	2.83	.33	2.31	.45	1.68	.11
ST 411	2.92	.27				
ST 405	3.00	.59				
ST 413	3.17	.35				
ST 407	3.25	.48				
ST 399	3.42	.47				
ST 408	3.42	.38				
ST 409	3.58	.35	3.15	.49	1.04	.31
ST 414	3.58	.56	4.47	.45	−1.36	.19
ST 403	3.67	.37				
ST 412	3.67	.24				
ST 415	3.67	.47				
ST 390	3.75	.40	3.79	.41	−.09	.93
ST 391	4.00	.28	3.27	.47	1.85	.08
ST 392	4.08	.22	3.88	.45	.58	.57
ST 406	4.58	.43				
ST 404	5.25	.40				

Table 7.13
Substantive Tests Phase: Task Structure—Ownership Equity

	1996 Study		1988 Study		Two-Sample t Tests	
Task	Mean	Coefficient of Variation	Mean	Coefficient of Variation	t statistic	p value
ST 134	1.73	.55	1.39	.60	1.25	.22
ST 136	2.27	.49				
ST 142	2.40	.56				
ST 138	2.47	.57	2.06	.55	1.02	.32
ST 137	2.53	.54				
ST 135	3.00	.52				
ST 144	3.13	.45				
ST 140	3.33	.43	2.76	.53	1.35	.19
ST 143	3.60	.58	2.76	.51	1.46	.16
ST 141	3.67	.53	3.39	.48	.50	.62
ST 145	3.87	.42				
ST 139	4.33	.30	3.67	.43	1.64	.11
ST 133	4.53	.34	4.08	.41	.96	.34

Table 7.14
Substantive Tests Phase: Task Structure—Summary of Tasks by Subphase

Subphase of SubstantiveTests	1996 Study			1988 Study		
	Overall Mean (COV)	Range of Means		Overall Mean (COV)	Range of Means	
		Low	High		Low	High
General and AR Procedures (Tasks in Table 7.4)	4.70 (.38)	4.07	5.80	5.24 (.34)	4.35	6.18
Cash (Tasks in Table 7.5)	2.23 (.55)	1.60	3.20	2.07 (.60)	1.20	3.63
Revenue and Receipt Cycle (Tasks in Table 7.6)	2.94 (.56)	1.73	4.73	2.82 (.59)	1.67	4.94
Purchasing and Disbursements Cycle (Tasks in Table 7.7)	3.02 (.54)	1.47	5.73	2.70 (.58)	1.82	4.71
Inventory (Tasks in Table 7.8)	3.46 (.48)	1.58	5.08	3.33 (.53)	1.90	5.61
Fixed Assets (Tasks in Table 7.9)	3.63 (.52)	1.60	6.20	2.87 (.60)	1.29	4.27
Payroll (Tasks in Table 7.10)	3.31 (.51)	1.87	5.00	3.14 (.53)	1.84	4.67
Investments (Tasks in Table 7.11)	3.36 (.48)	1.58	5.08	2.83 (.60)	1.39	4.77
Indebtedness (Tasks in Table 7.12)	3.15 (.49)	1.67	5.25	2.75 (.60)	1.27	4.47
Ownership Equity (Tasks in Table 7.13)	3.14 (.32)	1.73	4.53	2.88 (.58)	1.39	4.08

Table 7.15
Forming Opinion Phase: Task Structure

	1996 Study		1988 Study		Two-Sample t Tests	
Task	Mean	Coefficient of Variation	Mean	Coefficient of Variation	t statistic	p value
FO 265	4.07	.43	5.47	.35	−2.65	.01
FO 274	4.20	.42	5.64	.37	−2.56	.02
FO 281	4.33	.59				
FO 277	4.40	.51				
FO 273	4.47	.41				
FO 288	4.47	.47	6.29	.32	−2.96	.01
FO 272	4.60	.43	5.70	.36	−1.85	.08
FO 286	4.73	.43	5.80	.36	−1.74	.10
FO 263	4.93	.37	6.24	.28	−2.46	.02
FO 266	5.00	.46				
FO 269	5.00	.47				
FO 264	5.07	.46	6.39	.25	−2.05	.06
FO 289	5.40	.42	6.39	.36	−1.46	.16
FO 275	5.47	.40				
FO 268	5.53	.39				
FO 267	5.60	.40	6.59	.24	−1.60	.13
FO 278	5.67	.39				
FO 270	5.73	.40	6.29	.25	−.88	.39
FO 282	5.80	.46				
FO 276	5.87	.35				
FO 280	5.93	.35	6.96	.20	−1.81	.09
FO 287	5.93	.33	6.39	.31	−.78	.44
FO 271	6.00	.36	6.63	.24	−1.04	.31
FO 279	6.27	.33	6.63	.22	−.63	.54
FO 285	6.40	.33	6.94	.25	−.89	.38
FO 283	6.53	.31				
FO 284	6.73	.30				

Table 7.16
Financial Statements Reporting Phase: Task Structure

	1996 Study			1988 Study		Two-Sample *t* Tests	
Task	Mean	Coefficient of Variation	Mean	Coefficient of Variation	*t* statistic	*p* value
FR 421	2.58	.51	3.71	.49	−2.46	.02
FR 419	3.33	.62	5.65	.36	−3.51	.00
FR 424	3.50	.38	4.84	.42	−2.81	.01
FR 417	3.58	.45	5.41	.37	−3.32	.00
FR 416	3.83	.65	6.02	.31	−2.86	.01
FR 418	3.92	.50	5.71	.33	−2.85	.01
FR 428	4.00	.49	4.86	.42	−1.35	.19
FR 427	4.25	.39				
FR 426	4.33	.43	4.53	.50	−.31	.76
FR 425	4.50	.42	5.82	.32	−2.17	.05
FR 420	4.67	.45	5.55	.36	−1.32	.21
FR 422	4.67	.28	5.39	.36	−1.54	.14
FR 432	4.92	.38	6.71	.22	−3.19	.01
FR 433	5.00	.35	6.12	.26	−2.02	.06
FR 429	5.25	.26	6.12	.25	−1.95	.07
FR 423	5.42	.38	6.02	.31	−.92	.37
FR 430	5.58	.30	6.22	.27	−1.18	.25
FR 431	5.75	.32	6.06	.30	−.55	.59

Table 7.17
Orientation Phase: Experience

Task	1996 Study				1988 Study
	Mean Years of Experience	Coefficient of Variation	Mean Supervised Instances	Coefficient of Variation	Median Professional Rank
OR 27	2.73	.59	2.64	1.18	Senior
OR 29	2.33	.45	2.29	.74	
OR 55	3.13	.32	2.85	.70	Senior
OR 56	3.40	.35	3.23	.84	
OR 54	2.93	.40	2.54	.52	Senior
OR 7	2.00	.57	2.14	.75	Senior
OR 36	3.20	.66	2.62	1.32	Senior
OR 21	3.47	.42	3.15	1.03	Senior
OR 35	3.27	.37	2.92	.65	
OR 40	2.93	.40	2.62	.71	
OR 46	2.40	.49	2.08	.60	Staff
OR 33	3.07	.38	3.39	.56	
OR 8	2.00	.46	2.14	.87	
OR 38	3.47	.45	3.31	.97	Senior
OR 9	3.33	.48	3.23	.97	
OR 48	2.93	.54	2.54	.80	Senior
OR 2	2.07	.59	2.58	.69	
OR 26	4.37	.39	3.85	.82	Senior
OR 34	2.87	.39	2.85	.62	
OR 1	2.20	.62	3.00	.88	
OR 50	3.33	.31	3.46	.78	
OR 19	3.13	.38	2.31	.51	Senior
OR 24	3.80	.40	3.31	.61	Senior
OR 16	3.53	.53	2.58	.78	Senior
OR 52	4.73	.34	4.92	.74	
OR 49	3.60	.31	3.69	.74	Senior
OR 5	3.60	.36	3.92	.63	
OR 53	3.87	.29	3.92	.66	Senior
OR 57	3.87	.29	4.46	.80	
OR 37	4.60	.33	5.00	.76	
OR 43	4.07	.35	4.54	1.00	
OR 51	3.80	.28	4.38	.74	
OR 39	3.20	.38	2.92	.70	Senior
OR 20	3.60	.25	2.69	.72	
OR 22	3.93	.31	3.15	.67	Senior
OR 3	3.67	.30	4.00	.64	Senior
OR 58	4.27	.26	4.00	.57	
OR 15	4.13	.46	3.92	.95	Manager
OR 45	3.07	.34	2.85	.65	Senior

Table 7.17 (continued)
Orientation Phase: Experience

	1996 Study				1988 Study
Task	Mean Years of Experience	Coefficient of Variation	Mean Supervised Instances	Coefficient of Variation	Median Professional Rank
OR 23	4.53	.36	3.69	.89	Senior
OR 31	4.00	.30	4.00	.60	Senior
OR 41	3.47	.32	3.46	.80	
OR 42	3.40	.35	3.00	.93	Senior
OR 30	3.87	.39	3.08	.57	Manager
OR 4	3.87	.32	4.77	.59	
OR 44	3.93	.28	4.08	.67	
OR 11	5.13	.31	3.77	1.01	Manager
OR 18	3.67	.47	3.15	.77	Manager
OR 28	3.87	.29	2.54	.73	Manager
OR 6	3.53	.37	4.00	.59	Senior
OR 10	5.53	.21	4.92	.71	
OR 32	4.27	.27	3.69	.49	Senior
OR 47	4.33	.33	4.00	.69	Senior
OR 14	4.40	.35	3.85	.78	Manager
OR 17	4.53	.39	4.15	.88	Manager
OR 13	3.33	.42	2.77	.72	Senior
OR 25	4.97	.28	3.92	.49	Manager
OR 12	1.64	.91	2.00	1.04	Senior

Table 7.18
Control Structure Phase: Experience

	1996 Study				1988 Study
Task	Mean Years of Experience	Coefficient of Variation	Mean Supervised Instances	Coefficient of Variation	Median Professional Rank
CS 169	1.37	.56	1.87	.57	Assistant
CS 170	1.23	.51	1.96	.49	
CS 167	1.70	.67	2.21	.62	Staff
CS 149	1.97	.68	2.10	.51	Staff
CS 161	1.27	.58	2.29	.60	
CS 162	2.17	.68	3.07	.70	Staff
CS 164	2.18	.58	3.27	.68	Staff
CS 168	1.70	.59	2.36	.57	Staff
CS 163	1.83	.41	3.13	.71	Staff
CS 165	2.39	.54	3.57	.62	Staff
CS 182	2.83	.39	3.27	.57	
CS 180	2.43	.64	2.40	.77	Staff
CS 184	2.97	.42	3.53	.49	
CS 148	1.83	.62	2.57	.56	Staff
CS 183	3.03	.43	3.47	.50	Senior
CS 147	2.20	.60	2.67	.69	Senior
CS 171	2.23	.40	2.79	.57	Staff
CS 166	2.23	.59	2.73	.61	Staff
CS 185	3.50	.45	4.20	.58	Senior
CS 186	3.17	.45	3.87	.62	
CS 189	3.17	.41	4.27	.56	Senior
CS 155	2.25	.62	2.43	.48	
CS 160	2.37	.28	3.27	.67	Staff
CS 172	2.03	.40	2.64	.53	Staff
CS 158	2.57	.49	3.13	.74	Senior
CS 146	2.43	.52	3.04	.44	Senior
CS 154	2.30	.59	2.67	.58	Staff
CS 157	2.57	.54	3.00	.73	Senior
CS 174	3.57	.35	4.33	.63	
CS 192	3.23	.41	4.00	.55	Senior
CS 188	3.30	.39	4.13	.57	Senior
CS 156	2.90	.51	3.20	.71	Senior
CS 159	3.23	.32	4.20	.65	Senior
CS 187	3.10	.38	4.00	.57	Senior
CS 181	3.37	.48	3.27	.55	Senior
CS 175	3.43	.31	3.87	.59	Senior
CS 176	3.63	.39	4.40	.69	Senior

Table 7.18 (continued)
Control Structure Phase: Experience

	1996 Study				1988 Study
Task	Mean Years of Experience	Coefficient of Variation	Mean Supervised Instances	Coefficient of Variation	Median Professional Rank
CS 153	2.70	.50	2.80	.69	
CS 178	3.70	.37	4.00	.60	
CS 190	3.77	.30	4.14	.57	Senior
CS 177	3.70	.34	4.07	.73	Senior
CS 191	3.90	.31	4.00	.61	Senior
CS 173	4.17	.32	4.47	.65	
CS 193	4.37	.31	4.47	.52	Senior
CS 150	3.03	.46	4.20	.73	
CS 151	3.70	.37	5.00	.55	
CS 179	3.83	.42	4.47	.71	Senior
CS 152	4.03	.33	4.86	.48	

Table 7.19
Tests of Controls Phase: Experience

Task	1996 Study				1988 Study
	Mean Years of Experience	Coefficient of Variation	Mean Supervised Instances	Coefficient of Variation	Median Professional Rank
TC 293	1.25	.64	2.19	.43	Assistant
TC 297	.96	.52	1.81	.55	Assistant
TC 325	2.19	.47	3.46	.43	Staff
TC 295	1.32	.55	2.04	.47	
TC 292	1.39	.53	2.12	.61	
TC 296	1.32	.55	2.04	.55	
TC 311	1.42	.61	3.13	.79	Assistant
TC 290	1.54	.55	2.88	.87	
TC 300	2.39	.49	3.19	.38	
TC 310	2.18	.42	3.42	.68	Senior
TC 294	1.46	.51	2.27	.53	
TC 305	2.82	.47	4.11	.51	Senior
TC 307	2.32	.53	3.73	.63	
TC 309	2.18	.42	3.58	.63	Senior
TC 299	2.11	.46	3.19	.74	Senior
TC 298	2.18	.46	3.35	.73	
TC 308	2.25	.42	3.73	.64	Senior
TC 302	1.75	.56	2.81	.59	
TC 303	2.39	.40	4.39	.76	
TC 319	2.35	.42	4.27	.82	
TC 301	2.46	.51	3.54	.47	
TC 327	3.04	.38	5.27	.92	
TC 323	2.50	.33	4.21	.87	
TC 322	2.50	.49	4.87	1.03	
TC 312	2.50	.54	4.54	1.12	Senior
TC 324	4.27	.55	7.88	1.28	
TC 326	3.27	.40	5.65	.85	
TC 317	3.12	.34	5.50	.89	
TC 306	2.75	.44	4.54	.57	Senior
TC 320	2.88	.45	5.42	.84	
TC 315	2.88	.45	4.87	1.02	Senior
TC 316	3.29	.45	5.12	.97	Senior
TC 318	3.12	.38	5.58	.87	Senior
TC 304	3.04	.47	5.27	.72	Senior
TC 314	2.54	.41	4.38	.83	
TC 313	2.88	.55	4.81	.99	Senior
TC 321	4.04	.59	8.19	1.22	
TC 291	2.32	.48	3.32	.69	Senior

Table 7.20
Substantive Tests Phase: Experience—General and Analytical Review Procedures

	1996 Study				1988 Study
Task	Mean Years of Experience	Coefficient of Variation	Mean Supervised Instances	Coefficient of Variation	Median Professional Rank
ST 65	3.40	.31	3.08	.76	Senior
ST 64	2.93	.27	3.00	.74	Staff
ST 63	3.27	.34	3.00	.77	Senior
ST 59	3.07	.29	3.50	.72	Senior
ST 61	3.67	.34	3.39	.55	Senior
ST 60	3.53	.35	4.46	.60	
ST 62	4.07	.25	5.00	.71	

Table 7.21
Substantive Tests Phase: Experience—Cash

Task	1996 Study				1988 Study
	Mean Years of Experience	Coefficient of Variation	Mean Supervised Instances	Coefficient of Variation	Median Professional Rank
ST 68	1.00	.56	1.46	.87	Assistant
ST 72	1.14	.58	1.58	.78	Assistant
ST 73	1.00	.39	1.25	.60	Assistant
ST 74	1.00	.39	1.33	.58	
ST 80	1.00	.38	1.39	.47	Assistant
ST 81	1.00	.39	1.25	.60	Assistant
ST 83	1.07	.43	1.46	.77	
ST 78	1.00	.38	1.23	.59	Assistant
ST 66	1.53	.42	2.21	.89	Staff
ST 69	.93	.64	1.79	.70	
ST 77	1.00	.38	1.46	.66	Assistant
ST 82	1.20	.35	2.08	.67	Assistant
ST 71	1.60	.57	2.00	.71	
ST 75	1.20	.56	2.00	.65	Assistant
ST 79	1.13	.46	1.69	.78	Assistant
ST 67	1.47	.44	2.36	.83	Assistant
ST 70	1.07	.56	1.71	.77	Assistant
ST 84	1.20	.47	2.07	.74	
ST 76	1.33	.54	2.00	.73	Assistant
ST 85	2.00	.71	2.23	.82	Staff

Table 7.22
Substantive Tests Phase: Experience—Revenue and Receipt Cycle

	1996 Study				1988 Study
Task	Mean Years of Experience	Coefficient of Variation	Mean Supervised Instances	Coefficient of Variation	Median Professional Rank
ST 103	1.14	.47	1.39	.81	
ST 109	1.07	.43	1.54	.82	
ST 110	1.07	.43	1.50	.90	
ST 93	1.47	.35	2.14	.89	Assistant
ST 107	1.27	.47	1.50	.97	Assistant
ST 108	1.13	.46	1.50	.82	
ST 96	1.20	.47	1.57	.78	
ST 106	1.07	.43	1.50	.82	
ST 105	1.13	.46	1.50	.68	
ST 94	1.33	.37	1.93	.72	
ST 98	1.53	.42	1.71	.66	Assistant
ST 99	1.47	.35	1.86	.70	
ST 101	1.80	.31	2.21	.83	Assistant
ST 86	2.13	.43	2.57	.74	Staff
ST 104	1.27	.36	1.64	.57	
ST 92	1.60	.40	1.93	.72	Assistant
ST 90	2.00	.27	2.00	.68	Assistant
ST 91	1.60	.40	2.07	.81	Assistant
ST 97	2.13	.30	2.36	.74	Staff
ST 111	1.67	.29	2.00	.62	Assistant
ST 112	1.73	.26	2.07	.58	Staff
ST 89	2.07	.22	2.71	.70	Staff
ST 114	2.00	.42	2.50	.71	
ST 100	1.67	.37	2.21	.83	Assistant
ST 115	2.13	.61	2.46	.75	
ST 88	2.60	.46	2.69	.73	Staff
ST 102	1.87	.34	2.14	.57	
ST 95	2.07	.56	2.08	.67	Staff
ST 116	2.87	.45	2.77	.78	Senior
ST 87	2.80	.56	2.92	1.10	Senior
ST 113	2.33	.31	2.64	.64	

Table 7.23
Substantive Tests Phase: Experience—Purchasing and Disbursements Cycle

	1996 Study				1988 Study
Task	Mean Years of Experience	Coefficient of Variation	Mean Supervised Instances	Coefficient of Variation	Median Professional Rank
ST 199	.90	.52	1.29	.64	
ST 200	.83	.63	1.21	.66	
ST 224	.97	.57	1.50	.77	
ST 228	1.03	.47	1.86	.87	Assistant
ST 202	1.23	.59	1.47	.57	Assistant
ST 204	1.23	.51	1.71	.53	
ST 216	2.10	.49	2.07	.67	
ST 223	.97	.57	1.71	.66	
ST 225	.90	.52	1.64	.74	Assistant
ST 226	.90	.52	1.79	.88	
ST 206	1.10	.49	1.57	.74	
ST 209	1.17	.50	2.29	.87	Assistant
ST 210	1.07	.58	2.36	.83	Assistant
ST 213	1.03	.70	1.64	.70	
ST 211	.93	.53	1.93	.83	
ST 219	1.23	.67	1.93	.87	Assistant
ST 222	1.17	.68	1.79	.67	
ST 212	1.00	.68	1.79	.91	
ST 220	1.30	.65	2.21	.76	
ST 208	1.57	.43	2.40	.72	Assistant
ST 201	1.37	.56	1.93	.52	Assistant
ST 205	1.37	.49	1.86	.55	
ST 203	1.37	.56	1.86	.55	
ST 214	1.17	.75	1.71	.70	
ST 227	1.77	.49	2.71	.53	
ST 215	1.23	.59	2.21	.80	
ST 221	1.23	.73	2.07	.55	
ST 194	1.90	.49	2.27	.54	Staff
ST 217	1.63	.52	2.00	.65	Assistant
ST 196	1.83	.52	2.40	.94	Assistant
ST 197	1.63	.62	2.29	.53	
ST 198	1.50	.58	2.57	.60	
ST 230	1.77	.53	2.50	.60	
ST 195	3.03	.40	3.60	.69	Senior
ST 218	1.63	.62	2.57	.69	
ST 207	2.03	.38	2.47	.53	Staff
ST 231	2.57	.30	2.73	.53	
ST 232	2.97	.30	3.87	.60	
ST 229	2.83	.28	3.07	.50	

Table 7.24
Substantive Tests Phase: Experience—Inventory

	1996 Study				1988 Study
Task	Mean Years of Experience	Coefficient of Variation	Mean Supervised Instances	Coefficient of Variation	Median Professional Rank
ST 348	1.08	.48	1.64	.56	
ST 332	1.73	.48	2.79	.39	Assistant
ST 347	1.21	.60	1.91	.55	Assistant
ST 338	1.19	.58	2.13	.60	Assistant
ST 339	1.19	.58	2.04	.58	Assistant
ST 361	1.50	.53	2.46	.42	Assistant
ST 362	1.50	.53	2.46	.42	Assistant
ST 351	1.54	.51	2.09	.75	Assistant
ST 334	1.54	.49	2.38	.53	Assistant
ST 340	1.58	.55	2.29	.55	Assistant
ST 335	1.46	.51	2.29	.55	Assistant
ST 346	1.54	.51	2.18	.54	
ST 337	1.39	.61	2.29	.55	Assistant
ST 349	1.92	.47	2.27	.59	
ST 328	1.96	.37	3.04	.35	Staff
ST 352	1.88	.53	2.54	.64	Staff
ST 331	1.89	.41	3.04	.47	
ST 330	2.04	.32	3.13	.44	
ST 353	1.79	.47	2.64	.49	Assistant
ST 356	2.33	.46	3.36	.50	Staff
ST 336	1.46	.51	2.54	.50	Assistant
ST 342	1.73	.48	2.71	.37	
ST 357	2.00	.52	3.27	.48	
ST 329	2.19	.39	3.71	.61	Senior
ST 343	1.81	.50	2.29	.58	Staff
ST 344	1.58	.55	2.54	.44	
ST 354	2.25	.34	3.18	.46	Staff
ST 333	2.12	.34	3.21	.37	Staff
ST 350	2.25	.43	3.36	.50	Staff
ST 355	2.58	.31	3.54	.43	
ST 359	2.67	.29	3.82	.47	Staff
ST 360	2.08	.38	3.27	.53	Staff
ST 358	2.50	.50	3.54	.44	Senior
ST 345	2.35	.38	3.21	.42	
ST 364	2.67	.40	3.36	.50	
ST 341	2.12	.39	2.88	.42	
ST 363	2.92	.34	4.18	.57	

Table 7.25
Substantive Tests Phase: Experience—Fixed Assets

| Task | 1996 Study | | | | 1988 Study |
	Mean Years of Experience	Coefficient of Variation	Mean Supervised Instances	Coefficient of Variation	Median Professional Rank
ST 237	.90	.52	1.36	.68	Assistant
ST 248	1.03	.59	2.07	.81	Assistant
ST 252	.90	.52	1.50	.68	Assistant
ST 247	1.23	.59	2.00	.78	Assistant
ST 253	1.10	.69	1.93	.94	
ST 238	1.17	.60	1.71	.66	Assistant
ST 239	1.17	.60	1.79	.63	Assistant
ST 250	1.63	.62	2.50	.64	Assistant
ST 254	1.43	.63	2.47	.72	
ST 235	1.63	.62	2.36	.59	Assistant
ST 236	1.50	.63	2.14	.51	Assistant
ST 255	2.10	.51	2.87	.54	
ST 233	1.77	.53	2.71	.57	
ST 241	1.63	.57	2.57	.54	
ST 259	1.70	.56	2.64	.74	Assistant
ST 234	2.30	.54	3.14	.76	Staff
ST 245	2.23	.44	2.93	.64	
ST 258	2.37	.40	2.87	.67	
ST 251	2.03	.55	3.07	.47	Staff
ST 256	2.50	.48	3.07	.53	
ST 262	2.57	.40	2.80	.53	
ST 261	2.23	.33	2.71	.47	
ST 246	3.03	.38	3.20	.49	
ST 257	2.63	.41	3.53	.51	Staff
ST 260	2.63	.29	2.93	.57	
ST 240	2.03	.50	2.80	.65	
ST 249	2.63	.43	3.14	.43	Staff
ST 243	3.10	.44	4.07	.62	
ST 242	2.83	.38	3.87	.65	Staff
ST 244	3.70	.33	4.00	.63	

Table 7.26
Substantive Tests Phase: Experience—Payroll and Related Costs

| Task | 1996 Study | | | | 1988 Study |
	Mean Years of Experience	Coefficient of Variation	Mean Supervised Instances	Coefficient of Variation	Median Professional Rank
ST 129	1.00	.38	1.21	.66	
ST 125	1.07	.43	1.43	1.02	
ST 130	1.07	.43	1.50	.90	
ST 128	1.00	.38	1.50	.82	Assistant
ST 127	1.13	.46	1.57	.78	
ST 122	1.80	.52	2.29	.63	Assistant
ST 124	1.40	.45	2.21	1.09	
ST 123	1.53	.48	2.00	.65	Assistant
ST 131	1.20	.47	1.54	.98	
ST 117	1.67	.49	2.00	.61	
ST 119	2.27	.39	2.57	.71	Staff
ST 120	2.13	.35	2.21	.73	
ST 121	2.40	.54	2.54	.75	Staff
ST 118	2.80	.53	2.92	.97	Staff
ST 132	3.33	.43	3.73	.81	Senior
ST 126	3.07	.50	4.00	1.14	Senior

Table 7.27
Substantive Tests Phase: Experience—Investments

| Task | 1996 Study | | | | 1988 Study |
	Mean Years of Experience	Coefficient of Variation	Mean Supervised Instances	Coefficient of Variation	Median Professional Rank
ST 370	1.08	.62	2.00	.71	Assistant
ST 372	1.29	.48	1.91	.60	Assistant
ST 374	1.29	.58	2.09	.69	Assistant
ST 375	1.38	.64	2.46	.61	
ST 381	1.42	.47	2.18	.49	Assistant
ST 382	1.50	.45	2.18	.49	Assistant
ST 371	1.58	.63	2.73	.66	
ST 383	1.58	.42	2.36	.51	Assistant
ST 385	1.63	.48	2.82	.55	
ST 384	1.33	.58	2.54	.48	
ST 380	2.17	.39	3.18	.56	Staff
ST 379	1.83	.51	2.73	.47	Assistant
ST 388	1.75	.43	3.00	.47	
ST 366	2.21	.52	3.36	.74	Staff
ST 365	2.21	.52	3.27	.76	Senior
ST 368	1.88	.40	2.82	.52	Staff
ST 387	2.00	.48	2.91	.47	
ST 377	2.08	.43	3.18	.48	
ST 386	1.88	.48	3.27	.82	Senior
ST 367	2.63	.49	3.91	.68	Senior
ST 369	2.08	.48	3.27	.79	Staff
ST 376	2.08	.43	2.91	.52	
ST 378	2.75	.44	4.09	.62	
ST 389	2.75	.27	4.18	.59	Staff
ST 373	2.42	.41	3.82	.64	

Table 7.28
Substantive Tests Phase: Experience—Indebtedness

	1996 Study				1988 Study
Task	Mean Years of Experience	Coefficient of Variation	Mean Supervised Instances	Coefficient of Variation	Median Professional Rank
ST 393	1.08	.73	1.73	.58	Assistant
ST 394	1.46	.61	1.82	.54	Assistant
ST 395	1.33	.49	2.18	.57	
ST 400	1.29	.75	1.91	.44	
ST 396	1.42	.47	2.18	.57	
ST 401	1.46	.61	1.91	.44	
ST 398	1.17	.62	1.91	.60	Assistant
ST 397	1.58	.42	2.27	.59	
ST 402	1.75	.55	2.36	.61	
ST 410	2.08	.38	3.09	.47	Assistant
ST 411	1.67	.59	2.73	.59	
ST 405	1.75	.43	2.73	.55	
ST 413	1.92	.47	2.82	.50	
ST 407	1.75	.49	2.46	.59	
ST 399	2.17	.48	3.18	.82	
ST 408	1.92	.47	2.73	.49	
ST 409	2.33	.33	3.64	.68	Staff
ST 414	2.54	.37	3.73	.58	Senior
ST 403	2.25	.43	3.82	.67	
ST 412	1.92	.52	3.00	.49	
ST 415	2.58	.26	3.91	.66	
ST 390	2.42	.45	3.46	.74	Staff
ST 391	1.92	.47	3.00	.49	Staff
ST 392	2.00	.48	3.00	.49	Staff
ST 406	2.33	.42	4.00	.99	
ST 404	2.83	.33	4.18	.92	

Table 7.29
Substantive Tests Phase: Experience—Ownership Equity

| Task | 1996 Study | | | | 1988 Study |
	Mean Years of Experience	Coefficient of Variation	Mean Supervised Instances	Coefficient of Variation	Median Professional Rank
ST 134	1.13	.46	1.31	1.01	Assistant
ST 136	1.93	.60	2.14	.89	
ST 142	1.64	.51	2.07	.88	
ST 138	1.73	.60	2.14	.87	Assistant
ST 137	1.47	.51	2.29	.78	
ST 135	1.73	.51	1.86	.66	
ST 144	2.07	.44	2.29	.72	
ST 140	2.14	.40	2.21	.62	Assistant
ST 143	2.29	.32	2.14	.82	Staff
ST 141	2.14	.40	2.36	.77	Staff
ST 145	3.07	.39	3.00	1.03	
ST 139	3.07	.43	3.08	.97	Staff
ST 133	2.93	.46	3.62	.98	Senior

Table 7.30
Substantive Tests Phase: Experience—Summary of Tasks by
Subphase

Subphase of Substantive Tests	1996 Study Years of Experience			1996 Study Supervised Instances			1988 Study
	Overall Mean (COV)	Range of Means		Overall Mean (COV)	Range of Means		Median Rank
General and AR Procedures (Tasks in Table 7.20)	3.42 (.32)	2.93	4.07	3.62 (.71)	3.00	5.00	Senior
Cash (Tasks in Table 7.21)	1.20 (.56)	.93	2.00	1.74 (.76)	1.23	2.36	Asst.
Revenue and Receipt Cycle (Tasks in Table 7.22)	1.72 (.51)	1.07	2.87	2.05 (.78)	1.39	2.92	Asst.
Purchasing and Disbursements Cycle (Tasks in Table 7.23)	1.47 (.64)	.83	3.03	2.13 (.72)	1.21	3.87	Asst.
Inventory (Tasks in Table 7.24)	1.87 (.49)	1.08	2.92	2.80 (.53)	1.64	4.18	Staff
Fixed Assets (Tasks in Table 7.25)	1.99 (.59)	.90	3.70	2.71 (.66)	1.36	4.07	Asst.
Payroll (Tasks in Table 7.26)	1.80 (.65)	1.00	3.33	2.17 (.97)	1.21	4.00	Staff
Investments (Tasks in Table 7.27)	1.87 (.52)	1.08	2.75	2.93 (.64)	1.91	4.18	Asst.
Indebtedness (Tasks in Table 7.28)	1.88 (.51)	1.08	2.83	2.84 (.70)	1.73	4.18	Staff
Ownership Equity (Tasks in Table 7.29)	2.10 (.53)	1.13	3.07	2.34 (.90)	1.31	3.62	Staff

Table 7.31
Forming Opinion Phase: Experience

	1996 Study				1988 Study
Task	Mean Years of Experience	Coefficient of Variation	Mean Supervised Instances	Coefficient of Variation	Median Professional Rank
FO 265	4.37	.27	5.07	.64	Manager
FO 274	4.23	.31	4.80	.65	Senior
FO 281	4.37	.30	4.40	.48	
FO 277	5.17	.43	4.73	.62	
FO 273	4.77	.25	5.27	.63	
FO 288	6.43	.49	4.87	.51	Manager
FO 272	4.50	.29	5.13	.59	Manager
FO 286	4.70	.29	4.20	.46	Manager
FO 263	4.83	.27	6.73	.61	Manager
FO 266	4.83	.29	6.00	.61	
FO 269	4.97	.25	6.33	.59	
FO 264	4.90	.27	6.80	.60	Manager
FO 289	6.90	.46	5.80	.55	Partner
FO 275	5.03	.30	5.07	.63	
FO 268	6.10	.39	6.20	.83	
FO 267	5.50	.30	6.53	.52	Manager
FO 278	6.03	.48	5.27	.60	
FO 270	4.97	.32	6.00	.55	Manager
FO 282	6.50	.41	5.47	.53	
FO 276	5.17	.22	5.87	.52	
FO 280	6.23	.45	4.93	.66	Manager
FO 287	5.77	.39	4.73	.33	Manager
FO 271	4.97	.31	6.27	.61	Manager
FO 279	5.37	.40	5.33	.51	Manager
FO 285	6.63	.36	5.47	.58	Manager
FO 283	5.77	.35	5.60	.43	
FO 284	7.10	.39	5.47	.57	

Table 7.32
Financial Statements Reporting Phase: Experience

Task	1996 Study				1988 Study
	Mean Years of Experience	Coefficient of Variation	Mean Supervised Instances	Coefficient of Variation	Median Professional Rank
FR 421	3.17	.26	4.50	.56	Senior
FR 419	3.50	.29	5.17	.69	Manager
FR 424	3.33	.39	4.92	.78	Senior
FR 417	3.08	.35	4.42	.62	Manager
FR 416	3.42	.32	5.33	.70	Manager
FR 418	3.29	.35	4.82	.80	Manager
FR 428	3.83	.37	5.17	1.01	Manager
FR 427	3.75	.38	5.00	.81	
FR 426	3.58	.37	5.50	.99	Senior
FR 425	4.08	.24	5.83	.87	Manager
FR 420	3.42	.26	4.58	.77	Manager
FR 422	3.42	.26	4.75	.74	Manager
FR 432	4.67	.23	6.25	.82	Manager
FR 433	4.08	.32	6.08	.87	Manager
FR 429	4.21	.25	6.08	.86	Manager
FR 423	4.33	.27	6.33	.77	Manager
FR 430	4.13	.29	5.75	.93	Manager
FR 431	4.13	.30	5.75	.92	Manager

Table 7.33
Orientation Phase: Decision Aids

Task	1996 Study					1988 Study				
	% of Subjects Choosing					% of Subjects Choosing				
	AU	DSS	KES	HP	Median	AU	DSS	KES	HP	Median
OR 27	13	20	0	67	HP	6	16	8	70	HP
OR 29	33	20	0	47	DSS					
OR 55	13	13	0	74	HP	8	12	10	70	HP
OR 56	20	20	7	53	HP					
OR 54	7	7	0	86	HP	2	14	8	76	HP
OR 7	0	0	0	100	HP	2	4	0	94	HP
OR 36	13	13	7	67	HP	17	6	2	75	HP
OR 21	20	27	13	40	KES	10	51	16	23	DSS
OR 35	7	33	20	40	KES					
OR 40	21	21	0	58	HP					
OR 46	20	13	7	60	HP	29	19	8	44	KES
OR 33	7	50	14	29	DSS					
OR 8	7	13	0	80	HP					
OR 38	20	7	0	73	HP	0	4	16	80	HP
OR 9	13	27	7	53	HP					
OR 48	27	20	13	40	KES	0	13	21	67	HP
OR 2	13	7	7	73	HP					
OR 26	13	27	7	53	HP	2	8	22	67	HP
OR 34	7	27	13	53	HP					
OR 1	13	7	7	73	HP					
OR 50	20	13	20	47	KES					
OR 19	13	27	0	60	HP	2	12	16	69	HP
OR 24	13	20	7	60	HP	0	6	16	78	HP
OR 16	13	13	0	74	HP	4	4	6	85	HP
OR 52	0	27	7	66	HP					
OR 49	13	20	7	60	HP	0	4	17	79	HP
OR 5	7	33	27	33	KES					
OR 53	0	27	7	66	HP	0	6	29	65	HP
OR 57	7	20	20	53	HP					
OR 37	7	20	33	40	KES					
OR 43	0	20	7	73	HP					
OR 51	7	27	20	46	KES					
OR 39	7	13	0	80	HP	0	4	16	80	HP
OR 20	13	27	0	60	HP					
OR 22	13	27	13	47	KES	8	42	19	31	DSS/KES
OR 3	7	13	0	80	HP	0	4	10	85	HP
OR 58	7	13	7	73	HP					
OR 15	13	20	0	67	HP	0	4	8	88	HP
OR 45	0	20	0	80	HP	0	2	18	80	HP
OR 23	20	20	13	47	KES	4	12	18	65	HP
OR 31	0	14	21	64	HP	0	2	20	78	HP
OR 41	7	20	13	60	HP					
OR 42	7	7	13	73	HP	0	2	14	84	HP
OR 30	0	13	0	87	HP	0	0	6	94	HP

Table 7.33 (continued)
Orientation Phase: Decision Aids

Task	1996 Study					1988 Study				
	% of Subjects Choosing				Median	% of Subjects Choosing				Median
	AU	DSS	KES	HP		AU	DSS	KES	HP	
OR 4	7	20	13	60	HP					
OR 44	13	7	7	73	HP					
OR 11	0	7	0	93	HP	0	0	2	98	HP
OR 18	0	21	0	79	HP	0	6	6	88	HP
OR 28	7	20	0	73	HP	0	4	8	88	HP
OR 6	0	20	27	53	HP	0	14	12	74	HP
OR 10	0	0	0	100	HP					
OR 32	0	13	20	67	HP	0	8	10	82	HP
OR 47	7	13	7	73	HP	0	2	12	86	HP
OR 14	0	7	13	80	HP	0	6	15	79	HP
OR 17	0	27	0	73	HP	0	0	6	94	HP
OR 13	0	7	0	93	HP	4	4	11	81	HP
OR 25	0	13	0	87	HP	0	0	6	94	HP
OR 12	0	0	0	100	HP	2	0	0	98	HP

Table 7.34
Control Structure Phase: Decision Aids

Task	1996 Study					1988 Study				
	% of Subjects Choosing					% of Subjects Choosing				
	AU	DSS	KES	HP	Median	AU	DSS	KES	HP	Median
CS 169	7	7	13	73	HP	8	6	0	86	HP
CS 170	0	14	14	72	HP					
CS 167	7	0	27	66	HP	0	6	6	88	HP
CS 149	27	20	20	33	KES	6	18	18	58	HP
CS 161	0	7	7	86	HP					
CS 162	0	27	20	53	HP	4	16	16	64	HP
CS 164	0	29	21	50	KES/HP	2	12	20	65	HP
CS 168	7	7	20	66	HP	0	8	10	82	HP
CS 163	0	29	21	50	KES/HP	2	12	14	72	HP
CS 165	0	15	31	54	HP	4	10	18	68	HP
CS 182	7	20	20	53	HP					
CS 180	13	13	7	67	HP	4	11	6	79	HP
CS 184	7	20	20	53	HP					
CS 148	7	20	7	66	HP	2	8	15	75	HP
CS 183	0	20	20	60	HP	0	6	30	64	HP
CS 147	7	7	0	86	HP	0	2	2	96	HP
CS 171	0	7	13	80	HP	0	6	6	88	HP
CS 166	0	7	27	66	HP	0	10	22	67	HP
CS 185	0	40	13	47	KES	0	8	29	63	HP
CS 186	7	33	20	40	KES					
CS 189	7	27	20	46	KES	0	10	33	56	HP
CS 155	7	14	29	50	KES/HP					
CS 160	13	27	7	53	HP	6	6	17	71	HP
CS 172	0	7	13	80	HP	2	4	4	90	HP
CS 158	7	20	33	40	KES	2	8	16	74	HP
CS 146	0	13	20	67	HP	0	15	33	52	HP
CS 154	7	20	27	46	KES	0	6	31	63	HP
CS 157	7	20	33	40	KES	0	14	24	61	HP
CS 174	7	26	7	60	HP					
CS 192	7	13	7	73	HP	0	2	4	94	HP
CS 188	0	27	20	53	HP	0	6	31	63	HP
CS 156	7	20	27	47	KES	0	8	31	61	HP
CS 159	0	27	40	33	KES	0	13	23	65	HP
CS 187	0	27	20	53	HP	0	10	25	65	HP
CS 181	7	7	13	73	HP	0	4	17	79	HP
CS 175	0	13	7	80	HP	0	2	12	86	HP
CS 176	0	13	13	73	HP	0	2	12	86	HP
CS 153	0	7	27	67	HP					
CS 178	7	13	7	73	HP					

Table 7.34 (continued)
Control Structure Phase: Decision Aids

Task	1996 Study					1988 Study				
	% of Subjects Choosing					% of Subjects Choosing				
	AU	DSS	KES	HP	Median	AU	DSS	KES	HP	Median
CS 190	0	27	0	73	HP	0	4	10	86	HP
CS 177	0	7	0	93	HP	0	4	6	90	HP
CS 191	0	13	0	87	HP	0	4	6	90	HP
CS 173	0	7	0	93	HP					
CS 193	0	13	7	80	HP	0	2	8	90	HP
CS 150	0	33	13	54	HP					
CS 151	0	33	7	60	HP					
CS 179	0	7	0	93	HP	0	4	6	90	HP
CS 152	0	13	20	67	HP					

Table 7.35
Tests of Controls Phase: Decision Aids

	1996 Study					1988 Study				
	% of Subjects Choosing					% of Subjects Choosing				
Task	AU	DSS	KES	HP	Median	AU	DSS	KES	HP	Median
TC 293	29	21	14	36	DSS/KES	4	17	11	68	HP
TC 297	22	7	7	64	HP	0	8	2	90	HP
TC 325	62	23	0	15	AU	29	38	4	29	DSS
TC 295	31	0	0	69	HP					
TC 292	14	14	29	43	KES					
TC 296	14	0	22	64	HP					
TC 311	8	8	0	84	HP	2	4	2	92	HP
TC 290	0	7	29	64	HP					
TC 300	35	7	29	29	KES					
TC 310	29	29	14	29	DSS	0	8	15	77	HP
TC 294	7	7	14	72	HP					
TC 305	43	36	14	7	DSS	33	20	10	37	DSS
TC 307	14	22	14	50	KES/HP					
TC 309	21	15	21	43	KES	2	8	14	76	HP
TC 299	14	7	43	36	KES	0	4	22	73	HP
TC 298	14	21	36	29	KES					
TC 308	21	21	21	36	KES	12	35	12	41	KES
TC 302	8	8	15	69	HP					
TC 303	0	14	22	64	HP					
TC 319	0	8	15	77	HP					
TC 301	7	14	22	57	HP					
TC 327	0	15	0	85	HP					
TC 323	0	8	8	84	HP					
TC 322	0	0	15	85	HP					
TC 312	0	8	31	61	HP	0	12	20	67	HP
TC 324	0	0	0	100	HP					
TC 326	8	15	15	62	HP					
TC 317	0	8	31	61	HP					
TC 306	0	0	14	86	HP	0	6	10	84	HP
TC 320	0	8	8	84	HP					
TC 315	0	8	17	75	HP	2	6	12	80	HP
TC 316	0	17	0	83	HP	2	10	14	74	HP
TC 318	0	8	23	69	HP	0	6	16	78	HP
TC 304	0	23	8	69	HP	0	4	10	86	HP
TC 314	0	8	8	84	HP					
TC 313	0	8	8	84	HP	0	2	8	90	HP
TC 321	0	8	8	84	HP					
TC 291	0	0	14	86	HP	0	2	8	90	HP

Table 7.36
Substantive Tests Phase: Decision Aids—General and Analytical Review Procedures

Task	1996 Study					1988 Study				
	% of Subjects Choosing				Median	% of Subjects Choosing				Median
	AU	DSS	KES	HP		AU	DSS	KES	HP	
ST 65	33	13	7	47	KES	12	41	10	37	DSS
ST 64	33	13	7	47	KES	12	53	10	24	DSS
ST 63	27	13	7	53	HP	13	47	13	27	DSS
ST 59	0	13	13	74	HP	0	12	14	74	HP
ST 61	7	13	0	80	HP	0	8	6	86	HP
ST 60	7	20	7	66	HP					
ST 62	0	7	7	86	HP					

Table 7.37
Substantive Tests Phase: Decision Aids—Cash

Task	1996 Study					1988 Study				
	% of Subjects Choosing					% of Subjects Choosing				
	AU	DSS	KES	HP	Median	AU	DSS	KES	HP	Median
ST 68	40	7	7	46	KES	78	4	2	16	AU
ST 72	7	7	0	86	HP	6	0	0	94	HP
ST 73	13	7	0	80	HP	4	0	0	96	HP
ST 74	20	7	0	73	HP					
ST 80	27	7	0	66	HP	22	2	0	76	HP
ST 81	33	0	0	67	HP	57	4	0	39	AU
ST 83	7	0	0	93	HP					
ST 78	13	7	0	80	HP	18	2	0	80	HP
ST 66	13	13	7	67	HP	0	2	4	94	HP
ST 69	20	13	0	67	HP					
ST 77	7	7	0	86	HP	2	0	0	98	HP
ST 82	13	7	0	80	HP	8	2	0	90	HP
ST 71	13	7	0	80	HP					
ST 75	0	7	0	93	HP	0	0	0	100	HP
ST 79	0	13	0	87	HP	2	2	0	96	HP
ST 67	29	14	7	50	KES/HP	25	22	0	53	HP
ST 70	13	7	0	80	HP	8	6	0	86	HP
ST 84	7	13	0	80	HP					
ST 76	0	7	0	93	HP	0	2	0	98	HP
ST 85	13	13	0	74	HP	0	4	8	88	HP

Table 7.38
Substantive Tests Phase: Decision Aids—Revenue and Receipt Cycle

	1996 Study					1988 Study				
	% of Subjects Choosing					% of Subjects Choosing				
Task	AU	DSS	KES	HP	Median	AU	DSS	KES	HP	Median
ST 103	33	0	0	67	HP					
ST 109	20	7	0	73	HP					
ST 110	20	7	0	73	HP					
ST 93	20	13	0	67	HP	33	16	2	49	KES
ST 107	13	7	0	80	HP	14	2	0	84	HP
ST 108	13	7	0	80	HP					
ST 96	20	0	0	80	HP					
ST 106	13	7	0	80	HP					
ST 105	13	0	0	87	HP					
ST 94	13	13	0	74	HP					
ST 98	7	7	0	86	HP	0	0	2	98	HP
ST 99	13	7	0	80	HP					
ST 101	13	7	0	80	HP	2	4	0	94	HP
ST 86	0	20	7	73	HP	0	0	4	96	HP
ST 104	7	0	0	93	HP					
ST 92	0	7	0	93	HP	0	2	0	98	HP
ST 90	21	29	0	50	KES/HP	39	43	6	12	DSS
ST 91	0	13	7	80	HP	10	2	4	84	HP
ST 97	7	7	0	86	HP	0	0	0	100	HP
ST 111	0	7	7	86	HP	0	4	0	96	HP
ST 112	0	7	7	86	HP	0	2	0	98	HP
ST 89	27	13	0	60	HP	18	23	4	55	HP
ST 114	7	7	0	86	HP					
ST 100	20	13	0	67	HP	63	8	2	27	AU
ST 115	7	13	0	80	HP					
ST 88	20	13	13	54	HP	20	47	10	23	DSS
ST 102	7	7	0	86	HP					
ST 95	0	7	0	93	HP	0	0	2	98	HP
ST 116	0	13	0	87	HP	0	4	8	88	HP
ST 87	7	7	7	80	HP	0	2	4	94	HP
ST 113	0	20	0	80	HP					

Table 7.39
Substantive Tests Phase: Decision Aids—Purchasing and Disbursements Cycle

Task	1996 Study					1988 Study				
	% of Subjects Choosing					% of Subjects Choosing				
	AU	DSS	KES	HP	Median	AU	DSS	KES	HP	Median
ST 199	64	0	0	36	AU					
ST 200	53	7	0	40	AU					
ST 224	53	7	13	27	AU					
ST 228	13	7	7	73	HP	2	0	0	98	HP
ST 202	66	20	7	7	AU	51	35	4	10	AU
ST 204	33	20	7	40	DSS					
ST 216	13	7	7	73	HP					
ST 223	7	7	7	80	HP					
ST 225	0	7	7	86	HP	4	0	0	96	HP
ST 226	0	0	7	93	HP					
ST 206	13	13	13	60	HP					
ST 209	20	7	7	66	HP	6	4	0	90	HP
ST 210	13	7	7	73	HP	8	2	0	90	HP
ST 213	0	7	7	86	HP					
ST 211	13	7	7	73	HP					
ST 219	40	7	7	46	KES	6	0	0	94	HP
ST 222	40	7	7	46	KES					
ST 212	26	7	7	60	HP					
ST 220	27	7	20	46	KES					
ST 208	27	20	13	40	KES	29	6	0	65	HP
ST 201	27	20	0	53	HP	31	29	0	41	DSS
ST 205	20	20	13	47	KES					
ST 203	20	13	13	54	HP					
ST 214	7	13	13	67	HP					
ST 227	0	13	7	80	HP					
ST 215	13	7	7	73	HP					
ST 221	26	7	7	60	HP					
ST 194	0	7	20	73	HP	0	0	4	96	HP
ST 217	0	14	7	79	HP	0	0	0	100	HP
ST 196	46	20	7	27	DSS	31	27	4	39	DSS
ST 197	33	13	0	54	HP					
ST 198	20	13	7	60	HP					
ST 230	7	13	7	73	HP					
ST 195	0	7	29	64	HP	0	4	8	88	HP
ST 218	13	20	7	60	HP					
ST 207	0	7	13	80	HP	0	2	0	98	HP
ST 231	0	20	13	67	HP					
ST 232	0	7	20	73	HP					
ST 229	0	13	13	74	HP					

Table 7.40
Substantive Tests Phase: Decision Aids—Inventory

Task	1996 Study					1988 Study				
	% of Subjects Choosing					% of Subjects Choosing				
	AU	DSS	KES	HP	Median	AU	DSS	KES	HP	Median
ST 348	67	0	0	33	AU					
ST 332	61	8	8	23	AU	51	39	2	8	AU
ST 347	17	8	8	67	HP	45	4	2	49	KES
ST 338	38	8	0	54	HP	59	8	0	33	AU
ST 339	31	15	0	54	HP	61	6	0	33	AU
ST 361	8	8	8	75	HP	16	4	2	78	HP
ST 362	17	8	0	75	HP	16	4	0	80	HP
ST 351	8	8	0	84	HP	16	0	0	84	HP
ST 334	0	23	15	62	HP	8	14	0	78	HP
ST 340	15	0	0	85	HP	2	0	0	98	HP
ST 335	0	8	8	84	HP	0	2	0	98	HP
ST 346	0	8	8	84	HP					
ST 337	8	30	8	54	HP	14	18	0	68	HP
ST 349	0	17	0	83	HP					
ST 328	8	8	15	69	HP	2	2	2	94	HP
ST 352	0	8	17	75	HP	6	2	2	90	HP
ST 331	23	31	8	38	DSS					
ST 330	15	23	23	39	KES					
ST 353	0	8	17	75	HP	2	4	2	92	HP
ST 356	8	8	8	75	HP	2	2	2	94	HP
ST 336	0	8	0	92	HP	4	0	2	94	HP
ST 342	0	0	8	92	HP					
ST 357	0	8	8	84	HP					
ST 329	8	15	15	62	HP	0	8	6	86	HP
ST 343	15	0	0	85	HP	0	0	2	98	HP
ST 344	0	8	0	92	HP					
ST 354	8	17	17	58	HP	8	17	12	63	HP
ST 333	15	15	15	54	HP	20	29	6	45	KES
ST 350	0	8	0	92	HP	2	0	2	96	HP
ST 355	0	8	25	67	HP					
ST 359	0	17	8	75	HP	4	4	2	90	HP
ST 360	8	8	8	75	HP	35	18	2	45	DSS
ST 358	0	8	0	92	HP	0	2	2	96	HP
ST 345	8	8	17	67	HP					
ST 364	0	8	0	92	HP					
ST 341	0	0	0	100	HP					
ST 363	0	17	25	58	HP					

Table 7.41
Substantive Tests Phase: Decision Aids—Fixed Assets

Task	1996 Study					1988 Study				
	% of Subjects Choosing					% of Subjects Choosing				
	AU	DSS	KES	HP	Median	AU	DSS	KES	HP	Median
ST 237	20	7	7	66	HP	21	4	0	74	HP
ST 248	73	7	13	7	AU	92	2	2	4	AU
ST 252	0	0	7	93	HP	0	2	0	98	HP
ST 247	20	20	7	53	HP	10	2	0	88	HP
ST 253	0	0	7	93	HP					
ST 238	0	13	7	80	HP	0	2	0	98	HP
ST 239	7	7	7	80	HP	0	2	0	98	HP
ST 250	67	13	0	20	AU	49	6	2	43	DSS
ST 254	0	7	7	86	HP					
ST 235	40	27	6	27	DSS	49	22	2	27	DSS
ST 236	27	27	6	40	DSS	27	35	2	35	DSS
ST 255	7	7	26	60	HP					
ST 233	0	7	7	86	HP					
ST 241	0	13	7	80	HP					
ST 259	7	13	13	67	HP	0	2	2	96	HP
ST 234	0	0	7	93	HP	0	2	13	85	HP
ST 245	0	7	7	86	HP					
ST 258	0	13	20	67	HP					
ST 251	13	7	20	60	HP	2	6	2	90	HP
ST 256	13	13	27	47	KES					
ST 262	0	13	7	80	HP					
ST 261	0	7	7	86	HP					
ST 246	0	7	7	86	HP					
ST 257	0	7	7	86	HP	0	2	2	96	HP
ST 260	0	13	13	74	HP					
ST 240	7	7	13	73	HP					
ST 249	0	20	27	53	HP	0	6	4	90	HP
ST 243	0	13	20	67	HP					
ST 242	0	20	13	67	HP	0	8	2	90	HP
ST 244	0	13	20	67	HP					

Table 7.42
Substantive Tests Phase: Decision Aids—Payroll and Related Costs

	1996 Study					1988 Study				
	% of Subjects Choosing					% of Subjects Choosing				
Task	AU	DSS	KES	HP	Median	AU	DSS	KES	HP	Median
ST 129	26	7	7	60	HP					
ST 125	7	7	7	80	HP					
ST 130	13	7	7	73	HP					
ST 128	13	7	7	73	HP	0	2	0	98	HP
ST 127	20	7	7	66	HP					
ST 122	7	20	7	66	HP	14	10	2	74	HP
ST 124	7	7	7	80	HP					
ST 123	13	7	7	73	HP	23	10	4	63	HP
ST 131	0	7	0	93	HP					
ST 117	0	7	0	93	HP					
ST 119	7	26	7	60	HP	24	37	6	33	DSS
ST 120	7	20	0	73	HP					
ST 121	13	20	0	67	HP	12	21	4	63	HP
ST 118	0	7	7	86	HP	0	4	12	84	HP
ST 132	0	14	0	86	HP	0	6	15	79	HP
ST 126	0	7	7	86	HP	8	4	6	82	HP

Table 7.43
Substantive Tests Phase: Decision Aids—Investments

Task	1996 Study					1988 Study				
	% of Subjects Choosing				Median	% of Subjects Choosing				Median
	AU	DSS	KES	HP		AU	DSS	KES	HP	
ST 370	33	0	0	67	HP	14	8	0	78	HP
ST 372	17	8	8	67	HP	8	2	4	86	HP
ST 374	42	25	0	33	DSS	33	6	4	56	HP
ST 375	33	17	8	42	DSS/KES					
ST 381	0	8	17	75	HP	0	2	0	98	HP
ST 382	8	8	17	67	HP	2	4	0	94	HP
ST 371	0	0	17	83	HP					
ST 383	8	8	8	75	HP	6	4	2	88	HP
ST 385	17	33	0	50	KES/HP					
ST 384	8	8	0	84	HP					
ST 380	0	36	0	64	HP	6	6	2	86	HP
ST 379	8	8	17	67	HP	6	10	4	80	HP
ST 388	0	8	0	92	HP					
ST 366	0	17	8	75	HP	2	2	10	86	HP
ST 365	0	8	17	75	HP	2	4	12	82	HP
ST 368	8	25	8	59	HP	21	31	2	46	DSS
ST 387	8	8	0	84	HP					
ST 377	0	9	27	64	HP					
ST 386	0	8	0	92	HP	2	0	4	94	HP
ST 367	0	0	0	100	HP	2	0	2	96	HP
ST 369	0	17	25	58	HP	10	18	2	69	HP
ST 376	8	33	0	59	HP					
ST 378	0	8	17	75	HP					
ST 389	0	17	8	75	HP	2	4	13	81	HP
ST 373	0	17	0	83	HP					

Table 7.44
Substantive Tests Phase: Decision Aids—Indebtedness

Task	1996 Study					1988 Study				
	% of Subjects Choosing				Median	% of Subjects Choosing				Median
	AU	DSS	KES	HP		AU	DSS	KES	HP	
ST 393	25	0	0	75	HP	20	2	0	78	HP
ST 394	25	0	8	67	HP	10	4	0	86	HP
ST 395	17	17	0	66	HP					
ST 400	0	8	17	75	HP					
ST 396	17	0	17	66	HP					
ST 401	0	8	8	84	HP					
ST 398	0	9	9	82	HP	2	0	0	98	HP
ST 397	8	0	0	92	HP					
ST 402	0	8	0	92	HP					
ST 410	33	25	8	33	DSS	51	6	4	39	AU
ST 411	0	17	17	66	HP					
ST 405	0	8	17	75	HP					
ST 413	17	17	0	66	HP					
ST 407	0	8	8	84	HP					
ST 399	0	8	0	92	HP					
ST 408	8	17	25	50	KES/HP					
ST 409	17	17	17	50	KES/HP	16	4	4	76	HP
ST 414	8	8	8	75	HP	0	4	8	88	HP
ST 403	0	33	25	42	KES					
ST 412	8	8	17	67	HP					
ST 415	0	0	17	83	HP					
ST 390	0	17	17	66	HP	2	2	10	86	HP
ST 391	8	25	17	50	KES/HP	23	23	2	52	HP
ST 392	8	33	25	33	KES	20	31	4	45	DSS
ST 406	0	17	17	66	HP					
ST 404	8	0	0	92	HP					

Table 7.45
Substantive Tests Phase: Decision Aids—Ownership Entity

	1996 Study					1988 Study				
	% of Subjects Choosing					% of Subjects Choosing				
Task	AU	DSS	KES	HP	Median	AU	DSS	KES	HP	Median
ST 134	21	0	0	79	HP	18	2	0	80	HP
ST 136	7	7	0	86	HP					
ST 142	13	7	0	80	HP					
ST 138	7	7	0	86	HP	0	0	0	100	HP
ST 137	0	14	0	86	HP					
ST 135	7	7	0	86	HP					
ST 144	7	7	0	86	HP					
ST 140	0	13	0	87	HP	0	0	2	98	HP
ST 143	7	7	0	86	HP	0	0	4	96	HP
ST 141	0	13	0	87	HP	0	0	0	100	HP
ST 145	0	20	7	73	HP					
ST 139	0	7	0	93	HP	10	6	2	82	HP
ST 133	0	7	7	86	HP	0	2	13	85	HP

Table 7.46
Substantive Tests Phase: Decision Aids—Summary of Tasks by Subphase

Subphase of Substantive Tests	1996 Study				1988 Study			
	% of Subjects Choosing				% of Subjects Choosing			
	AU	DSS	KES	HP	AU	DSS	KES	HP
General and AR Procedures (Tasks in Table 7.36)	15	13	7	65	5	27	15	53
Cash (Tasks in Table 7.37)	14	8	1	77	12	3	1	84
Revenue and Receipt Cycle (Tasks in Table 7.38)	11	9	2	78	13	8	2	77
Purchasing and Disbursements Cycle (Tasks in Table 7.39)	19	11	9	61	11	6	2	81
Inventory (Tasks in Table 7.40)	11	11	8	70	16	9	2	73
Fixed Assets (Tasks in Table 7.41)	10	11	11	68	12	5	3	80
Payroll (Tasks in Table 7.42)	8	11	5	76	7	9	4	80
Investments (Tasks in Table 7.43)	8	13	8	71	9	6	4	81
Indebtedness (Tasks in Table 7.44)	8	12	11	69	13	7	3	77
Ownership Equity (Tasks in Table 7.45)	5	9	1	85	4	1	4	91

Table 7.47
Forming Opinion Phase: Decision Aids

Task	1996 Study					1988 Study				
	% of Subjects Choosing					% of Subjects Choosing				
	AU	DSS	KES	HP	Median	AU	DSS	KES	HP	Median
FO 265	0	13	20	67	HP	0	2	6	92	HP
FO 274	7	20	7	66	HP	8	12	6	73	HP
FO 281	0	13	0	87	HP					
FO 277	0	7	7	86	HP					
FO 273	7	13	13	67	HP					
FO 288	0	0	27	73	HP	0	0	8	92	HP
FO 272	7	13	20	60	HP	2	2	4	92	HP
FO 286	7	0	0	93	HP	0	0	4	96	HP
FO 263	0	13	27	60	HP	0	2	8	90	HP
FO 266	0	7	27	66	HP					
FO 269	0	7	33	60	HP					
FO 264	0	7	20	73	HP	0	4	8	88	HP
FO 289	0	0	20	80	HP	0	0	8	92	HP
FO 275	0	0	7	93	HP					
FO 268	0	0	13	87	HP					
FO 267	0	0	20	80	HP	0	0	10	90	HP
FO 278	0	7	20	73	HP					
FO 270	0	0	13	87	HP	0	0	8	92	HP
FO 282	0	0	13	87	HP					
FO 276	0	0	7	93	HP					
FO 280	0	0	20	80	HP	0	0	4	96	HP
FO 287	0	0	13	87	HP	0	0	4	96	HP
FO 271	0	0	20	80	HP	0	0	4	96	HP
FO 279	0	0	20	80	HP	0	0	6	94	HP
FO 285	0	0	20	80	HP	0	0	6	94	HP
FO 283	0	0	13	87	HP					
FO 284	0	0	20	80	HP					

Table 7.48
Financial Statements Reporting Phase: Decision Aids

Task	1996 Study % of Subjects Choosing AU	DSS	KES	HP	Median	1988 Study % of Subjects Choosing AU	DSS	KES	HP	Median
FR 421	8	8	25	59	HP	0	6	12	82	HP
FR 419	0	25	25	50	KES/HP	0	8	14	78	HP
FR 424	8	25	0	67	HP	0	6	8	86	HP
FR 417	0	8	25	67	HP	0	0	4	96	HP
FR 416	0	8	25	67	HP	0	8	14	78	HP
FR 418	8	8	17	67	HP	0	4	4	92	HP
FR 428	0	17	8	75	HP	0	4	8	88	HP
FR 427	0	25	25	50	KES/HP					
FR 426	8	25	0	67	HP	8	6	4	82	HP
FR 425	0	17	25	58	HP	0	4	8	88	HP
FR 420	0	17	0	83	HP	0	4	4	92	HP
FR 422	0	17	25	58	HP	0	2	8	90	HP
FR 432	0	0	0	100	HP	0	0	6	94	HP
FR 433	0	8	17	75	HP	0	0	8	92	HP
FR 429	0	0	8	92	HP	0	2	10	88	HP
FR 423	0	17	8	75	HP	0	4	6	90	HP
FR 430	0	0	8	92	HP	0	4	6	90	HP
FR 431	0	8	0	92	HP	0	2	6	92	HP

Chapter 8

Aggregate Results

In this chapter we first present descriptive data for each of the audit phases and for the audit taken as a whole. The data analysis shows the relative position of each of the phases of the audit concerning task structure, experience requirements, and decision aids. In the second section, we present a discussion of the statistical methods used for analysis of the data at the aggregate level and by audit phase.[1] In the third section, we present the results of a statistical analysis for an investigation of the hypotheses at the aggregate audit phase level and for the audit tasks taken as a whole. All the analyses are performed in comparison with a previous study.[2] That study was based on data collected in 1988. Since data were collected in 1996 for the current study, the comparative analysis provides indications of changes over an eight-year period. Conclusions and implications of the results in this chapter and Chapter 7 are discussed in the final chapter.

AGGREGATE DESCRIPTIVE DATA

To show the pattern of results by each of the audit phases and in the aggregate, three tables were prepared; one each for task structure classifications, knowledge base demands, and decision aids,

---

1. Detailed data analysis at the individual task level is provided in Chapter 7.

2. See M. J. Abdolmohammadi, 1999, "A Comprehensive Taxonomy of Task Structure and Knowledge Base Demands in Auditing," *Behavioral Research in Accounting* 11, pp. 51–92.

respectively. The descriptive data analyses are presented in Tables 8.1 to 8.3 and are discussed below.

TASK STRUCTURE CLASSIFICATION

Table 8.1 presents task structure classifications by the current study in comparison with the 1988 study. The phases of the audit are listed along with the number of tasks in each of the phases. Note that the number of tasks in each phase is different between the 1988 study and the 1996 study. As discussed in Chapter 5, the current study expanded the audit task inventory. The total number of observations for each phase and in total are also provided in the table. This is the number of tasks in each phase multiplied by the number of participants responding minus the number of missing data. For example, the 866 observations for the Orientation phase is derived by multiplying 58 tasks by 15 participating auditors minus four missing data.[3] The means, medians, and coefficients of variation (COVs) are also provided in Table 8.1. The rationale for the selection of the mean, median, and the COV is that they are appropriate for the interval data in task structure (scale from 1 to 9). Consequently, the final column was prepared to provide a formal test to compare the data in this study and the 1988 data using the parametric t test. The column provides the t statistics and their significance levels for the comparative analysis.

Overall, audit tasks in the aggregate can be viewed as semistructured for the current study (mean 3.92, median 4) and the 1988 study (mean 3.96, median 4). The t statistic of -1.11 indicates that the overall results were not significantly different between the two studies. However, there are variations across audit phases and between the two studies within phases. For example, considering the 1996 data while the tasks in the Substantive Tests phase (mean 3.20, median 3) can be viewed as more structured than the aggregate, the Orientation and Forming Opinions phases are at the higher end of the semistructured category (means of 5.09 and 5.34 and medians of 5 and 5, respectively). Furthermore, the relatively high coefficients of variation (ranging from .41 for the Forming Opinion phase to .53 for the Substantive Tests phase) indicate either significant disagreement

---

3. Because of the differences in missing data for each of the response modes (i.e., task structure, experience level, supervised instances, professional rank, and decision aids), the number of observations for each phase in Tables 8.2 and 8.3 may be slightly different than the observations for corresponding phases listed in Table 8.1.

Table 8.1
Task Structure Classification   Scale: 1–9 (Structured/Unstructured)

Audit Phase	No. of Tasks		Observations		1996 Structure			1988 Structure			1996/1988 Comparison	
	1996	1988	1996	1988	Mean	Med.	COV	Mean	Med.	COV	t stat	Sig.
Orientation	58	45	866	2,181	5.09	5	.43	5.38	5	.42	-3.17	.002
Control Structure	48	41	718	2000	4.72	4	.42	4.33	4	.44	4.55	.000
Tests of Controls	38	34	510	1653	4.29	4	.49	4.36	5	.44	-0.66	.510
Substantive Tests	244	171	3,412	8,343	3.20	3	.53	2.94	3	.60	7.44	.000
Forming Opinions	27	23	405	1,117	5.34	5	.41	6.24	6	.31	-7.34	.000
Financial Reporting	18	18	216	882	4.39	4	.44	5.52	5	.36	-7.67	.000
Aggregate	433	332	6,127	16,176	3.92	4	.53	3.96	4	.56	-1.11	.270

Note: COV = coefficient of variation; AU = Automation; Med. = median; DSS = decision support system; KES = knowledge-based expert system; HP = human processing ; t stat = t statistic for two-sample t test; Sig. = significance.

between subjects and/or significant variation between specific tasks within each of the audit phases.

The 1988 data present generally similar results, but some important differences too. The aggregate means and medians are not significantly different between the 1988 and 1996 studies. However, while the Tests of Controls phase present no significant differences between the two studies, the Control Structure phase indicates a statistically significant difference: the 1996 task structure (mean 4.72, median 4) is significantly less structured than the 1988 study (mean 4.33, median 4) at the .000 level. This difference may not be considered to be practically significant, however, since the two means and medians indicate a semistructured classification (4 to 6 rating) for both studies. The same can be said about the Orientation and Substantive Tests phases where statistical differences were observed, but the general classifications are not that different in practical terms.

The exceptions are the Forming Opinions and Financial Reporting phases where the 1996 data indicate significantly (statistically and practically speaking) more structured ratings than the 1988 data. An explanation may be that using new audit decision aids accounting firms have developed more structured approaches for the tasks in these phases (see the comparative decision aids data presented later in the section that supports this argument).

The COVs indicate the interauditor variations in their assessments of task structure. These variations range from a low of .31 for Forming Opinions to .60 for Substantive Tests in the 1988 data. The 1996 data indicate some what less variability: the COVs range from .41 for Forming Opinions to .53 for Substantive Tests. Note however, that the phases with the lowest and highest COVs are the same between the two studies.

KNOWLEDGE BASE REQUIREMENT

Summary descriptive data for the knowledge required to perform the tasks in the aggregate and by audit phase are presented in Table 8.2. The data collected in this study related to years of experience and the number of supervised instances of practice before one is qualified to perform each task independently. These measures were not used in the 1988 study where only the required professional rank was used as a surrogate for knowledge base to perform the tasks. Consequently, while the data are provided for both the 1988 and 1996 studies, these data can not be directly and statistically compared.

Table 8.2
Required Knowledge

Scale: Years of experience; Number of supervised instances;
Professional rank (assistant, staff, senior, manager, partner)

Audit Phase	1996 Years of Experience			1996 Supervised Instances			1988 Rank
	Mean	Med.	COV	Mean	Med.	COV	
Orientation	3.56	3	.43	3.35	2	.79	Senior
Control Structure	2.81	3	.52	3.41	3	.65	Senior
Tests of Controls	2.38	2	.57	4.07	3	.99	Senior
Substantive Tests	1.80	2	.59	2.45	2	.73	Assistant
Forming Opinions	5.41	5	.39	5.49	5	.58	Manager
Financial Reporting	3.75	4	.32	5.35	4	.81	Manager
Aggregate	2.52	2	.66	3.15	2	.84	Staff

Note: COV = coefficient of variation; Med. = median.

The data in Table 8.2 indicate that on average, an auditor with a professional rank of staff (in an assistant, staff, senior, manager, and partner classification), who possesses 2.52 years of experience, and had performed the task 3.15 times under supervision is qualified to perform the audit. However, analysis by audit phase indicates that while only an average 1.8 years of experience, 2.45 instances of supervised practice, and the professional rank of assistant are needed for performing the Substantive Tests phase, 5.41 years of experience, 5.49 instances of supervised practice, and the professional rank of manager are needed for the Forming Opinion phase. The experience levels indicated for performing other phases are somewhere between these two end points: 3.56 years of experience is needed for performing the Orientation phase, 2.81 years for the Control Structure phase, 2.38 years for the Tests of Controls phase, and 3.75 years for the Financial Reporting phase of the audit. Similarly, over 5 instances of supervised task performance, and the professional rank of manager are needed for the Financial Reporting phase. However, only three to four instances of supervised task performance, and the professional rank of senior are needed for performing the tasks in the

Orientation, Control Structure, and Tests of Controls phases of the audit.

Similar to the task structure assessments, the COV for the years of experience responses indicate significant variation in auditors' knowledge base judgments. The COVs range from .32 for the Financial Reporting phase to .59 for the Substantive Tests phase with an overall .66 COV for the aggregate tasks. The judgment variations between auditors is even higher for the instances of supervised practice. It ranges from .58 for Forming Opinions to .99 for Tests of Controls with an overall .84 COV for the aggregate tasks. These results indicate that auditors have better agreement concerning broader measures of knowledge base such as years of experience (and professional rank) than more refined measures such as the number of supervised instances of practice.

DECISION AID CHOICES

A summary of the decision aid choices by auditors in the 1988 and 1996 studies are presented in Table 8.3. The data indicate that a majority of all tasks were viewed as being strictly subject to human

Table 8.3
Decision Aids Selected

| Audit Phase | Percentage of Responses Indicating: | | | | | | | | Median | |
| | AU | | DSS | | KES | | HP | | | |
	1996	1988	1996	1988	1996	1988	1996	1988	1996	1988
Orientation	9	3	17	9	8	12	66	76	HP	HP
Control Structure	4	1	17	8	16	16	63	75	HP	HP
Tests of Controls	11	3	11	10	16	13	62	74	HP	HP
Substantive Tests	12	12	10	7	7	3	71	78	HP	HP
Forming Opinions	1	1	5	1	16	6	78	92	HP	HP
Financial Reporting	2	0	13	4	13	8	72	88	HP	HP
Aggregate	9	7	12	7	10	7	69	79	HP	HP

Note: AU = automation; DSS = decision support system; KES = knowledge-based expert system; HP = human processing.

processing. Overall, only 9% of all responses in 1996, and 7% in 1988, indicated automation followed by 12% and 7% indicating DSS, 10% and 7% for KES. The remaining 69% and 79% of responses indicated HP, in the 1996 and 1988 studies, respectively.

The overall results are generally mirrored between audit phases with some variation. For example, for the 1996 data within the Tests of Controls phase, the percentages of responses for the four choices of decision aids (i.e., automation, DSS, KES, and HP) were 11%, 11%, 16%, and 62% while the choices for the Forming Opinion phase were 1%, 5%, 16%, and 78%, respectively. Similarly, for the 1988 data, the choices were 3%, 10%, 13%, and 74% for the decision aid choices within the Tests of Controls phase while the choices for the Forming Opinion phase were 1%, 1%, 6%, and 92%, respectively.

The phase for which subjects indicated the largest percentage for automation is the Substantive Tests phase in both the 1996 and the 1988 studies with 12% of the responses. This is followed by Tests of Controls phase with 11% in 1996, but only 3% in 1988. The Orientation phase, likewise, received 9% of the responses in AU in 1996 as compared with only 3% in 1988. These phases seem to be the ones with the greatest increase in perceived opportunities for automation over the time period studied. The changes in percentages of automation for other phases are negligible. The phases with the largest percentages selected for the DSS development are the Orientation and Control Structure phases with 17% each as compared with 9% and 8% choices in 1988. This is followed by Financial Reporting (13% in 1996 as compared with 4% in 1988), Tests of Controls (11% in 1996 compared with 10% in 1988), and Substantive Tests (10% in 1996 compared with 7% in 1988). The Forming Opinions phase had only 5% of the responses in 1996 and 1% in 1988 indicating DSS.

For KES development, three phases tied with 16% of responses in 1996. These phases were Control Structure, Tests of Controls, and Forming Opinions. The comparable data from 1988 were 16%, 13%, and 6%, respectively. Thus, KES choices increased significantly for the Forming Opinion phase. Other phases, with the exception of the Orientation phase also show some increase: Financial Reporting (13% in 1996 compared with 8% in 1988) and Substantive Tests (7% in 1996 compared with only 3% in 1988). The Orientation phase indicated a significant drop in KES choice (from 12% in 1988 to 8% in 1996).

An interesting pattern emerges from Table 8.3 for a comparison between 1996 and 1988 data. For all phases of the audit, the auditors in 1996 had more decision aid responses (i.e., less for HP responses) than the auditors in the 1988 study. There has been a trend in the auditing profession to adopt more decision aids for performing more audit tasks, but the data clearly show that there are still many tasks that are viewed as strictly human processing tasks. The proportions of responses indicating suitability for automation, DSS, and KES are still small in comparison with the proportions selected for HP. The phase with the smallest percentage of HP responses was Tests of Controls (62% in 1996 compared with 74% in 1988) while Forming Opinions phase had the highest percentage of HP responses (78% in 1996 compared with 92% in 1988). Thus, although a larger proportion of responses support decision aid development, still 69% of the responses in 1996 (as compared with 79% of the responses in 1988) indicated a need for strictly human processing.

STATISTICAL TESTS FOR THE LINKAGE BETWEEN TASK STRUCTURE, KNOWLEDGE BASE, AND DECISION AIDS

Figure 8.1 presents the linkages between task structure (as an independent variable) and years of experience, supervised instances of practice, professional rank, and decision aids, each as a separate

Figure 8.1
Task Structure, Experience Level, and Decision Aids–
Data Type and Statistical Tests

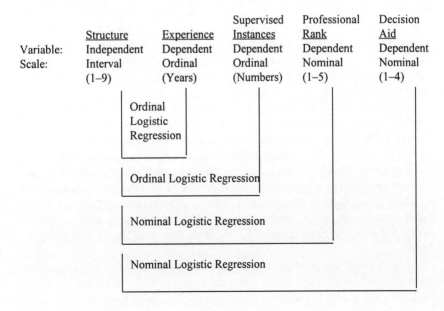

dependent variable. A simple measure of the strength of the linkage between these variables is the correlation coefficient. We present these coefficients for all three linkages. To test the significance of these linkages, we performed a battery of logistic regressions. The type of the logistic model selected depended on the type of the dependent variable as explained below.

As described earlier, a scale of 1 to 9 was used to collect data for task structure. By definition, this range can be considered an interval scale. The scale used for years of experience and supervised instances of practice on the other hand, are assumed to be ordinal in nature. The ordinal scale implies that while a higher number indicates more experience than a lower number, the difference may not necessarily be in an interval or a ratio scale. The scale used to collect data for the professional rank and decision aid choices are clearly categorical or nominal in nature.

Consequently, the ordinal logistic regression model was used to investigate the task structure/experience and the task-structure/supervised-instances relationships. On the other hand, nominal logistic regression models were used to investigate the relationship between task-structure and professional rank as well as the relationship between task-structure and decision-aids. Details of the results are presented in the next sections.

STATISTICAL TESTS BY AUDIT PHASE AND IN THE AGGREGATE

The results of the correlation analysis and logistic regression for the relationship between task structure and knowledge base measures are reported in Table 8.4. The data are organized by audit phases and in the aggregate for three measures of the knowledge base: experience in years, number of supervised instances of practice, and professional rank. The audit phases are listed in Column 1. The statistics related to a test of the relationship between task structure and experience ($H_{3\text{-}1a}$) are listed in Columns 2 through 4. Similar statistics are provided for the relationships between task structure and supervised instances ($H_{3\text{-}1b}$) in Columns 5 through 7 as well as task structure and professional rank ($H_{3\text{-}1c}$) in Columns 8 through 10. The results reported in Table 8.4 provide statistically significant support for all three hypotheses as described below.

Table 8.4
Relationship between Task Structure and Knowledge Base

1	Task Structure and Experience in Years			Task Structure and Supervised Instances			Task Structure and Professional Rank		
	2	3	4	5	6	7	8	9	10
Phase	Correlation Coefficient	O-Logit G statistic	p value	Correlation Coefficient	O-Logit G statistic	p value	Correlation Coefficient	N-Logit G statistic	p value
Orientation	.45	214.18	.000	.17	34.40	.000	.55	766.78	.000
Control Structure	.43	172.98	.000	.31	71.50	.000	.45	480.72	.000
Tests of Controls	.39	81.76	.000	.47	85.45	.000	.56	618.45	.000
Substantive Tests	.49	866.72	.000	.38	454.53	.000	.61	3,678.81	.000
Forming Opinions	.14	34.14	.000	.23	21.36	.000	.38	180.67	.000
Financial Reporting	.41	35.25	.000	.49	37.70	.000	.51	261.03	.000
Aggregate	.52	2175.78	.000	.40	992.57	.000	.70	10,489.30	.000

Note: O-Logit is the Ordinal Logistic Regression used for ordinal data in the dependent variable. N-Logit is the Nominal Logistic Regression used for nominal data in the dependent variable. G statistic is the statistic generated by the logistic regression. p value indicates the significance of the G statistic.

TASK STRUCTURE AND EXPERIENCE RELATIONSHIP (H₃₋₁ₐ)

The correlation coefficients reported for task structure and experience level are all positive. The correlation coefficient is .52 for audit tasks taken as a whole. As reported, the ordinal logistic model indicated a G statistic of 2175.78, which is significant at the .000 level. Similarly, all the correlation coefficients and G statistics were positive and significant for each of the audit phases. This result implies that, in general, the less structured the task, the more years of audit experience are required to perform it. The major outlier is the Forming Opinion phase. While the result is statistically significant, the correlation coefficient is only .14, indicating that the relationship between the task structure and experience is not as strong in this phase as it is in other phases. As reported in Chapter 7, regardless of the level of the task structure, subjects selected relatively high levels of experience to perform the tasks in this phase.

TASK STRUCTURE AND SUPERVISED INSTANCES RELATIONSHIP (H₃₋₁ᵦ)

Task structure and supervised instances of practice present qualitatively similar results to the task structure and experience relationship: all correlation coefficients are positive and the G statistics are all significant at the .000 level. This result implies that, in general, the less structured the task, the more supervised instances of practice are required before the task can be performed independently. However, there were some differences among audit phases. While the correlation coefficients were weaker than the task structure/experience hypothesis (H₃₋₁ₐ) for the Orientation, Control Structure, and Substantive Tests phases, they were stronger for the Tests of Controls, Forming Opinions and Financial Reporting phases. Overall, the correlation coefficient for this hypothesis was .40 as compared with .52 for the task-structure/experience hypothesis. Nevertheless, the ordinal logistic G statistic of 992.57 for this hypothesis is highly significant at the .000 level.

TASK STRUCTURE AND PROFESSIONAL RANK RELATIONSHIP (H₃₋₁c)

Task structure and professional rank present stronger results than the previous two relationships (i.e., H₃₋₁ₐ and H₃₋₁ᵦ). All correlation coefficients are positive and are greater than the coefficients in H$_{3\text{-}1a}$ and H$_{3\text{-}1b}$. This is true for the aggregate data where the .70 coefficient (G statistic = 10,489.30, significant at the .000 level) here compares favorably with the .40 for the task structure/supervised instances and the .52 for the task structure/experience relationships. This is the pattern for all phases of the audit without any exception. Furthermore, the G statistics are all significant at the .000 level. This result implies that, in general, the less structured the task, the higher the professional rank that is required to perform the task. Nevertheless, there were some differences among audit phases. Similar to the data for H$_{3\text{-}1a}$ and H$_{3\text{-}1b}$, the Forming Opinion phase with a coefficient of .38 had the smallest correlation coefficient of all phases while the correlation coefficients for the Substantive Tests phase was the highest at .61.

TASK STRUCTURE AND DECISION AIDS RELATIONSHIP

We present three sets of analyses to describe the relationship between task structure and decision aids. The first is a correlation coefficient analysis for task structure and decision aids by audit phase and in the aggregate for the 1996 and 1988 data. This analysis presents descriptive data, as well as a general test of H$_{4\text{-}2}$. The second set of analyses focuses on the decision aid data where all HP choices are deleted, thus a test of H$_{4\text{-}1}$ is provided in which it is shown that regardless of the level of structure, some tasks are classified as non-programmable. Finally, for the programmable tasks (i.e., the tasks for which AU, DSS, or KES was indicated), we present a more refined test of the relationship between task structure and decision aids (i.e., H$_{4\text{-}2}$).

General Correlational Analysis

The correlational analysis by phase of the audit and in the aggregate is reported in Table 8.5 for the 1996 and 1988 data. All correlation coefficients are positive and significant using the nominal logistic regression as indicated by the highly significant G statistics. Thus, the data provide overall support for H$_{4\text{-}2}$.

An interesting observation is that there are consistently greater correlations for the 1996 data for all phases of the audit and in the aggregate than for the 1988 data. For example, the correlation coefficient for the Forming Opinions phase was only .08 in 1988 while it is .22 for the 1996 data. Similarly the Orientation phase rendered a correlation coefficient of .28 in 1988 compared with .40 in 1996.

Table 8.5
Relationship between Task Structure and Decision Aids
Aggregate: All Tasks

1	Task Structure and Decision Aids – 1996 Data			Task Structure and Decision Aids – 1988 Data		
Phase	2 Correlation Coefficient	3 N-Logit G statistic	4 p value	5 Correlation Coefficient	6 N-Logit G statistic	7 p value
Orientation	0.40	144.72	0.000	0.28	209.37	0.000
Control Structure	0.24	47.99	0.000	0.13	61.27	0.000
Tests of Controls	0.38	106.57	0.000	0.19	76.66	0.000
Substantive Tests	0.14	219.88	0.000	0.12	493.84	0.000
Forming Opinions	0.22	35.69	0.000	0.08	11.46	0.009
Financial Reporting	0.17	17.30	0.001	0.09	14.94	0.002
Aggregate	0.21	487.25	0.000	0.19	1,218.10	0.000

Note: N-Logit is the Nominal Logistic Regression used for nominal data in the dependent variable. *G* statistic is the statistic generated by the logistic regression. *p* value indicates the significance of the *G* statistic.

Consequently, the aggregate correlation coefficient was .19 in 1988 as compared with .21 in 1996.

A major problem with these correlation coefficients is that they explain only a small portion of the variations in the dependent variable (the decision aid choices) based on the variations in the independent variable (task structure). The R^2s are approximately .04 for 1988 and 1996 aggregate data. This indicates that using all of the data for a test of H_{4-2} renders weak support for the hypothesis; the independent variable explains only 4% of the variation in perceived level of decision aid suitability. Thus, there is a need for stratifying the tasks into programmable and nonprogrammable tasks for a more accurate test of the task structure/decision aid relationship. This is because the weak correlation coefficients are the result of the selection of a majority of tasks in each phase for strictly human processing regardless of their task structure classification as reported earlier.

Programmable and Nonprogrammable Hypothesis (H$_{4-1}$)

The auditors' responses concerning applicable decision aids for various tasks were analyzed as follows. First, the median of the responses for each task was calculated. If the median was 4 (corresponding to HP), the task was considered to be nonprogrammable. For tasks with a median decision aid of less than 4, at least half of the auditors had selected some form of a decision aid (i.e., AU, DSS, or KES) to be applicable for performing the task. These tasks were classified as programmable. The results are presented in Table 8.6. Consistent with previous tables, these results are organized by various phases of the audit and in the aggregate.

The aggregate results indicate that overall, auditors in the 1996 study perceived 16% of the tasks as applicable for decision aid use as compared with only 11% in 1988. This evidence can be interpreted in two ways. The first is that the accounting firms have invested heavily in technology in the past decade, thus more tasks were selected as candidates for decision aids. The second explanation may be that the tasks in the 1996 study were defined in a more detailed manner compared with the 1988 study (i.e., 433 tasks versus 332 tasks). The more detailed nature of the tasks may have resulted in a greater

Table 8.6
Programmable and Nonprogrammable Tasks

	1996 Data			1988 Data		
1	2	3	4	5	6	7
Phase	Prog.	Non-prog.	Total	Prog.	Non-prog.	Total
Orientation	11 19%	47 81%	58	3 7%	42 93%	45
Control Structure	12 25%	36 75%	48	0 0%	41 100%	41
Tests of Controls	11 30%	27 70%	38	3 9%	31 91%	34
Substantive Tests	35 14%	209 86%	244	29 17%	142 83%	171
Forming Opinions	0 0%	27 100%	27	0 0%	23 100%	23
Financial Reporting	2 11%	16 89%	18	0 0%	18 100%	18
Aggregate	71 16%	362 84%	433	35 11%	297 89%	332

Note: Prog. is programmable, non-prog. is nonprogrammable.

number of them being selected as applicable for decision aid use. Alternatively, a higher percentage of the added tasks may have been deemed suitable for decision aid development, thus rendering the overall percentage of suitable tasks in the 1996 study higher than in the 1988 study.

The results of the analysis at the audit phase level are generally consistent with the results at the aggregate level with two exceptions. While no tasks were selected as programmable in the Forming Opinion phase, the proportion of the tasks selected in other phases with the exception of the Substantive Tests phase are consistently larger for the 1996 data than for the 1988 data. For example, 19% of the tasks in the Orientation phase for the 1996 data were viewed as programmable as compared with only 7% for the 1988 data. In the case of the Control Structure phase, decision aids were selected for 25% of the tasks in the 1996 data while no task was selected as programmable in 1988. However, the Substantive Tests phase of the audit rendered only 14% of the tasks for which decision aids were selected by auditors in 1996 as compared with 17% in 1988. In connection with the data for the Control Structure and Tests of Controls phases for which significantly larger proportions of the tasks were selected for decision aids in 1996 compared to 1988, this data may reflect the emphasis in recent years on the control structure and tests of controls at the expense of tests of details.

The results reported in Table 8.6 provide strong support for H_{4-1}. They indicate that for a majority of the tasks (84 percent in 1996 and 89 percent in 1988), no decision aid was selected by a majority of auditors as applicable to perform the tasks regardless of their level of structure (i.e., they are nonprogrammable). Thus, we test the task structure/decision aid type hypothesis (H_{4-2}), for only the programmable tasks in the next section.

A Test of the Relationship between Programmable Tasks and Decision Aid Type (H_{4-2})

Table 8.7 presents the results of the correlation analysis and the significance of the relationship between task structure and decision aids for the programmable tasks. The correlations are generally larger in this table as compared with Table 8.5 resulting in higher R^2s, thus explaining a larger proportion of the variation in the

Table 8.7
Relationship between Task Structure and Decision Aids:
Programmable Tasks Only

1 Phase	Task Structure and Decision Aids – 1996 Data			Task Structure and Decision Aids – 1988 Data		
	2 Correlation Coefficient	3 N-Logit *G* statistic	4 *p* value	5 Correlation Coefficient	6 N-Logit *G* statistic	7 *p* value
Orientation	.55	59.87	.000	.39	33.87	.000
Control Structure	.24	15.72	.001	NA	NA	NA
Tests of Controls	.39	39.11	.000	.29	18.63	.000
Substantive Tests	.28	80.79	.000	.34	273.44	.000
Forming Opinions	NA	NA	NA	NA	NA	NA
Financial Reporting	-.27	7.26	.027	NA	NA	NA
Aggregate	.36	198.89	.000	.35	337.52	.000

Note: O-Logit is the Ordinal Logistic Regression used for ordinal data in the dependent variable. N-Logit is the Nominal Logistic Regression used for nominal data in the dependent variable. *G* statistic is the statistic generated by the logistic regression. *p*-value is the significance of the *G* statistic. NA = not applicable.

dependent variable (decision aid choice). For example, the overall correlations of .36 and .35 for the 1996 and 1988 data translate into 13% and 12% of the variations being explained as compared with approximately 4% in Table 8.5. The major exception to this rule is the negative correlation coefficient of -.27 for the Financial Reporting phase. As the significance level of .027 indicates, this correlation was not as significant as others, and since there were only two programmable tasks in this phase (see Table 8.6), the generalizability of the result should be interpreted cautiously.

SUMMARY

For the aggregate data by audit phase and for the audit tasks taken as a whole, strong support was found for all hypotheses. Namely, the correlation coefficients were all positive and the logistic regressions were statistically significant for the task-structure/experience, task-structure/supervised-instances, task-structure/professional rank, and task-structure/decision-aids relationships. For the latter relationship, the tasks were further classified into programmable and nonprogrammable, and the correlational tests were performed for programmable tasks only. The results were stronger in support of the task structure/decision aid type hypothesis for this subset of tasks. However, significant variations were observed between audit phases and within each of the phases. These differences are due to task specific nature of the audit process as analyzed in Chapter 7. Further summary and conclusions from the study are discussed in Chapter 9.

Chapter 9

Summary and Conclusions

In this chapter we first present a summary of the results from the study. This is followed by a number of observations regarding the implications of the results for audit research and practice. In the final section, we discuss the limitations of our study and provide a list of issues for practice and research considerations.

SUMMARY

Based on calls in recent years for identification of task-specific knowledge base in auditing, we conducted this large scale study with four broad objectives. These objectives and the outcome from the research are summarized below.

An Inventory of Audit Tasks

The first objective was to develop a comprehensive inventory of detailed audit tasks. This objective was achieved by compilation of 433 audit tasks based on a review of several audit manuals, auditing texts, and professional standards and manuals. This detailed list of audit tasks is presented in Chapter 5.

This is the most refined inventory of detailed audit tasks found in the professional and academic literature. In an early study of the 14 largest accounting firms, a 28-step audit process was documented in

1986.[1] This list was further refined into a 60 distinct audit steps a year later by other researchers.[2] In the same year, Abdolmohammadi undertook a study to document a more detailed inventory of audit tasks. His refined list of 332 detailed audit tasks was classified into six audit phases, each of which had several subphases. The results of this study were published in 1999.[3] The current study further refined Abdolmohammadi's inventory of audit tasks by providing a list of 433 audit tasks classified into six audit phases and many subphases as reported in Chapter 5. Details of the method of compilation are provided in Chapter 6. While many of these tasks were exactly the same as those in the earlier study, others were either new in this study or were tasks that were subdivided into more detailed tasks. Comparative analyses are provided in this book between the two studies for the tasks that were exactly the same in both studies.

Task Structure

The second objective of this research was to classify the detailed audit tasks by their levels of task structure. This objective was accomplished by having a sample of 44 managers and partners from several offices of the then Big Six and a regional accounting firm classify the tasks by their levels of task structure. The framework used for task structure classification was a popular framework from the management science literature.[4] This model of the decision process had been investigated and adapted to the auditing literature by researchers in the 1980s.[5] A discussion of the details of this model as well as other frameworks is provided in Chapter 2.

---

1. See B. E. Cushing and J. K. Loebbecke, 1986, "Comparison of Audit Methodologies of Large Accounting Firms," *Studies in Accounting Research No. 26* (Sarasota, Fla.: American Accounting Association).

2. See W. C. Chow, A. H. McNamee, and R. D. Plumlee, 1987, "Practitioners' Perceptions of Audit Step Difficulty and Criticalness: Implications for Audit Research," *Auditing: A Journal of Practice and Theory* 6 (2), pp. 123–133.

3. See M. J. Abdolmohammadi. 1999, "A Comprehensive Taxonomy of Task Structure and Knowledge Base Demands in Auditing," *Behavioral Research in Accounting* 11, pp. 51–92.

4. See H. Simon, 1960, *The New Science of Management* (New York: Harper and Row).

5. See M. J. Abdolmohammadi and A. Wright, 1987, "An Examination of the Effects of Experience and Task Complexity on Audit Judgments," *The Accounting Review* 62 (1), pp. 1–13.

This model was presented and explained in non-technical terms to the highly experienced managers and partners who participated in this study (see the appendix to Chapter 6). The scale used to collect task structure data was a Likert scale ranging from 1 to 9 (structured to unstructured). Detailed task-level statistics are provided in Chapter 7. Aggregate data by audit phase and for the audit taken as a whole are presented in Chapter 8. These chapters present the data collected for this study in comparison with the data collected in 1988 for the tasks that were exactly the same in both studies. At the individual task level, the t statistic was used to investigate the significance of the differences between the two studies.

Task-specific analyses reported in Chapter 7 (Tables 7.1 to 7.16) present detailed task structure data within each of the audit phases. The Orientation, Control Structure, and Tests of Control phases of the audit indicated that structure ratings have generally remained stable over time. Only isolated differences were observed for these audit phases. The Substantive Tests phase indicated significant differences between 1996 and 1988 data for approximately 15% of the comparable tasks. Most of these tasks were perceived to be less structured in 1996 than in 1988. On the other hand, 25% of the comparable tasks in the Forming Opinion phase and 50% in the Financial Reporting phase indicated that the tasks have become more structured in 1996 than in 1988. This result could be related to the increasing use of decision aids in these phases in recent years. An interesting observation from the task structure data is that in general, as the assessed degree of task structure increases, the coefficient of variation decreases indicating that there is more consensus among auditors for less structured tasks than for more structured tasks.

The aggregate results by audit phase are presented in Chapter 8 (Table 8.1). These results indicate that task structure ratings range from an average of 3.20 for Substantive Tests to 5.34 for Forming Opinions. Comparable data from the 1988 study were 2.94 and 6.24, respectively, which indicated statistically significant differences. Thus, as reported earlier, the substantive test tasks have become less structured, while the Forming Opinion tasks have become more structured. Other phases of the audit, except for the Tests of Controls, also indicated changes over time of becoming either less or more structured over the eight-year period from 1988 to 1996. However, significant variations among respondents were also observed as reflected in the coefficients of variations within these audit phases. Consequently, the average structure ratings of all tasks in the whole audit indicated no significant difference between the two study years.

Knowledge Base

The third objective of the study was to provide detailed task-specific knowledge base demands for task performance. Many studies have emphasized the importance of task-specific knowledge.[6] We collected two types of data from the highly experienced subjects (managers and partners) in the 1996 study. The first was audit experience in years and the second was the number of supervised instances of practice before an auditor is considered to be knowledgeable enough to perform the task independently. In the 1988 study data were collected only on the professional rank needed to perform each task. All three types of data are presented in Chapters 7 at the detailed task level and in Chapter 8 for the aggregate results.

Tables 7.17 to 7.32 provide details of the knowledge base demands for each of the audit tasks within the phases of the audit. A general observation here is that for the years of experience variable, the coefficient of variation decreases for higher levels of experience as compared to lower levels. This observation is consistent with the same observation for task structure. The coefficients of variation for the supervised instances of practice are more randomly distributed to warrant a conclusion about an inverse relationship between the response variable and its coefficient of variation. The median professional rank data from the 1988 study are also presented in these detailed tables.

The aggregate results presented in Chapter 8 (Table 8.2) indicate that an overall average of 2.52 years of experience and 3.15 times of supervised instances of practice as well as a professional rank of staff

---

6. For example, see M. J. Abdolmohammadi and A. Wright, 1987, "An Examination of the Effects of Experience and Task Complexity on Audit Judgments," pp. 1–13; A. H. Ashton, 1991, "Experience and Error Frequency Knowledge as Potential Determinants of Audit Expertise," *The Accounting Review* 66 (2), pp. 218–239; J. Bédard and M. T. H. Chi, 1993, "Expertise in Auditing," *Auditing: A Journal of Practice and Theory* 12 (Supplement), pp. 21–45; S. E. Bonner, 1990, "Experience Effects in Auditing: The Role of Task-Specific Knowledge," *The Accounting Review* 65 (1), pp. 72–92; S. Bonner and B. Lewis, 1990, "Determinants of Auditor Expertise," *Journal of Accounting Research* 28 (Supplement), pp. 1–20; S. Bonner and N. Pennington, 1991, "Cognitive Processes and Knowledge as Determinants of Auditor Expertise," *Journal of Accounting Literature* 10, pp. 1–50; D. M. Frederick and R. Libby, 1986, "Expertise and Auditors' Judgments of Conjunctive Events," *Journal of Accounting Research* 24 (2), pp. 270–290; and R. Libby, 1995, "The Role of Knowledge and Memory in Audit Judgment," in R. H. Ashton and A. H. Ashton (eds.), *Judgment and Decision Making Research in Accounting and Auditing* (New York: Cambridge University Press), pp. 176–206.

are needed to perform all audit tasks. However, significant variations between various phases of the audit were also observed as reflected in the mean and medians of various phases. For example, on one extreme, on average only about two years of experience, 2.45 instances of practice and a professional rank of assistant were required to perform the tasks in the Substantive Test phase. On the other extreme, the Forming Opinion phase required an average of 5.41 years of experience, 5.49 instances of supervised practice and a professional rank of manager to perform the tasks. These results show that the overall average knowledge base is insufficient for performing tasks of varying structure in various audit phases.

Decision Aids Responses

The fourth objective of this research was to provide data on applicable decision aids for detailed audit tasks. The data were collected based on the argument in the literature that decision aid development in auditing is, in part, dependent on the structure of the task under investigation.[7] The auditing literature has interpreted this argument to mean that while routine tasks can be automated, decision support systems and knowledge-based expert systems are useful for more complex audit tasks.[8] Similar data were collected in the 1988 study.

Decision aids responses for detailed audit tasks are presented in Chapter 7 (Tables 7.33 to 7.48) while aggregate results are presented in Chapter 8 (Table 8.3). A general observation from the detailed data is that for a majority of audit tasks, the highly experienced participants assessed complete human processing as the method for performing the task. This observation was generally consistent for both the 1996 and 1988 data. However, while only a limited number of tasks were deemed to benefit from decision aids (i.e., automation, decision support, or

---

7. See P. G. W. Keen and M. S. Scott-Morton, 1978, *Decision Support Systems: An Organizational Perspective* (Reading, Mass: Addison-Wesley).

8. See M. J. Abdolmohammadi, 1987, "Decision Support and Expert Systems in Auditing: A Review and Research Directions," *Accounting and Business Research* 17 (66), pp. 173–185; W. F., Messier Jr., 1995, "Research in and Development of Audit Decision Aids," in R. H. Ashton and A. H. Ashton (eds.), *Judgment and Decision Making Research in Accounting and Auditing* (New York: Cambridge University Press), pp. 207–228; W. F. Messier, Jr. and J. V. Hansen, 1984, "Expert Systems in Accounting and Auditing: A Framework and Review," in S. Moriarity and E. Joyce (eds.), *Decision Making and Accounting: Current Research* (University of Oklahoma), pp. 182–202; W. F. Messier Jr. and J. V. Hansen, 1987, "Expert Systems in Auditing: The State of the Art," *Auditing: A Journal of Practice and Theory* 7 (1), pp. 94–105.

expert systems) in both studies, relatively more of the comparable tasks were selected for decision aids in 1996 than in 1988. For example, while only 11% of the comparable tasks in the Orientation phase were deemed applicable for decision aids use in 1996, this proportion was significantly larger than the 9% of the same tasks in the 1988 study.

Similarly, while 26% of the comparable tasks in the Control Structure, 41% in the Tests of Controls, and 6% in the Financial Reporting phases were selected for decision aids in 1996, the rates for the same sets of tasks from the 1988 study were respectively 0%, 18%, and 0%. This result may be a reflection of the impact that computer technology has had on practice in recent years. However, the results indicate a smaller number of the comparable tasks in the Substantive Tests phase chosen for decision aids development in 1996 (15%) as compared with 1988 (20%). For example, the Inventory subphase received less decision aids selection in 1996 than in 1988. These results may be affected by the strategic audit approaches of late that do not emphasize tests of details. Finally, the Forming Opinion phase did not indicate any difference between the two years: 100% of the tasks were selected for strictly human processing in both years.

Tests of Research Hypotheses

The final objective in this study was to investigate the relationships between task structure as an independent variable and knowledge base and decision aids as dependent variables. Three hypotheses relating to the inverse relation between task structure and audit experience defined in years of experience (H_{3-1a}), supervised instances of practice (H_{3-1b}) and professional rank (H_{3-1c}) were tested. These hypotheses were developed in Chapter 3 based on the pertinent literature. As reported in Chapter 8 (Table 8.4), all three hypotheses were supported at highly significant levels for all phases of the audit and in the aggregate.

Also tested was the relationship between task structure and decision aids. Two hypotheses were tested. The first hypothesis (H_{4-1}) reflects the idea that regardless of the level of structure, some tasks would be classified as programmable and others as nonprogrammable. The second hypothesis (H_{4-2}) predicts a positive correlation between task structure and decision aid type for the programmable subset of the tasks. These hypotheses were developed in Chapter 4 based on the pertinent literature. Both hypotheses were supported at highly significant levels at the audit phase and aggregate levels as shown in Tables 8.5 to 8.7.

IMPLICATIONS

The results of the study have several important practice and research implications. First, the detailed audit tasks in Chapter 5 and their task structure classification and knowledge base demands can be used by practitioners and academics alike in practice and research situations in which it is critical to know the requisite knowledge for task performance. For example, audit experience, supervised instances of practice and professional rank data can be used as benchmarks to assess an auditor's level of knowledge for task performance. This information can be used to assign tasks to auditors in professional settings. It can also be used by researchers for assigning auditors to experiential tasks in expertise/specialization studies.

The coefficients of variation can serve as a further guide for the purpose of staff assignment to audit tasks and for subject selection for behavioral research. For tasks where there is wide variation in responses, it may not be sufficient to assign staff on the basis of average knowledge base alone. Audit researchers must also be cautious in using the average experience level for behavioral studies. Rather, the experience level for staff assignment or subject assignment in behavioral research for tasks with high coefficients of variation may have to be chosen from the high end of the experience spectrum of responses for that task. For example, the upper level of knowledge base can be used for expertise classification, while the lower bound of the range can be used to identify the level below novice level. Those with experience levels within the range can be viewed as novices.

Additionally, the data provide practitioners and behavioral researchers three measures of knowledge base that might be helpful in various settings. For staff assignment and behavioral research on certain tasks, general audit experience in years may be sufficient. Examples are tasks in the Tests of Controls phase of the audit. Other tasks may require instances of practice for performance regardless of the auditor's years of experience. Examples include highly complex tasks such as those in commercial real estate valuation. In many other tasks, the professional rank may be a good surrogate for knowledge base. For example, higher-rank auditors are assigned to review the work of lower level auditors in many audit situations. Researchers may want to include questions in their research instrument asking auditor-subjects specifically about the number of times they have performed a task in addition to the number of years they have been an auditor or their professional rank.

Second, the task structure and knowledge base data have benefits for audit courses and staff training in accounting firms. Students can benefit from these data where a clear understanding of the nature of audit tasks and the requisite knowledge to perform them can be communicated. In practice, structured tasks with a low level of knowledge base requirement can be assigned to less experienced auditors while less structured tasks require more knowledgeable auditors. It is for these tasks that there is a need for more and better training programs. A recent review article reported auditors performed poorly in experimental studies using relatively complex tasks, because they had not had good opportunities to acquire knowledge.[9] Years of experience, number of supervised instances of practice, professional rank, as well as adequate formal training may be the key to superior performance.

The researchers further argued that, "tasks that receive a large amount of feedback but show poor performance by experts (e.g., developing specific expectations about the balance of each account) are those with virtually no instruction because there are no well-developed theories of task performance. The lack of theories prohibits learning from outcome feedback."[10] The detailed task structure and knowledge base demands provided in this book should assist practitioners and researchers to develop such theories.

Third, the decision aids data are helpful for research and development of decision aids in auditing. A previous study reported that despite the heavy emphasis on decision aid development in auditing in recent years, there is no systematic model to identify audit tasks for decision aid development.[11] Such developments are still done largely on a one-task-at-a-time basis. In this study we collected decision aid choices of highly experienced auditors for a comprehensive inventory of audit tasks. This list can be consulted by researchers and decision aid developers for future work.

---

9. See S. E. Bonner and N. Pennington, 1991, "Cognitive Processes and Knowledge as Determinants of Auditor Expertise," *Journal of Accounting Literature* 10, p. 27.

10. Ibid., p. 36.

11. See M. J. Abdolmohammadi, 1991a, "Factors Affecting Auditor's Perceptions of Applicable Decision Aids for Various Audit Tasks," *Contemporary Accounting Research* 7 (2), pp. 535–548 and M. J. Abdolmohammadi, 1991b, "A Test of the Relationship between Task Structure and Decision Aid Type in Auditing" in L. A. Ponemon and D. R. L. Gabhart (eds.), *Auditing Advances in Applied Behavioral Research*, (New York: Springer-Verlag Publishing), pp. 131–142.

LIMITATIONS AND FUTURE RESEARCH DIRECTIONS

The magnitude of this research required participation of only managers and partners to assess the detailed tasks. This was necessary because managers and partners are the only group of auditors with sufficient amount of knowledge and experience with all audit tasks to be able to evaluate the tasks under investigation on the necessary dimensions. These professionals are extremely busy and their participation in a study such as ours is on the basis of availability and interest. Consequently, we had no way of randomly selecting the respondents, who were chosen through a contact partner in each of the participating offices. To the extent that lack of random selection can affect our results, caution must be exercised in interpreting the data.

Also, given the large number of audit tasks (433 in all), we divided the tasks into three approximately equal groups or versions in the current study. This was based on the experience from the 1988 study in which all 332 tasks were presented to the participating auditors, requiring approximately three hours of response time. To reduce the time requirement and possible fatigue, each auditor in the 1996 study received only one version, and thus only a third of the total tasks. Nevertheless, the time required to respond to all parts of each of the versions of the task instrument was approximately 90 minutes. This required a major commitment from highly busy professional auditors. A consequence of this time demand was that despite the great assistance we received from our contacts, we had only 14 or 15 subjects for each of the three versions of the task instrument. The sample size, while sufficient for statistical analysis, was nevertheless a limitation. For example, while the audit phases and aggregate tests resulted in highly significant logistic regression statistics, many task-specific statistics were either insignificant or significant at marginal levels such as the .10 level. The difference may be due to the fact that for the aggregate data, or for audit phase level analysis, there were large numbers of combined observations, but for analysis at the task level there were only 14 or 15 observations corresponding to the number of participants. Future studies may be needed to tackle a much smaller number of tasks, with a larger group of auditors to investigate the issues further. Such studies are particularly needed for tasks for which we found particularly large coefficients of variation.

A related issue is that due to small sample sizes, we could not investigate the effects of a number of potentially confounding variables. For example, while it was desirable to investigate the effects of professional rank (i.e., manager versus partner) on the results, there were very few partners per each version to allow a meaningful comparison with managers. Similarly, we collected data to independently classify audit firms by their audit methodology and the use of high technology in their audits. Unfortunately, the number of partcipants was too small to allow partition for analysis of the data for these variables. The same is true for audit specialty. We simply did not have enough data to afford partition by these demographic variables.

One area of analysis in which the use of demographic variables was particularly desirable was the decision aids data. For a majority of audit tasks, strict human processing was selected as the appropriate way of performing the task. While more tasks were selected for decision aids development in 1996 than in 1988, it is not clear why so many tasks were considered to be subject to strictly human processing in both the 1996 and 1988 studies. An earlier study reported that the choice of decision aid type for a task may be dependent on a number of factors such as the auditors' electronic data processing specialty, rank, and audit firm methodology.[12] We could not test these propositions in the current study due to the small sample sizes. We should note, however, that in a study with 134 auditors and only 30 audit tasks (all in the risk assessment area), researchers also found a majority of the tasks to be deemed subject to strict human processing, not any kind of decision aids.[13] In that study the researchers reported that for the few tasks for which the median decision aid was other than strictly human processing, a statistically significant contingency was found between task structure and decision aids. This is the result that was also found in our studies. Future research is particularly needed to better understand the nature of the audit tasks that auditors consider subject to human processing as compared with those for which some kind of decision aid can be utilized.

While the sample size limitation prevented us from delving into the effects of these demographic variables, we believe that the sample sizes were large enough for data analysis at the aggregate and detailed task levels that we performed. It is our hope that these results will assist researchers and professionals alike to better understand the nature of the detailed audit tasks, and the knowledge base required to perform the tasks. As explained earlier, this understanding should (1) foster better staff assignment in practice and subject assignment in behavioral research, (2) assist in the development of better theories of

---

12. Ibid.

13. See M. J. Abdolmohammadi and W. J. Read, 1996, "An Investigation of the Relationship between Task Structure and Task Programmability in Audit Risk Assessment," *Asia-Pacific Journal of Accounting* 3 (1), pp. 137–154.

training, and more training material and programs for the unstructured tasks that have resulted in poor performance by auditors in behavioral research, and (3) assist in the research and development efforts for decision aids that can enhance auditor efficiency and effectiveness in today's competitive environment.

References

Abdolmohammadi, M. J. 1987. "Decision Support and Expert Systems in Auditing: A Review and Research Directions." *Accounting and Business Research* 17(66), pp. 173-185.

Abdolmohammadi, M. J. 1991a. "Factors Affecting Auditor's Perceptions of Applicable Decision Aids for Various Audit Tasks." *Contemporary Accounting Research* 7 (2), pp. 535–548.

Abdolmohammadi, M. J. 1991b. "A Test of the Relationship between Task Structure and Decision Aid Type in Auditing." In L. A. Ponemon and D. R. L. Gabhart, eds., *Auditing: Advances in Applied Behavioral Research.* New York: Springer-Verlag Publishing, pp. 131-142.

Abdolmohammadi, M. J. 1999. "A Comprehensive Taxonomy of Task Structure and Knowledge Base Demands in Auditing." *Behavioral Research in Accounting* 11, pp. 51–92.

Abdolmohammadi, M. J., and M. S. Bazaz. 1991. "Identification of Tasks for Expert Systems Development in Auditing." *Expert Systems with Applications* 3 (1), pp. 99–108.

Abdolmohammadi, M. J., and R. J. McQuade. *Accounting Theory and Methods of Professional Research,* New York: McGraw-Hill, forthcoming.

Abdolmohammadi, M. J., and W. J. Read. 1996. "An Investigation of the Relationship between Task Structure and Task Programmability in Audit Risk Assessment." *Asia-Pacific Journal of Accounting* 3 (1), pp. 137-154.

Abdolmohammadi, M. J., J. Searfoss, and J. Shanteau. 1997. "A Framework for Analysis of Characteristics of Audit Experts" (working paper, Bentley College)

Abdolmohammadi, M. J., and J. Shanteau. 1992. "Personal Attributes of Expert Auditors." *Organizational Behavior and Human Decision Processes* 5 (2), pp. 158-172.

Abdolmohammadi, M. J., and A. Wright. 1987. "An Examination of the Effects of Experience and Task Complexity on Audit Judgments." *The Accounting Review* 62 (1), pp. 1–13.

Aldersley, S. J. 1988. Discussant's Response to "Using and Evaluating Audit Decision Aids." In R. P. Srivastava and J. E. Rebele, eds., *AuditingSymposium IX: Proceedings of the 1988 Touche Ross/University of Kansas Symposium on Auditing Problems.* Lawrence, Kans.: University of Kansas Printing Service, pp. 26–31.

Arens, A. A., and J. K. Loebbecke. 1994. *Auditing: An Integrated Approach.*Upper Saddle River, N.J: Prentice-Hall.

Ashton, A. H. 1991. "Experience and Error Frequency Knowledge as Potential Determinants of Audit Expertise." *The Accounting Review* 66 (2), pp. 218–239.

Ashton, R. H. 1982. *Human Information Processing in Accounting.* Sarasota, Florida: American Accounting Association.

Ashton, R. H., and J. J. Willingham. 1988. "Using and Evaluating Audit Decision Aids". In R. P. Srivastava and J. E. Rebele, eds., *AuditingSymposium IX: Proceedings of the 1988 Touche Ross/University of Kansas Symposium on Auditing Problems.* Lawrence, Kans.: University of Kansas Printing Service, pp. 1–25.

Bailey, A. D., Jr., G. L. Duke, J. Gerlach, C. Ko., R. D. Meservy, and A. B. Whinston. 1985. "TICOM and the Analysis of Internal Controls." *The Accounting Review* 60 (2), pp. 186–201.

Beckman, T. 1991. "Selecting Expert Systems Application." *AI Expert* (February), pp. 42–48.

Bédard, J., and M. T. H. Chi. 1993. "Expertise in Auditing." *Auditing: A Journal of Practice and Theory* 12 (Supplement), pp. 21–45.

Bell, T., G. S. Ribar, and J. Verchio. 1990. "Neural Nets versus Logistic Regression: A Comparison of Each Model's Ability to Predict Commercial Bank Failures." In R. P. Srivastava, ed., *Auditing Symposium X: Proceedings of the 1990 Deloitte and Touche/ University of Kansas Symposium on Auditing Problems.* Lawrence, Kans.: University of Kansas Printing Service.

Benbasat, I., and B. R. Nault. 1988. "Empirical Research in Decision Support and Expert Systems: An Examination of Research to Date and Emerging Topics." In A. Bailey, ed., *Auditor Productivity in the Year 2000: 1987 Proceedings of the Arthur Young Professors' Roundtable*, pp. 255–303.

Billings, R. S., and S. A. Marcus. 1983. "Measures of Compensatory and Noncompensatory Models of Decision Behavior: Process Tracing Versus Policy Capturing." *Organizational Behavior and Human Performance* 31 (1), pp. 331–352.

Bonner, S. E. 1990. "Experience Effects in Auditing: The Role of Task-Specific Knowledge." *The Accounting Review* 65 (1), pp. 72–92.

Bonner, S. E. 1994. "A Model of the Effects of Audit Task Complexity." *Accounting, Organizations and Society* 19 (3), pp. 213–234.

Bonner, S., and B. Lewis. 1990. "Determinants of Auditor Expertise." *Journal of Accounting Research* 28 (Supplement), pp. 1–20.

Bonner, S., R. Libby, and M. W. Nelson. 1996. "Using Decision Aids to Improve Auditors' Conditional Probability Judgments." *The AccountingReview* 71 (2), pp. 221–240.

Bonner, S., and N. Pennington. 1991. "Cognitive Processes and Knowledge as Determinants of Auditor Expertise." *Journal of Accounting Literature* 10, pp. 1–50.

Bonner, S., and P. Walker. 1994. "The Effects of Instruction and Experience on the Acquisition of Auditing Knowledge." *The Accounting Review* 69 (1), pp. 157–178.

Bowrin, A. R. 1998. "Review and Synthesis of Audit Structure Literature." *Journal of Accounting Literature* 17, pp. 40–71.

Brown, C. E. 1991. "Expert Systems in Public Accounting: Current Practice and Future Directions." *Expert Systems with Applications* 3, pp. 3–18.

Brown, C. E., and D. S. Murphy. 1990. "The Use of Auditing Expert Systems in Public Accounting." *Journal of Information Systems* 4 (3), pp. 63–72.

Brown, D. and M. M. Eining. 1996. "The Role of Decision Aids in Accounting: A Synthesis of Prior Research." *Advances in Accounting Information Systems* 4, pp. 305–332.

Campbell, D. J. 1988. "Task Complexity: A Review and Analysis." *Academy of Management Review* 13 (1), pp. 40–52.

Canadian Institute of Chartered Accountants. 1994. *CICA Handbook, Volume I and II.* Toronto: The Canadian Institute of Chartered Accountants.

Choo, F. 1989. "Expert-Novice Differences in Judgment/Decision Making Research." *Journal of Accounting Literature* 8, pp. 106–136.

Chow, W. C., A. H. McNamee, and R. D. Plumlee, 1987. "Practitioners' Perceptions of Audit Step Difficulty and Criticalness: Implications for Audit Research." *Auditing: A Journal of Practice and Theory* 6 (2), pp. 123–133.

Coopers and Lybrand. 1991. *Bridging the GAAP: Accounting in Canada and the United States, 1991–92 Edition.* Canada: Coopers and Lybrand.

Cox, E. P. III. 1980. "The Optimal Number of Response Alternatives for a Scale: A Review." *Journal of Marketing Research* 17 (November), pp. 407–422.

Cushing, B. E., and J. K. Loebbecke. 1984. "The Implications of Structured Audit Methodologies." *The Auditor's Report* 8 (Summer), pp. 1, 10, 13.

Cushing, B. E., and J. K. Loebbecke. 1986. "Comparison of Audit Methodologies of Large Accounting Firms." *Studies in Accounting Research No. 26.* Sarasota, Fla.: American Accounting Association.

Davis, J. S., and I. Solomon. 1989. "Experience, Expertise, and Expert-Performance Research in Accounting." *Journal of Accounting Literature* 8, pp. 150–164.

Eining, M. M., and P. B. Dorr. 1991. "The Impact of Expert System Usage on Experiential Learning in an Auditing Setting." *Journal of Information Systems* (Spring), pp. 1–16.

Elliott, R. K., and J. A. Kielich. 1985. "Expert Systems for Accountants." *Journal of Accountancy* (September), pp. 126–134.

Felix, Jr., W. L., and W. R. Kinney Jr. 1982. "Research in the Auditor's Opinion Formulation Process: State of the Art." *The Accounting Review* 57 (2), pp. 245–271.

Frederick, D. M., and R. Libby. 1986. "Expertise and Auditors' Judgments of Conjunctive Events." *Journal of Accounting Research* 24 (2), pp. 270–290.

Gill, G. 1995. "Early Expert Systems: Where Are They Now." *MIS Quarterly* 19 (1), pp. 51–81.

Goodall, R., and A. Skinner. 1994. *Professional Engagement Manual.* Toronto: The Canadian Institute of Chartered Accountants.

Gorry, G. A., and M. S. Scott-Morton. 1971. "A Framework for Management Information Systems." *Sloan Management Review* (Fall), pp. 55–70.

Graham, L. E. 1990. "A Technological Response to the Changing Audit Environment." *The Auditor's Report* (Summer), pp. 10, 15.

Grease, C. E. 1984. "Accounting for Change." *World* 18, pp. 16–17.

Han, I., and J. Choi. 1995. "Selection of Appropriate Tasks for Expert System Development in Auditing" (working paper).

Hansen, J. V., and W. F. Messier Jr. 1986. "A Preliminary Test of EDP-Expert." *Auditing: A Journal of Practice and Theory* 6 (1), pp. 109–123.

Karan, V., U. S. Murthy, and A. S. Vinze. 1995. "Assessing the Suitability of Judgmental Auditing Tasks for Expert Systems Development: An Empirical Approach." *Expert Systems with Applications* 9, pp. 441–55.

Keen, P. G. W., and M. S. Scott-Morton. 1978. *Decision Support Systems: An Organizational Perspective.* Reading, Mass: Addison-Wesley.

Keith, J. R. 1985. "Expert Systems in Auditing: A Practitioner'sPerspective." Presented at the 1985 Price Waterhouse Auditing Symposium, Lake Tahoe.

Kida, T., J. Cohen, and L. Paquette. 1990. "The Effect of Cue Categorization and Modeling Techniques on the Assessment of Cue Importance." *Decision Sciences* 21, pp. 357–372.

Kim, C., and M. Khoury. 1987. "Task Complexity and Contingent Information Processing in the Case of Couple's Decision Making." *Academy of Marketing Science* 15 (3), pp. 32–43.

Kinney, W. 1986. "Audit Technology and Preference for Auditing Standards." *Journal of Accounting and Economics,* 8 (1) pp. 73–89.

Lenard, M. J., P. Alam, and G. R. Madey. 1995. "The Application of Neural Networks and a Qualitative Response Model to the Auditor's Going Concern Uncertainty Decision," *Decision Sciences* 26 (2), pp. 209–227.

Libby, R. 1995. "The Role of Knowledge and Memory in Audit Judgment." In R. H. Ashton and A. H. Ashton, eds., *Judgment and Decision Making Research in Accounting and Auditing.* New York: Cambridge University Press, pp. 176–206.

Libby, R. and J. Luft 1993. "Determinants of Judgment Performance in Accounting Settings: Ability, Knowledge, Motivation, and Environment," *Accounting, Organizations and Society* 18 (5), pp. 425–450.

Libby, R. and H. T. Tan. 1994. "Modeling the Determinants of Audit Expertise," *Accounting, Organizations and Society* 19, pp. 701–716.

Mackay, J., S. Barr, and M. Kletke. 1992. "An Empirical Investigation of the Effects of Decision Aids on Problem-Solving Processes." *Decision Sciences* 23, pp. 648–672.

March, J., and H. Simon. 1958. *Organizations.* New York: Wiley.

Meigs, W. B., O. R. Whittington, R. F. Meigs, and W. P. Lam. 1987. *Principles of Auditing,* 3d Canadian ed. Homewood, Ill.: Irwin.

Messier, W. F., Jr., 1995. "Research in and Development of Audit Decision Aids." In R. H. Ashton and A. H. Ashton, eds., *Judgment and Decision Making Research in Accounting and Auditing.* New York: Cambridge University Press, pp. 207–228.

Messier, W. F., Jr., and J. V. Hansen. 1984. "Expert Systems in Accounting and Auditing: A Framework and Review." In S. Moriarity and E. Joyce, eds., *Decision Making and Accounting: Current Research.* University of Oklahoma, pp. 182–202.

Messier, W. F., Jr., and J. V. Hansen. 1987. "Expert Systems in Auditing: The State of the Art." *Auditing: A Journal of Practice and Theory* 7 (1), pp. 94–105.

Murphy, D. 1990. "Expert System Use and the Development of Expertise in Auditing: A Preliminary Investigation." *Journal of Information Systems* 4 (3), pp. 18–35.

Neves, D. M., and J. R. Anderson. 1981. "Knowledge Compilation: Mechanisms for the Automatization of Cognitive Skills." In J. R. Anderson, ed., *Cognitive Skills and Their Acquisition.* Hillsdale, N.J.: Lawrence Erlbaum Associates.

Paquette, L., and T. Kida. 1988. "The Effects of Decision Strategy and Task Complexity on Decision Performance." *Organizational Behavior and Human Decision Processes* 41, pp. 128–142.

Payne, J. 1976. "Task Complexity and Contingent Processing in Decision-Making: An Information Search and Protocol Analysis." *Organizational Behavior and Human Processing* 16, pp. 300–316.

Payne, J., J. Bettman, and E. Johnson. 1988. "Adaptive Strategy Selection and Decision Making," *Journal of Experimental Psychology* 14 (3), pp. 534–552.

Pieptea, D. R., and E. Anderson. 1987. "Price and Value of Decision Support Systems." *MIS Quarterly* 11 (4), pp. 514–527.

Prawitt, D. 1995. "Staffing Assignments for Judgment-Oriented Audit Tasks: The Effects of Structured Audit Technology." *The Accounting Review* 70 (3), pp. 443–465.

Qureshi, A. A., J. K. Shim, and J. G. Siegel. 1998. "Artificial Intelligence in Accounting and Business." *The National Public Accountant* 43 (7), pp. 13-16.

Salterio, S. 1994, "Researching for Accounting Precedents: Learning, Efficiency, and Effectiveness," *Contemporary Accounting Research* 11 (Fall), pp. 515–542.

Sankar, C. S. 1990. "A Framework to Integrate Applications, Management, and Movement of Information," *Information Management Review* 5 (3), pp. 55–67.

Shanteau, J. 1993. "Discussion of Expertise in Auditing." *Auditing: A Journal of Practice and Theory* 12 (Supplement), pp. 51–56.

Simon, H. 1960. *The New Science of Management.* New York: Harper and Row.

Simon, H. 1973. "The Structure of Ill-Structured Problems." *Artificial Intelligence*, pp. 181–201.

Solomon I., and M. D. Shields. 1995. "Judgment and Decision Making Research in Auditing." In R. H. Ashton and A. H. Ashton, eds., *Judgment and Decision Making Research in Accounting and Auditing.* New York: Cambridge University Press, pp. 137–175.

Sutton, S., V. Arnold, and T. Arnold. 1995. "Toward an Understanding of the Philosophical Foundations for Ethical Development of Audit Expert Systems." *Research on Auditing Ethics* 1, pp. 61–74.

Sutton, S., R. Young, and P. McKenzie. 1994. "An Analysis of Potential Legal Liability Incurred through Audit Expert Systems." *Intelligent Systems in Accounting, Finance and Management* 4, pp. 191–204.

Tan, H. T., and R. Libby. 1997. "Tacit Managerial versus Technical Knowledge as Determinants of Audit Expertise in the Field," *Journal of Accounting Research* 35 (1), pp. 97–113.

Turban, E. 1990. *Decision Support and Expert Systems.* New York: Macmillan.

Ursic, M. L., and J. G. Helgeson. 1990. "The Impact of Choice Phase and Task Complexity on Consumer Decision Making. " *Journal of Business Research* 21, pp. 69–90.

Wood, R. E. 1986. "Task Complexity: Definition of the Construct." *Organizational Behavior and Human Decision Processes* 37, pp. 60–82.

Yuthas, K., and J. Dillard. 1996. "An Integrative Model of Audit Expert System Development." *Advances in Accounting Information Systems* 4, pp. 55–79.

Index

About the Authors

MOHAMMAD J. ABDOLMOHAMMADI is John E. Rhodes Professor of Accountancy at Bentley College, Waltham, Massachusetts. He taught previously at Indiana University, Boston University, and the University of Illinois at Chicago. He publishes regularly and widely in the journals of his field.

CATHERINE A. USOFF is Associate Professor of Accounting, Bentley College. She specializes in behavioral auditing and accounting education research, and has published a number of papers in these fields in the professional and academic journals serving them.